BRODY

The Triumph and Tragedy of Wrestling's Rebel

LARRY MATYSIK AND
BARBARA GOODISH

ECW Press

Published by ECW PRESS
2120 Queen Street East, Suite 200, Toronto, Ontario, Canada M4E 1E2

LIBRARY AND ARCHIVES CANADA CATALOGUING IN PUBLICATION

Matysik, Larry
Brody : the triumph and tragedy of wrestling's rebel / Larry Matysik and Barbara Goodish.

ISBN-13: 978-1-55022-760-4
ISBN-10: 1-55022-760-2

1. Brody, Bruiser, 1946-1988. 2. Wrestler — United
States — Biography.
I. Goodish, Barbara II. Title.

GV1196.B76M38 2007   796.812092   C2006-906801-1

Editor: Michael Holmes
Cover and Text Design: Tania Craan
Typesetting: Mary Bowness
Photo Insert and Production: Rachel Brooks
Cover Photo: Jeanne Rohner
Printing: Printcrafters

This book is set in Adobe Garamond and Trajan

The thoughts expressed by Matysik and Goodish are the material of the individual author.

DISTRIBUTION
CANADA: Jaguar Book Group, 100 Armstrong Ave., Georgetown, ON L7G 5S4
UNITED STATES: Independent Publishers Group, 814 North Franklin St.,
Chicago, IL 60610

PRINTED AND BOUND IN CANADA

ECW PRESS
ecwpress.com

CONTENTS

Acknowledgements and
A Note on Style and Illustrations

Many deserve thanks when a book such as *Brody: The Triumph and Tragedy of Wrestling's Rebel* comes together. Frank Goodish was a unique personality in his own right, and he created an unforgettable character in Bruiser Brody. Those who honestly understood both sides of this complicated man made valuable contributions to the book. Thus, we offer thanks to many, but especially to the following individuals.

Pete Ortega opened his heart to share with us his friendship with Frank. Pete and his wife Rowe knew who Frank really was. Ronnie and Dede Middleton also described the private side of Frank they had come to know. Thanks also to Gerry Cohen and William and Mary Kirkwood.

Those in wrestling who actually were friends of Frank Goodish were generous with their time and knowledge. They didn't get detoured just telling "tall tales," but offered fact, analysis, and affection for a friend.

Thanks to Buck Robley, Gary Hart, and Stan Hansen, who were incredibly open about their experiences. Bobby Jaggers and Terry Funk added so much about Frank. They helped us capture who he was and explain his place in a crazy business.

Victor Quinones was completely open and intense about what he knew and why the terrible tragedy happened.

Dave Meltzer had a different perspective from which to consider Frank, and Jim Ross explained another aspect of Frank's personality. Matt Farmer furnished excellent research about Frank's in-ring record. Mel Hutnick, a wise attorney, was always able to suggest new and objective insights. Charles Holmes, with his computer expertise, and Kelly Matysik, with her photographic skill, were invaluable. Pat Matysik was a sharp proofreader and critic.

Michael Holmes of ECW Press has been much more than just an editor. Michael believed in this book from day one and had great advice, guidance, and friendship to provide.

Most of all, thanks go to the many dedicated fans who kept Bruiser Brody, the other part of Frank Goodish, alive. It is their passion that has made Brody a legend. Frank Goodish would want to tell them, "Thanks." So do we.

* * *

When Barbara Goodish and I began writing *Brody*, the biggest question was how to make clear who was talking. Michael Holmes, our editor with ECW Press, walked us through the process and we hope the result makes it easy for everyone to follow and understand the story of this very complex and entertaining character.

Chapters featuring the specific recollections of Barbara, Frank's wife, are prefaced with her name.

The excellent photographs come from the collection of Barbara Goodish, as well as from Roger Deem, Mike Gratchner, Hal LaPorte, J.R. Obrecht, and Linda Roufa. The cover photo is by Jeanne Rohner.

Parts of this tale are difficult and dark, while others are fun and, hopefully, informative. Putting it all together was tremendously satisfying for both of us. Our fondest hope is that you will find it just as compelling.

Larry Matysik, 2007

* * *

For Geoff and for Millie, Gayle, Gloria and Kathy — B.G.

As always, for Pat and for Kelly — L.M.

FOREWORD

by Dave Meltzer

When you look back at both the wrestler and the person Frank "Bruiser Brody" Goodish was, it becomes clear just how much wrestling has changed in the past 19 years. Looking back reveals a crazy picture.

In the 1980s, Bruiser Brody represented a fascinating dichotomy. True fans of wrestling recognized him as one of the three or four biggest stars in the game. Not only was he a legend in Japan, at a time when the popularity and standard of wrestling in that country far exceeded that in the United States, but he was a superstar wherever he wrestled in America as well. Brody was a genuine drawing card, whether it was for the various promoters trying to survive Vince McMahon's (and later Jim Crockett Jr.'s) national onslaught, or for small, independent promoters looking for a big name to spice their gates.

But because he never appeared in the post-1984 World Wrestling Federation, a large percentage of casual fans never really got to know him. With this book readers will get to know him very well.

When Brody died, I recall a newspaper reporter from Chicago, who was a big fan, saying he wanted to write Brody's obituary. He understood that Brody was one of the world's biggest stars, but his editors couldn't see how that was possible. Sure, they argued, he may have wrestled in front of some big crowds in Chicago for Verne Gagne, but if he was such a big star, why wasn't he in the WWF?

It's almost impossible to adequately explain the role he filled to a fan accustomed to contemporary wrestling. Wrestling, in terms of traditional competitive sports, was no more "real" in those days than it is today. But it *was* presented in a more realistic manner. Accordingly, there was an inherent belief — whether true or not — that a pro wrestler's toughness truly mattered. It added to his aura, his stardom.

Today, nobody ever wonders whether wrestling is real, or asks who's going to be world champion or win a specific match. In the 1980s, however, those were the questions I was asked most frequently.

There was nobody better at projecting real danger than Brody. He was someone you just didn't mess with. When you watched him wrestle, you couldn't be sure, in fact, that a match *hadn't* become real. And that was always his goal.

He had a theory, for example, about throwing effective kicks. He'd lay in a few easy ones, so fans would get used to them, and because of how he worked, he was believable enough just doing that. Then, at the right moment, he'd land a hard kick that made a truly nasty thud. Now, Brody's kicks were no more devastating than the hard kicks thrown by today's wrestlers, but tell that to anyone who watched him back then. It was how he set the thing up — the unexpected power and his sense of timing — that unsettled fans, and made entire audiences unsure about what they'd just seen.

Today's wrestling doesn't reward believability in the same way; it doesn't generate the same emotion. Brody's understanding of how and when to throw his kick made the audiences of his day gasp and believe — even if everything they'd seen up to that point wasn't real — that the rules had just changed. And from that moment on, they would take his match seriously.

When Brody said in an interview he was mad or was going to beat someone up, people believed him. They remembered what they had seen, or at least what they thought they had seen, in the past. And he sure looked and behaved like someone who could and would hurt people at will. Brody was a rarity, even among wrestlers. He truly stood out. From the very first time you watched him on TV — because of his size, his look, his athleticism and, most of all, his ability to make fans believe — he was unforgettable. His impact was instant and lasting.

All of this made him a superstar everywhere he worked, even if many promoters didn't like him personally or trust him professionally.

Today, everyone has seen even bigger men leapfrog opponents and throw impressive dropkicks. But Brody would do his leapfrog and high dropkick spot in a way that left everyone in awe. He not only made fans believe that he was a badass, he also appeared athletically superior to all the other big men in the business. He could do a great main event, one that left people speechless after only three minutes — which is a hell of a feat — or, when the situation called for it, after a 60-minute marathon (another remarkable, though very different feat).

Nowhere was this more obvious than in Japan. Wrestling was huge there during Brody's heyday. Three different networks aired wrestling — in prime time. Week after week he was one of the biggest American stars on two of these three programs, for World Pro Wrestling and for either All Japan or New Japan. World Pro Wrestling featured tapes from the United States and was usually built around the most popular foreigners: Brody, The Road Warriors, Stan Hansen, Ric Flair, and the Von Erichs. These shows weren't drawing the 2.6 rating of today's *Smackdown*; they were pulling in numbers like *Survivor* or *CSI*, often in the 15 to 20 range. In Japanese culture, Brody's stardom rivaled the fame of contemporary sports icons like Tiger Woods, LeBron James, Ray Lewis, or Alex Rodriguez. In Japan, he was a bigger star than Hulk Hogan — and Hogan himself was hugely popular there.

In the early 1980s, there was a group of American grapplers — Hansen, Andre the Giant, Hogan, Abdullah the Butcher, the Funk Brothers and, later, The Road Warriors — who battled for the spot as the biggest foreign name. At the time of his death in 1988, Brody had surpassed them all. In doing so, he made an impact on an entire generation of Japanese fans. And they've never forgotten him.

Some 15 years after Brody's death, Sylvester Terkay, a former NCAA wrestling champion whose main claim to fame as a pro wrestler is that he looks a lot like Brody, became an instant superstar in Japan when he came out of the dressing room doing the well-remembered Bruiser Brody ring entrance, swinging a chain. Older fans were moved to tears by the idea that Brody had finally come back. But when the bell rang, the illusion was shattered: Terkay could bark all he wanted, and he could try to emulate what he'd seen on tape (a true badass, Terkay later went into Mixed Martial Arts and actually had to leave because none of the top guys wanted to fight him), but no matter how well he copied Brody, he just couldn't project the same toughness in the ring. It probably wasn't fair to expect it from him. Even today, in 2007, the only guys who have that kind of presence are the world's top MMA fighters — guys like Chuck Liddell, Fedor Emelianenko, and Mirko Cro Cop.

Brody's unique appearance made him recognizable, but his ring style was even more impressive. He mixed the agility and fluidity of a smaller man with the look of a barbaric caveman and the aura of the toughest street fighter. In a country that loved Godzilla, King Kong, and Martial Arts, it was a potent combination. What completed the package was that this beastly-looking character was incredibly smart — hence his nickname, "The Intelligent Monster."

Brody played an important role in my career. When I started doing the *Wrestling Observer Newsletter* in 1982, I wasn't the first person to write about pro wrestling as it really was, nor the first to refuse to pretend that everything was real. But I *was* the first to gain a following for doing so. Wrestling never had a trade journal and because its essence was so deeply based in fabrication, someone who simply attempted to tell the truth about what was going on was able to carve out a niche inside the industry.

Very quickly, most of the top promoters and wrestlers subscribed to my publication — often using names of girlfriends or in-laws to hide their own identities. Of course, in the dressing rooms, almost every wrestler denied that he'd ever talked to me. And when my name did come up, what was said wasn't positive: I was bad for wrestling because I "exposed the business."

Brody had written sports journalism before getting into pro wrestling, and he must have looked at things differently. Even before we had ever met or even spoken, I'd hear about how he'd talk highly of me and the *Observer* — which in the culture of kayfabe was a real no-no. He'd even tell Japanese writers, guys who had been around the business far longer than I had, that I was a "real" journalist, and that they could learn something about how to cover wrestling from me. You might think they'd resent him for saying that — and maybe even hate me a bit for it. And maybe they did. But when I started going to Japan myself, the respect the reporters there showed me blew me away. Brody opened doors for me, convincing guys that I wasn't the enemy. He made wrestlers, brainwashed by the promoters who wanted to keep them from truly understanding their business, far more open to talking to me. When I started writing about wrestling, my weakness was that I had lived my life in the real world — one that was, and still is, very different from the world of wrestling. He and others like him taught me to expect deceit from the business, to look behind what was said, and not to accept anything at face value.

More importantly, Brody taught me about what wrestling really is for a wrestler. Neither art form, nor sport: it was a business. Wrestlers and promoters had only one common interest: working together to grow the product. On every other level, the two sides were locked into a seemingly unavoidable, mortal conflict. What was at stake was who got rich. Brody cost himself tons of money at different points in his career because he was unwilling to be a good boy when he felt he was getting screwed. At times, perhaps, worrying about being cheated by promoters hurt him needlessly. More often than not, however, his skepticism reflected not paranoia, but a deep understanding of the true nature of the wrestling game. Because, most of the time, he (and everyone like him) *was* being screwed.

As wrestling changed, his perspective was invaluable to me. Looking back, my luckiest break was being schooled by people who really knew the business and understood the personalities involved.

I wish I could adequately describe what it was like to see Bruiser Brody perform live. Unless you've seen him, I'm afraid my words will never really do him justice. Brody brought you into the match and made you scared. Scared for the well-being of his opponent, and, if he came out of the ring near you, for your own well-being, too.

Nobody ever got into Bruiser Brody's face and laughed. If they did, he'd knock them down — or out. But it rarely came to that, because when he took off into the crowd, people instinctively knew they should scatter. He performed a brawl like he was really in a brawl. He was intense and relentless. And he worked like a monster. He didn't do a patterned feed of the babyface's comeback, bumping, getting up and bumping again; and he was never what you'd call a smooth worker. But he was a more *effective* worker than just about anyone in the profession. When his beaten-down opponent made a comeback, he'd let the guy get in his blows, but he'd be hard to put down. It took a major effort just to get him to go to one knee. But doing so got an opponent over — he'd accomplished something. He made the guys he faced fight for their lives. You would think that would make for bad wrestling matches, but, actually, the opposite was true.

Like I said, Brody never came across as a "good worker," someone performing a role. But sometimes, in the early moments of a match, he'd do a few spots just to show that he could be. Nick Bockwinkel, for example, hated wrestling Brody — his idea of working was entirely different — but still freely admits that, as much as he didn't like facing him, he rates on the same level as Ray Stevens as a performer. And to Bockwinkel, who was one of the greats of his era, Stevens is the gold standard of a wrestler's ability.

When you watched him, Brody made you think he was double-crossing his opponent. Usually, but not always, he wasn't. When he wrestled, his unpredictability was palpable; danger was always in the air. Sometimes I think that Undertaker, who will tell you he learned a lot about how to work as a big man from Brody at his most vicious, captures some of what Brody had. Still, it's not the same, because although what he does works well for him, it's far more cartoonish than Brody's menace.

Bruiser Brody was 42 when he was murdered by Jose Gonzalez in the dressing room at Juan Loubriel Stadium in Bayamon. He was actually in better physical condition than he'd been in for probably two or three years, when the elbow and hip injuries that he kept quiet about had been starting to affect his performance. Since that time, I've always wondered how his life, his legacy, and the business itself would have changed if he hadn't been snuffed out.

At the time of this publication, Brody would be in his early sixties. One would assume he'd be out of wrestling completely, but I suppose it's possible he could still be working, in a coaching position, because for years the WWF had the big men they signed watch his tapes to learn how to get over using your size. But I like to think that he would have moved on into another field. He was smart with money, and if he had survived he would have had the opportunity for bigger money years than he'd have ever dreamed possible.

Either way, he would have had many more years in wrestling. And inevitably, at some point, he would have worked in the WWF. Generally speaking, while there were exceptions like Roddy Piper and Randy Savage, Hulk Hogan did his best business working with big men. Brody was, by reputation and in true ability, the best wrestler of his time. He may have gone on to headline WrestleMania, to be remembered by today's wrestling fans as a legend, mentioned in the same breath as Hot Rod or the Macho Man. Or he may have found Vince McMahon trying to change him, everything from his name to his gimmick. Maybe it would have been a success, and maybe it would have been a disaster. If the latter occurred, I don't think it would have taken long before he walked away.

In 1988 Brody seemed perfectly happy working for All Japan. He was the king of that market, and, between tours, worked around the world for companies both big and small. In the early 1990s, the men who worked All Japan considered it the plum job in all of wrestling. Giant Baba, who ran the promotion — after wcw and the wwf started signing most of the business's top names to exclusive full-time contracts — used his regulars more and more. Brody probably would have been working 28 weeks a year in Japan, earning perhaps more than $10,000 per week. It was also a low stress schedule by wrestling standards.

So, he might have headlined a WrestleMania with Hulk Hogan. Or stayed with All Japan, perhaps even working between tours for wcw. It's almost a given that he'd have had a run in ecw, where he surely would have fit the kind of living legend role Terry Funk did so much with. He was perfect for that fan base, and Paul Heyman truly loved him as a performer — even if Brody once violently threw him down (because he felt Heyman was violating kayfabe and needed to be taught a lesson). He probably would have walked out, and come back, more than once.

In late 1988, months after Brody died, Larry Matysik was offered the job as the first booker of wcw by Jim Herd. Jim Barnett eventually talked Herd out of it, and, as it turned out, Matysik never worked a day for wcw. There's little doubt in my mind that had Brody been alive, the situation may have turned out very differently. As much as 1989 is fondly remembered for the great series of Ric Flair and Ricky Steamboat matches, the bottom line is they didn't draw. In a different world, while I'm sure we would have still seen Flair vs. Steamboat, we would have also seen Flair vs. Brody. They would have been tough matches to book — but their few encounters had, historically, drawn big numbers wherever they'd taken place. All of which might have gotten wcw off on a completely different foot. There are so many variables, we'll just never know.

In the early 1990s, All Japan, which had already become very physical since Brody and Hansen set the standard, became even more brutal. Brody would have been in his mid-forties as the faster and harder style came in, when younger guys like Mitsuharu Misawa, Toshiaki Kawada, and Kenta Kobashi took over as the top Japanese stars. Hansen was able to work until he was 50, although he was forced, in his last few years, to save himself at house shows and only kick it up when TV cameras were rolling. At what point would this faster, harder style have taken its toll on Brody? We'll never know. But the day, inevitably, would have come.

In 1996, pro wrestling exploded in the U.S. In 1998, the Monday Night Wars peaked. Brody would have been 50. I think it's a safe bet he would have been looking to get out of All Japan a few years earlier. His timing couldn't have been worse for the WWF. With Hogan gone, his big money match was gone too. WCW had become the better fit. With Hogan working there in 1994, it would have made sense for Brody to follow. He also could have gone to FMW, where he would probably have had a sellout baseball stadium barbed wire match with Atsushi Onita. A run there would have lasted a year at most, but he might have been able to work WCW at the same time.

Could Brody have hung on until 1998? Would he have been a legitimate foe for guys like Bill Goldberg, Steve Austin, Undertaker, or The Rock? It's possible. Terry Funk was an effective star at the same age, and he had picked up far more injuries along the way. But Funk also reinvented himself. Brody would have had to push the envelope, but there was more money available to a top star than at any other time in wrestling history — his effort would have been rewarded handsomely.

With two major companies warring, I fully believe Brody would have gotten at least one big money U.S. offer. How effective he would have been is something else we'll never know. He may have been a highly paid face in the background of the NWO B-Team — getting $750,000 per year, only to be poorly used. Or he may have been the tough old brawler who turned into the top-level babyface everyone respected. Realistically, though, he probably would have been like Funk, coming in and going out, and working for every company at one time or another. He understood how to get over and would have understood how to work to keep himself over. There was so much money on the table that I fully believe he would have enjoyed a final, big run.

With Brody's death, wrestling and its fans were deprived of many possibilities — but this pales in comparison to what his friends and family lost. His son grew up without a father; his wife carried on without a husband. And even if justice had been served, nothing would bring Frank back. But the fact that there was no justice makes matters worse — everyone involved is left with a bitterness that won't ever be fully washed away.

In the past two decades wrestling has experienced a litany of tragedies. Many were the result of bad choices — deaths that can be directly linked to drug abuse; wrestlers used drugs to combat depression or physical pain, to get through a difficult schedule, or to bulk themselves up enough that people in charge, and the audience itself, would notice them or perceive them as a money player. And while these untimely deaths are no less sad to the families and friends of the men and women who have passed, they can at least be rationalized: if you play with fire, you risk getting burned. Other tragedies (like that of popular referee Brian Hildebrand, who died of cancer at a young age), though cruel, are at least a normal part of life.

In the modern era of professional wrestling, however, no tragedies are more difficult to accept than the murder of Bruiser Brody and the accidental death of Owen Hart. Both, simply, should never have happened. Nothing, no bitterness or long-held grudge, justifies killing someone. And no wrestling stunt should ever put a performer's life at risk. Barbara Goodish and Martha Hart have had to carry on knowing that their husbands' deaths were preventable — while wrestling fans have carried on wondering, *What if?*

At the end of the 20th century, a poll was conducted among Japan's approximately 500 active pro wrestlers: they were asked to name the greatest native and foreign stars of the 20th century. Out of every foreigner who ever worked in that part of the world, Brody was named the best by his peers. While it is, of course, a fantasy — one that's willingly believed — to the people who grew up with wrestling in Japan in the 1980s, he was simply one of the toughest men on the planet.

Now, however, the world is a very different place.

The pro wrestling shows that were once a fixture of Japanese network prime time programming are now broadcast at 2 a.m. — and are barely hanging on for dear life. There are many reasons for this, but most experts believe the popularity of mixed martial arts, as well as the fragmentation of the business between too many promotions, combined with terrible television time slots, are to blame. A whole new generation of Japanese children has grown up — kids who didn't watch pro wrestling every Friday and Saturday night with their parents.

In the U.S., pro wrestling has been transformed from a world dominated by individualists with unique styles to a homogenized group of well-built, good-looking guys who wrestle essentially the same way.

Puerto Rican wrestling, since Brody's death, has seen a number of odd turns. After he was acquitted in 1989 — the murder was ruled "self defense" — Jose Gonzalez returned to the ring as Invader I. And while wrestling has maintained, even to this day, a strong television fanbase, the WWC — which set records in 1984 when Brody and Hansen wrestled Carlos Colon and Abdullah the Butcher in stadium shows — never fully recovered from the murder. Over time, Invader I became the master of the heart punch — and it wasn't long, either, before he was back booking on the island. Some top stars, like Ric Flair and The Road Warriors, never returned to work for the WWC. Other big stars of the era vowed they'd never go back — but as time wore on, they forgot their promise. Many spoke about the uneasy feeling they had upon seeing Brody's killer as booker and top star.

Eventually, Victor Quinones broke away from the WWC and started up the IWA. Every Thanksgiving, he honored Frank Goodish with the annual Bruiser Brody Memorial Hardcore Weekend. A few years ago, Invader I had a falling out with Carlos Colon. Pressured to push Colon's sons as the WWC's top stars, he quit the company for good. After much soul searching, Quinones decided to hire Invader — even though he was going against the wishes of his booker, Savio Vega. Vega had worked with Brody in Japan, and was in the dressing room on the night of his murder.

Quinones justified the hiring like this: there were 40 families whose well being depended on his company staying alive. And the reality was that hiring Invader I to work big shows would be good for business. To his credit, he removed Brody's name from his hardcore weekend. He understood that having Invader I headline that show would be in bad taste — even for pro wrestling.

Still being run by Carlos Colon and Victor Jovica, WWC decided to pick up the "vigil." They actually had the gall to run a Brody Memorial event at Juan Loubriel Stadium — the same place where Brody was stabbed to death. The show bombed. Wrestlers who worked that night, to a man, noted that it just didn't feel right.

Last year, Quinones, who was Brody's best friend in Puerto Rico, began speaking regularly with Larry Matysik. The stress of running the IWA, which on good weeks could make $10,000, but on bad ones lose $20,000, had led Quinones to begin drinking heavily. While this book was being prepared, he died of a heart attack, at the age of 46.

In 1990, Atsushi Onita had an idea he thought would put his small promotion on the map. Because news of the death of Brody had dominated headlines in Japan for six straight weeks, Onita believed — rightly — that the wrestler most hated by the Japanese people was Invader I. Seeing dollar signs, he went to Puerto Rico and shot an angle where Invader I supposedly "stabbed" him in the chest — mimicking what happened to Brody. Onita did not have a television show at the time, but Japanese wrestling magazines and sports newspapers ran the shot of Invader I standing over him, blood pouring from his chest. He believed bringing Invader I to Japan would sell out one of the major baseball stadiums. But the angle backfired. The mainstream media brutalized Onita for even thinking of bringing in Brody's killer and exploiting the icon's death for profit. Fans hated the idea as well, and booed the usually popular Japanese wrestler at his next round of house shows. Onita had no choice but to drop the idea.

Jose Gonzalez's career lasted 18 years after Brody's death; he was a headliner the entire time. In 2006 at nearly 60 years of age, he announced his retirement. Vega and Invader I did an angle that saw Vega stab Invader I in the chest. When it aired on television, Vega stood over the fallen Gonzalez, blood everywhere.

The Puerto Rican government honored Invader I upon his retirement — for both 40 years in the ring and for consistently sending a positive message to Puerto Rican youths about the dangers of drugs. Seemingly, enough time had passed: what was once a black eye on the entire island was now largely forgotten. In truth, many younger fans didn't even realize what the stabbing angle with Vega signified. Still, those in the media who did remember were horrified — embarrassed that the man who had killed Bruiser Brody was being honored.

Invader I beat Vega in his retirement match. A sellout crowd at an outdoor baseball stadium — the IWA's biggest in many years — was on hand to watch Gonzalez retire as a hero, on his own terms and as one of Puerto Rico's greatest wrestling legends.

If Frank Goodish had been born into today's wrestling world, he wouldn't have had Japan — an income base that allowed him to play hardball with promoters. Being big, athletic and well-conditioned, he'd still be signed, immediately, after a WWE tryout. But they'd likely ask him to get a haircut — and to wrestle just like everyone else — which would mean he wouldn't be Bruiser Brody. That giant among stars was of a very different time, an entirely different world.

INTRODUCTION

by Jim Ross

In my 30 plus years in the often crazy world of pro wrestling I have never encountered a college-educated individual as simultaneously complex and simplistic as my friend Frank "Bruiser Brody" Goodish — arguably the greatest brawler ever to lace up a pair of wrestling boots.

My first job in wrestling coincided with Frank's. I was a rookie referee while my pal was a rookie wrestler working for the controversial "Cowboy" Bill Watts in Mid South Wrestling, and we spent many hours discussing our lives. Little has worked out as we predicted over 30 years ago.

Frank never fully trusted a wrestling promoter. Wrestlers had no contracts and were at the mercy of promoters who decided what to pay these road warriors and how often and where these men would wrestle. If a wrestler was off work for any reason, he simply did not get paid. Many promoters attempted to keep people with low self esteem or a lack of courage under their thumbs. Six-foot-five, three-hundred pound Frank did *not* fit under anyone's thumb. Through countless battles over money and violent disagreements over the creative direction of the Bruiser Brody persona, Frank and his obsession survived and achieved unparalleled success. He became known as fiercely independent, not to be trifled with, and just as intelligent as he was intimidating.

The business became the first "Cerebral Assassin's" passion. Driven by this, Bruiser Brody became one of the biggest stars in the history of wrestling. Fans in Japan still talk of Brody in reverential terms. Frank's wild matches on such platforms as WWE's 24/7 are must-see, as are the promos from this once-in-a-lifetime performer.

Then the passion betrayed Brody, allowing him to be senselessly murdered in a Puerto Rican locker room. His admitted killer never spent a day in jail.

Brody is a page-turner that addresses the life and death of one of wrestling's most controversial, talented, and influential performers. He was taken from his wife, his son, his friends and his fans much too soon. This story is long overdue. And once you read it, you will feel like you know Frank "Bruiser Brody" Goodish. And you will miss him as much as I do.

CHAPTER ONE

MURDER

Frank Goodish, famous internationally as professional wrestler Bruiser Brody, was murdered by Jose Huertas Gonzales on July 16, 1988, in Bayamon, Puerto Rico.

No motivation is sufficient and no excuse is acceptable. No matter what speculation floats on the Internet. No matter what lies are told or what rumors evolve. No matter whose agenda is being served.

There is no forgiving. There is no excuse. There is only one solitary fact.

Frank Goodish, Bruiser Brody, was murdered by Jose Huertas Gonzales on July 16, 1988, in Bayamon, Puerto Rico.

Once upon a time, however . . . The wrestling business in Puerto Rico was red hot. This was primarily thanks to Bruiser Brody, who ignited the explosion with his tag team partner Stan Hansen. Brody and Hansen came to San Juan and at least 28,000 emotional fans were on hand at Roberto Clemente Stadium to see the belligerent pair tackle Abdullah the Butcher and hometown hero Carlos Colon (who was, of course, part owner of the promotion) on June 2, 1984.

A rematch on September 15 drew another huge mob to see the violence. And still a third collision involving the quartet erupted October 15. All three features drew over 20,000 spectators each time. It was an amazing feat in a market that size, or, for that matter, in any market.

Over time, obviously, this kind of business could not be sustained, although Brody always made for a hot ticket. He had more than a few bloody engagements with Abdullah. As wrestling changed on the mainland and in Japan, Frank found himself picking up more dates in Puerto Rico for Colon and his business partner Victor Jovica.

By that time, though, Hansen had said "adios" to Puerto Rico. "I had had my fill and it just wasn't worth it," he maintains. "Dealing with them on their home turf was always a battle. A gringo is a gringo, and that's what we were. Frank felt he could handle it. He always believed he was invincible. I'd had more than enough, though."

Part of the problem was money. Checks bounced or were short. Kevin Von Erich, who had known Brody since Kevin was a small boy, remembers that once the Puerto Rican office "owed Frank big bucks. They hated him and were mad at him, but he had a lot of money coming."

Kevin's father Fritz, a powerful promoter from Dallas, where Frank started in the ring, got along well with Colon and, according to Kevin, brokered a deal so that Frank got a percentage of the money he was due in addition to his payoff on trips until the full amount was paid. "He wanted his money. Frank said 'That's mine' and my dad agreed," recalls Kevin. "Carlos was a good man and tried to work it out."

This does bring up a question, though: if Carlos was "a good man" and the promotion meant well, why did the checks bounce?

Buck Robley, a close friend and often a booker for Frank, explains, "Money was a problem. Checks bounced. It was always a fight for money, although the first couple years were good."

Bobby Jaggers (Jeaudoin), who met Brody when both were starting in the business, thought there might have been "heat" between Frank and the office over the method used to collect personal taxes from the wrestlers for Puerto Rico. Some suspected part of that money ended up in the office's pockets. "I know he went to the office and flat refused to let them take any money out or have him give money back. He said he'd pay his own taxes," Bobby notes.

Frank was always a planner, Buck remembers, and a few times he got checks from Colon just before leaving on a long trip. "Frank would take so much cash for expenses on the road, leave so much with his wife Barbara for the house, and put the rest away," says Buck. "Then the check would bounce, Barbara would have to get money from the savings, and Frank would just go ballistic. He would get the money eventually, but it was always a big argument."

An even bigger headache, perhaps, was the testy relationship between Frank and Jose Gonzales, the booker for Colon's and Jovica's World Wrestling Council. Victor Quinones, who worked in the company with Colon and Jovica, was the man who made all the details fit together in that operation.

Quinones pointed to 1976 in the World Wide Wrestling Federation as the year when "the seed of hatred was planted between Frank and Jose."

Brody was going into a long and profitable run against titleholder Bruno Sammartino. Frank understood he wasn't to sell anything for anyone until he squared off with Bruno, by order of Vince McMahon, Sr., who ran the company. Gonzales was led to believe that he was coming into the WWWF as an upcoming star who would be the replacement for the likes of Pedro Morales and Victor Rivera. The first part of that equation was accurate; the second was, obviously, incorrect.

The two were booked together often and Brody simply ate Gonzales for lunch. The volatile Brody was much bigger and clearly more charismatic, and when it came to the drive and hunger for success, Brody was in a league of his own. On one television taping when the two were paired, Gonzales complained to Gorilla Monsoon, Senior's assistant, about how Brody was manhandling him. To keep peace, Gorilla suggested they do a 50-50 match (both wrestlers getting a roughly equal amount of offense) for television.

Naturally, in the bout itself, Brody beat the daylights out of Gonzales and gave his foe nothing. Brody saw Jose Gonzales as little more than a mere job boy, who was about half of his size. How could Brody sell anything for someone like that and have any credibility as a challenger for the indestructible Bruno?

When Brody got to Puerto Rico years later, he found Jose Gonzales arrogant and in a position of power. Gonzales was both the booker for the World Wrestling Council and in main events as the masked Invader I. Frank was irritated but, as Quinones noted, "didn't put up with any of Jose's shit."

That was probably an understatement. Jack Brisco, a former world champion, says, "Frank would belittle Gonzales in front of the boys. He probably pushed over the line. Puerto Rico is such a little place. It's tough to stay there and make a living." Obviously, Brisco believes Brody cost Gonzales the respect of both the dressing room and the local talent.

Buck Robley agrees that Frank had no respect for Gonzales and that influenced how the big man treated him. "He intimidated that little midget!" scoffs Buck, applying the term "midget" to Gonzales because Jose was so small for a main event wrestler of that era. "Over the years, there was hatred building up and Frank got inside Jose's head. He would never answer to him.

"Frank would scream at Jose when he tried to give a finish in the dressing room and the midget would be so scared he wouldn't do anything," Robley says. "Then, all of a sudden, Frank would say 'It's okay. Don't worry about it.' But when he got in the ring, Frank would double cross Jose on the finish."

According to Buck, Frank never really tangled with Colon, except for demanding bad checks be addressed. "He was the money man. Don't mess with the money man," says Buck. "But the poor booker got the wrath of Frank. Frank would say he wasn't going to cut off his head [bleed] for that asshole."

Terry Funk, a friend of Frank's from the time Frank was in college at West Texas State, wrestled in Puerto Rico often and knew all the players quite well. "Frank could push harder than anyone I've ever seen, and Gonzales was certainly one of those he just ate up," says Funk. "Frank just belittled him."

Funk understood the problem with Gonzales. "Jose was not at all gifted as a booker. He only knew one way and didn't know how to change anything.

"It's tough to build a finish with the main event. Lots of egos, lots of talent. Everyone has to work together and have respect. If they don't want to do one thing, a good booker helps figure out something else," explains Funk, who was an imaginative booker in his own right. "I'd always be tweaking things, sometimes even when the guys went into the ring. It's an ongoing process, to have a great match. Sometimes it happens right in the ring!

"Frank always wanted to do the right thing for the money in the end," Funk goes on, "but he did not have respect for Jose. He would take over in the ring and change stuff. He'd take liberties in the ring. In the States, that didn't mean anything really. Hell, Frank did it to Verne Gagne [owner of the American Wrestling Association based in Minneapolis] all the time. But on that little island, everything is very macho."

Bobby Jaggers says, "Frank always told me Jose didn't know a thing about the psychology of the business. The big guy would say, 'Dory Jr. [Terry's older brother] and Terry must just puke when they come down here to work for him.'"

Robley adds, "Jose became the 'Yes man' for Carlos when Jose got the big push, but Frank knew better. He gave Jose no respect — and there was no reason he should have respect for Jose."

Frank was wary at times about his outings in Puerto Rico. He recognized that the relationships there were often uncomfortable. Once, he was slated in a match that had boxing great Joe Frazier as the special referee. Obviously, the finish would in some way involve the boxer, portrayed as a fed-up official, landing a punch on Brody. "If they want to double cross me, I'd be vulnerable," admitted Frank; this was especially true considering the power of Frazier.

"Here is a legitimate heavyweight professional boxer, with no glove on his hand, who really knows how to hit and me just giving him my jaw," a worried Frank said. "If they want to get me, he could wallop me and I'd end up a vegetable." Brody was as careful as could be, but nothing developed and the bout went fine with a worked punch.

Victor Quinones often ended up becoming the middle man for Colon, between Brody and Gonzales.

As Quinones got tighter with Frank, he would advise Colon: "Frank isn't going to do this, but he might do that." According to Quinones, Gonzales often wanted him to give Brody the finishes. Eventually this became a problem because Quinones had other duties the night of a card, so Colon and Jovica expected Gonzales to handle his own responsibilities.

Colon and Jovica kept the pressure on Gonzales as time went on, once telling Jose to order Frank "not to come to the matches wearing shorts," Quinones remembered. Of course, the shorts were part of Brody's public image, so any intelligent person knew exactly what would happen if Gonzales told him not to wear them.

Further internal pressure was on Gonzales after the drowning death of his young daughter near the start of 1988. "He was unbalanced, disturbed in the mind for a long time after that," said Quinones. "Jose suffered. He was insane."

But it wasn't all yelling and battling. Quinones was not the only one who remembered driving to matches in Puerto Rico with both Gonzales and Frank. The trips were relaxed, calm, and without trouble. There was even one such excursion only a day or two before that fateful evening.

Both Quinones and photographer "Fast Eddie" Gries recalled partying when both Frank and Gonzales were present. They said there was no trouble then. Of course, the talk wasn't about finishes and money. Nor was personal pride for Gonzales on the line at times like those.

And Buck Robley makes an interesting point when he suggests that the Puerto Rican office turned Brody into a babyface at Gonzales' suggestion — "So Jose wouldn't have to wrestle him and get beat up all the time."

In the shrinking wrestling world of 1988, Puerto Rico was one of the few paydays remaining, even if collecting that mediocre pay promptly and in total was occasionally in doubt. Those conditions often made Frank claim he wouldn't work there. Nonetheless, he felt that many of the problems in working the island had been put behind him, and he was fairly comfortable heading there that summer.

On July 16, the show was outdoors at the Juan Loubriel Stadium. It was a typically hot, oppressive, uncomfortable day in Puerto Rico. Frank went with Dutch Mantel and Tony Atlas to the facility. The babyfaces (including Frank) used one dressing room and the heels used the other, on opposite sides of the baseball field. Jaggers recalled that Frank took a look from one dugout and spotted Bobby peeking out from the other side, where the heels were housed. Figuring that most of the gathering crowd did not understand English, Frank yelled at Bobby to inquire whether or not Jaggers' wife had arrived yet. When Bobby acknowledged that she had, Frank said to tell her "hello" and "let's get together later." Then he disappeared back into the tunnel to the dressing room.

Inside was the typical milling about, grapplers at various stages of getting dressed and preparing. Frank noted a portrait that Atlas was painting of Chris and Mark Youngblood. He was impressed, and asked Tony about doing a painting of Frank's son Geoffrey. He dug out a picture of himself and his son to give to Atlas.

Gonzales, carrying a towel, walked by and asked Frank to come and talk with him in the bathroom. That was nothing unusual; many important wrestling meetings have taken place in the bathrooms of dressing rooms. Most promoters and bookers didn't take the time to talk with talent in an office or under respectful circumstances. The bathroom at a building was a handy location for giving instructions or trying to sell a wrestler on an idea, which perhaps showed how little esteem those in charge had for the people they employed.

It was private, and a normal enough place to meet, even on that horrible night in Puerto Rico. Gonzales and Brody were alone when the chaos erupted.

Various wrestlers in that dressing room recall hearing either a scream, or a scuffle followed by a scream. Memories play tricks with people, not only over the years but even at the very moment of a traumatic event. Anyone who has been at the scene of an accident, a tornado, or any emergency knows that time becomes skewed and thoughts jumbled.

The one agreed-upon fact was that Frank Goodish had been stabbed and was in desperate straits. Atlas got to the scene first. Most agree that Frank staggered out of the shower area under his own power before going down to the floor. Mantel has described Frank as "staring in disbelief," and he was undoubtedly in shock as well.

Frank was bleeding profusely; some noted that the blood was bubbling. This was an indication that a lung had been pierced. As it turned out, there was also internal hemorrhaging. Confusion reigned in the dressing room, with much yelling, mostly in Spanish. Gonzales was still in the room, by some accounts talking or arguing with Jovica. Atlas was staying close to Frank, who Tony knew was in trouble. Colon came and kneeled down. Frank told him to take care of his family. He said to tell Barbara, his wife, and Geoffrey, his young son, that he loved them.

The wait for an ambulance was agonizing, by most accounts well past twenty minutes and only after Quinones had appealed to a local radio station to broadcast that an ambulance was needed at the stadium.

It was that long before Gonzales even left the stadium. By the time the paramedics had Frank ready to move, almost an hour had passed since he had been attacked. Getting the big man up was almost impossible for the smaller attendants, and Atlas himself carried Frank up several steps to the ambulance, and rode to the hospital with him.

Amazingly enough, the show went on. Jose Gonzales returned and wrestled that night. What had he taken with him while he was gone? Where was the knife?

Police came to the dressing room. Mantel felt that the police thought, at first, that the incident was nothing but a staged angle. The knife that Gonzales had used had disappeared.

Atlas returned and was a complete wreck emotionally. The Youngbloods were on the edge of collapse. Tears were shed. The police either could not speak English or spoke English poorly, and they were starstruck by Colon and Gonzales.

When the heel side figured out what had happened — often after being told by their opponents in the ring — the shock spread. Jaggers retrieved and held onto Frank's briefcase until he could give it to Barbara days later. After the card, Atlas and Mantel tried to find out how Frank was doing at El Centro Medico. The answer was grim.

By 5:40 a.m. on July 17, Frank Goodish was dead.

Part of the problem was that Frank's blood was thin from all the aspirin he took to combat the pain of working. "They might have been able to save him with no aspirin," says Robley. In addition, in the opinion of all concerned — especially Barbara — the medical expertise and tools were substandard.

There was another show scheduled for July 17 in Mayaguez. That card never happened. Some guys had left the island. Others, both Puerto Rican and American, refused to participate. Atlas, Mantel, Jaggers, Dan Spivey, Sika, Ron Starr, and Dan Kroffat were in a hotel room when they finally made contact with the police and talked to detectives.

Miguel Perez Jr., Savio Vega (billed as TNT at the time), Hurricane Castillo, and Chicky Starr were among the Puerto Rican grapplers who stayed with the Americans. Jaggers said they were all together when they were told that Jose's brother had made the statement that he guessed that Brody would now pay his taxes and like it. "I want it known that the Puerto Rican boys stood with us," Bobby Jaggers says.

Atlas stayed at the police station for hours. He may well have been the

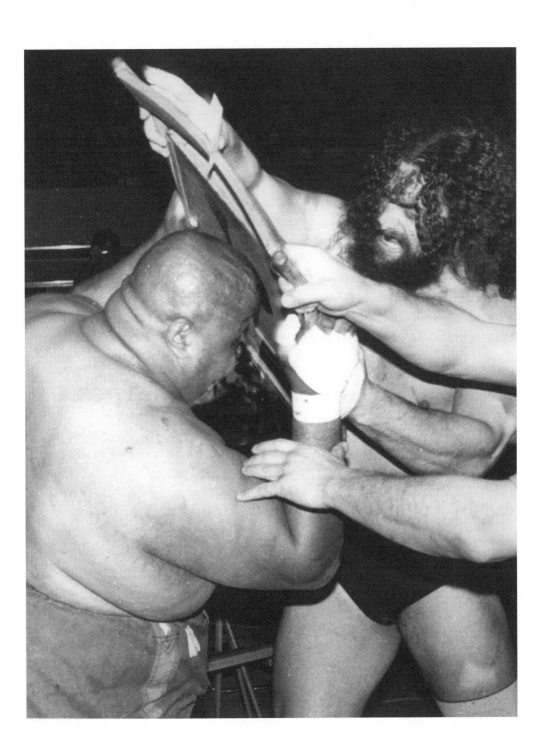

first person to point in the direction of Gonzales as the perpetrator. Sika went with Atlas at the insistence of the other wrestlers, who felt he could help protect him — just in case. None of the boys on the island trusted anyone at that point.

The wrestlers were very much aware when Frank's wife Barbara and young son Geoffrey arrived in Puerto Rico. Colon's wife had contacted Barbara, who was skeptical. Mantel talked to Barbara when she called in the middle of the night to find out if Frank was okay. Dutch had confirmed Frank was hurt "in an accident," which was a wise choice of words because it minimized fear and panic as much as possible. That phone call took place less than an hour before Frank passed away.

Jaggers recalls that Colon and his people "circled Barbara like the Mafia." Granted, she was in a terrible situation and decent people would want to look out for her. Still, it worried the boys. Bobby had immediately sent his family home after the murder. Fear was rampant, even among the so-called tough guys — many of whom, including Abdullah the Butcher, left the country quickly after the murder. Jaggers believes Abdullah might have felt he was next.

Quinones, in retrospect, felt that Colon and Jovica did not think Gonzales would go as far as he did, though he had been constantly pushed to settle the problem with Brody and take command of the dressing room. If, in fact, Frank's frustration about the withheld money upset them, it might also have been a factor in the pressure they put on Gonzales.

To what extent was the volatile Gonzales coerced? Quinones felt that Colon and Jovica were able to absolve themselves of any responsibility for the murder, no matter how much they had leaned on Gonzales.

They did, however, make a critical decision. "One was gone," said Quinones, "so they wanted to save the other." Apparently, that meant protect the killer and preserve the promotion — in any way they could.

Terry Funk admits "Carlos took the wrong route when they were dealing with Frank. But if that [the murder] had happened in my territory," he muses, taking a long pause, "I might have done what they did to save it [the promotion]."

The impact within the business was seismic. Many wrestlers vowed never to appear for WWC again, though in the end most went back, saying they needed to make money, even if it was just a pittance from a disreputable operation.

Frank Goodish would not have been surprised to see the vast majority jump off the edge of the cliff together, no matter what they had proclaimed. He would also have understood perfectly each wrestler's need to take care of himself and his family.

Gary Hart, a highly regarded booker in Texas and an ally of Brody, was not the only one who blasted some of those in Puerto Rico at the time of Gonzales' attack. Being helpless as the legal fiasco played itself out left many friends of Frank irate and frustrated because so many rumors and lies obscured the facts. "So many of them didn't have the balls to go to the prosecutor," Hart says of the wrestlers in Puerto Rico.

Hart continues: "Those who say Frank caused it himself by the way he treated some promoters are full of bullshit. Most of that never happened the way people say, and anyway it would be no excuse for murder.

"In my opinion, Gonzales tried to earn points by showing he could handle a tough guy and it got out of hand. Man to man, he had no chance. So two men got in a knife fight, but only one man had a knife," says Hart. "I think Carlos Colon was punished the most and deserved the least, considering what happened and how his business collapsed and he lost all respect."

Jaggers doesn't share this view. "I had to earn a living. I had a family," he says. "Don't blame the Youngbloods or anyone else. We tried. Lots of us talked to the investigators, but other things were going on. It wasn't safe."

"You have to remember one of the main concerns of every [wrestler], both American and Puerto Rican, on that rock, was the safety of Barbara and Geoffrey. We were watching over them the whole time and I don't even think she knew it, but Carlos and the office did and so did the police." He adds that he and wrestler Dan Kroffat had talked to the police inspector.

"Frank would have done that for any of us," says Jaggers. "Some of us never slept until she left the island.

"There are some assholes who were not there that want to play the tough card. Well, they can go to hell, because, like it or not, I was there. People say things without regard for other people's feelings. These guys (the wrestlers in Puerto Rico at the time) stood up for Frank, Barbara, and his son. The ones that are shooting off their mouths, not one of them ever got on a plane and did a damn thing," Jaggers insists.

"We did what we thought was right at the time. None of us are chickens or cowards," says Jaggers, who served in the "A" Battery of the 1/30 Artillery 1st Cavalry in Vietnam during the battles of Hue, Khe Saah, A-Shau Valley, and the Tet offensive.

"When I see Frank again, I will be able to look him in the eye. I've pretty much come to grips with it, except when I hear other people say what they would have done different. My question is, 'Why didn't you?'"

Even now, almost two decades after the dreadful moment, emotions are so raw that they still bleed for everyone who knew Frank Goodish or had a glimpse into his soul. The pitiful truth is that, most likely, no one could have done anything to change what happened.

Those who were half a world away were in shock, helpless, and angry. Those who were with him that dreadful day may have been worse off, in shock as well as gripped with paranoia and fear.

Frank's murder spurred Jaggers to leave professional wrestling for good. "I really miss Frank, but I think he helped me because his death gave me the balls to say 'enough is enough' and get on with my life. I thought wrestling was life and death until what happened to Frank. It just tore my heart out." Jaggers eventually wrestled in Florida, gave booker Dusty Rhodes two weeks' notice, and quit wrestling completely.

The investigation and subsequent legal proceedings were a fiasco. Now public knowledge, the actual coroner's report included toxicology information showing that Frank had no drugs or even alcohol in his system. The report concludes that the cause of death was, unmistakably, homicide.

There appeared to be no follow-up to the investigation. At one point, the prosecution actually called Frank's widow Barbara to see if she would locate witnesses. There were stories circulating of intimidation, even death threats, directed at possible witnesses. The trial date was changed at the last second, and the original charge of first degree murder had, inexplicably, been dropped to that of voluntary manslaughter.

When the trial finally happened, it is alleged that several witnesses were not even notified in time to appear; Barbara Goodish herself did not know the date in advance. Atlas has claimed he never heard from the prosecution and Mantel says his notification arrived the day after the trial.

There were no witnesses for the prosecution other than the two doctors who treated Frank. They repeated what he had told them had happened, but their testimony was dismissed as hearsay. Gonzales' defense crew brought up every fight or dispute Goodish had been involved in, with stories dating all the way back to college. With no witnesses to those events, why wasn't their testimony considered hearsay? Some stories were no more than rumors — perhaps even fiction — from wrestling lore.

Naturally, Colon and Jovica testified on behalf of Gonzales, their long-time friend and top star. They pulled whatever strings they could.

But the defense painted the victim as the bad guy. Frank Goodish, the victim, unable to defend himself, was actually put on trial. Echoes of those ugly sentiments, "One was gone; save the other," and "A gringo is a gringo" stirred the air.

Gonzales stated that he was defending himself against a much bigger man who had a "known reputation" for violence and was allegedly "crazed," a description that numerous wrestlers — had they been present — could have refuted. How did a knife appear in the dressing room, only to disappear later?

The jury returned with a verdict of "not guilty" because they had been led to believe the incident was a case of self-defense. This was a travesty of justice.

A final insult came a few years later when Gonzales attempted to work an angle based on the killing with Atsushi Onita. They tried to stage a match in Japan, where Bruiser Brody was revered as a legitimate "wrestling god." The Japanese media and fans reacted so horribly toward Onita that the entire disgusting idea was immediately dropped. Gonzales and Onita had thought they could make money by turning a real catastrophe into a wrestling angle. Fortunately, the public and the media had more class and intelligence than to accept such depravity.

J.J. Dillon, a wrestler and booker, worked on a tour that included Gonzales on the roster. "It was a creepy feeling having Gonzales around. It was like being with O.J. Simpson," Dillon remembers. "The trial was a joke. It was a charade. The man got away with murder."

Anyone who claims that Frank Goodish brought the attack upon himself — either because he argued with promoters, or because of the way he conducted business — has a seriously tenuous grasp on both morality and the idea of humanity. If one can "deserve" to be murdered, then how many promoters and bookers should have been murdered because they lied to the boys? Furthermore, if Brody's behavior was such a problem, why did the promoters keep booking him?

Barbara Goodish has spoken on these matters with eloquence and amazing restraint. The sheer terror, the total horror, of her husband's murder cannot be minimized, especially with all of the other disturbing factors surrounding the tragedy. But as strong as Barbara has been, she's human: a mother's fear and the need to keep a young child safe would guide any reasonable human being. Barbara's husband was gone; she was alone with their child. They needed to get away. To be safe.

Quinones spoke with me only days before he passed away unexpectedly on April 2, 2006. He said he wanted the truth to finally be known and asked that I quote him for this book. "Jose Gonzales got away with murder," he stated. "Carlos Colon and Victor Jovica got away with making Gonzales a murderer."

Stan Hansen, a strong and controlled person, admits with a quiver in his voice, "It's still hard for me to talk about this. Frank was stabbed . . . by that man.

"This was just beyond comprehension. Whatever the problem, was anything worth that?" he asks. "I know what I feel. I know what I know."

There are no excuses and no valid explanations.

Frank Goodish was murdered by Jose Huertas Gonzales on July 16, 1988, in Bayamon, Puerto Rico.

CHAPTER TWO

Barbara Remembers . . .
THE NIGHTMARE

Within eight days, I lost a child and a husband.

We had been happy to find out that I was pregnant as we had planned, but I suffered a miscarriage on July 8, 1988, just before we were all planning to go to Puerto Rico. Frank Goodish, my husband, known to most as wrestler Bruiser Brody, was booked to headline cards there. Our seven-year-old son Geoff and I were going to join Frank on this trip. But after the miscarriage, we decided it would be better if I recuperated safely at home.

On July 16, we talked in the afternoon. There was no problem and no hint of trouble. Frank felt like any problems — and there had certainly been some before — had been straightened out. He was comfortable dealing with "Little Victor" Quinones.

We didn't talk about anything out of the ordinary with the wrestling business. Maybe he let his guard down that night, because he was usually very careful. He often had a sixth sense about things like that, but he was quite relaxed. We planned to talk again the following Monday. He even asked me to make some appointments for him when he got back.

When Frank was on the road, it was standard procedure that I would not answer the phone if it rang late at night. If it was Frank, we had a code so I would know it was him. In the middle of the night, the phone began ringing. These were the days before answering machines were in every house, so I let it ring. It went on and on and on.

Finally I got mad and picked it up to give an earful to whoever was calling.

It was a woman who introduced herself as Nancy, the wife of Carlos Colon, the promoter in Puerto Rico. She informed me there had been an accident and that I should come to Puerto Rico at once. I actually did not take much notice, as a lot of women called trying to make trouble. We always thought that it was some promoter putting them up to it. That was one of the reasons I did not answer the phone at night.

I thought to myself that Frank would really get on my case if I just believed someone calling in the middle of the night and took off from home. So I called Frank's hotel room to tell him about the call. But I was put through to Dutch Mantel's room, and he told me that yes, there had been an accident and that I should come down immediately. I believed Dutch — nobody would be so cruel that they'd make up a wild story at this point; certainly not Dutch, who Frank truly liked.

After I had checked out the story Nancy had given me, she called back again trying to get me to believe it. This time, I did. I accepted her offer to pick me up at the airport. I knew I would need some sort of help to get around.

At about 3 a.m. I called the airlines, and I found a flight out at 6:30. I called my wonderful neighbor, Dede Middleton, who was kind enough to take me to the airport. She asked if I wanted to leave Geoff with her, but I knew that Frank would want to see him — we were a team. So we put Geoff, still asleep in his pajamas, in the back seat. I packed a change of clothes and we left with Dede.

At the airport, the agent at the counter was someone who knew Frank from all his traveling and he helped me get the right flight at a decent price. I did not have any money on me, but I found a credit card of Frank's that he had never used as he did not believe in them. I was so grateful that this gentleman knew Frank and helped me.

I dressed Geoff at the airport. I knew that Frank had a fear of hospitals and if he had to be in one, he would want his family there. During a plane change in Orlando, I called Nancy so she would know what flight we were on. We got on the plane, though, still not really knowing anything.

When I arrived at the airport in Puerto Rico, I was in a state of confusion. Geoff had no idea what was happening. Here I was waiting to be picked up at a ticket counter and trying to keep an eye on Geoff, who was seven, so I needed eyes in the back of my head to keep up with him. Then Abdullah the Butcher spotted me, walked up, and told me that Frank had died. He took off right away for his flight as he was leaving Puerto Rico as fast as he could.

There I was alone with a seven year old in the middle of the airport in a strange country. I had just been told my husband, my son's father, was dead.

I must have gone into shock, because after that everything became a blur. Nancy Colon finally found me. Luckily, she had her daughter with her, and that was someone for Geoff to relate to. She took me to the apartment where the Colons were staying (their house was having major work done at the time) so we could drop Geoff off as I had to go to the morgue to identify the body.

Nancy's son was playing basketball on a court with a bunch of kids, so Geoff got out of the car and started playing too. She left her kids in charge of Geoff. One of those children was probably Carlito, who wrestles today. I think back now and here I was leaving my son in a strange environment with people I didn't even know. I was in shock. I know there are some things I've blacked out.

Nancy turned out to be Canadian, and because she spoke English we could communicate well. Regardless of the situation, she turned out to be a really nice lady and she could translate for me, since she also spoke Spanish.

The morgue was horrible, just terrible. There was a door with a glass window and when you had to identify someone, they brought the body up to the window. It reminded me of going to see a baby in the hospital in the old days: they would bring the baby to the window for you to see. But that was a happy event, and this definitely was not.

They rolled Frank up on the other side of a big window. Then they wanted me to sign all these papers, but everything was in Spanish. They were all talking in Spanish as well and I refused to sign because I could not understand anything. Thank goodness, Nancy could translate for me.

After I identified the body, Nancy took me back to the apartment where we had dropped off Geoff. They wanted to give me a shot of whiskey to calm me down, because I now had to call his family. I dreaded it, but I wanted to get to them before the media did. I would have hated for his family to find out from the television. One of the worst things I have ever had to do was to call Frank's parents.

Later that night, after I had made some other calls, they took us to a hotel and checked us in. Reality finally raised its ugly head. There we were, Geoff and I, alone in a hotel room in this strange country. The last thing Nancy asked was how I wanted to handle the situation, in terms of taking possession of the body. What a question. We really were alone.

I finally got Geoff settled down — it had been a hell of a day for him too. I needed to think. I was in shock and my mind was working overtime. It was like Frank was standing next to me. I could almost see him, almost hear his voice saying, "You do what's best for you. You know what's best."

I still think that Frank would not have died if this had happened in the United States.

There was a horrendous crush of things to do. I called Pete Ortega, and then Larry Matysik, to ask if Frank had ever talked about cremation. He had. This is what you did in New Zealand, where I'm from. My mom had been cremated and my dad had told me that it was his wish as well. I knew this was the easiest, and I was also sure Frank would want to go home with us.

As I said before, I also know I've blocked out some things, but I don't blame the people of Puerto Rico for what happened. They didn't do this — they were Frank's fans. I realized he was a public figure.

Geoff helped me pick out the casket. We had gone to try to arrange a small service for him, but even the minister spoke Spanish; we could not find an English-speaking one.

I had told them that because he was being cremated, all we needed was the cheapest box to hold him in. That was Frank in my ear and saying, "Don't spend a lot of money — you'll need it." When we went to pick it up, the gentleman was very vocal. Of course, I couldn't understand the language. Nancy finally translated and told me that none of the cremation caskets were big enough for Frank.

Then they showed us the ones that would fit. They were the beautiful ones. Geoff picked out one that was blue with a pale blue lining — this little gentleman was being so strong. He said, "Dad will like this one because it is our favorite color." I had a hard time not completely losing it.

We tried to provide Geoff with other children to be around, to stay busy. I really didn't see Carlos much. Most of my contact was with Nancy.

After the funeral, I spent a couple of hours with the doctor at the hospital where Frank died. He was so kind to me. Despite my grief and shock, I had to know what had transpired in the last moments so I could go on. The doctor said that by the time he came into the operating theater, Frank was too far gone and he couldn't save him. The doctor had some last-minute words with him; the last words Frank uttered were my name and Geoff's.

Even today this is very hard for me to put in writing. I had filed it away in my head.

Naturally, I was given all the reports and papers even though they were written in Spanish. I also spent a day talking to the District Attorney. He told me they had been following me since I arrived, because this was a murder investigation and the wife is always looked at. Then they watched me because they thought I might be in danger too.

He also told me he did not think there would be any justice because of where it happened. He said it was a small town outside of the city limits where he had no jurisdiction and there were lots of politics. Now I know how right he was.

Before it was all said and done, the prosecutor was actually calling me to help track down his witnesses. I wasn't notified about the final trial date until the trial itself was already over.

When we got back home after Frank was cremated, *Entertainment Tonight* came to San Antonio and for a few days tried to talk me into an interview. I wasn't emotionally capable of dealing with the press, but somehow they discovered where we lived — because the gates were locked they actually called from just outside the house. Though I wouldn't speak with them, they did a nice piece on Frank and I appreciated that. My first priority was to keep Geoff safe. Eventually we had a memorial service at home in Boerne, Texas, but it was low-key. Only Stan Hansen, John Studd, and Larry Matysik were there from the wrestling world.

I bear no grudge. You must let negative things go or they'll destroy you. You might think you will live forever, but it is how you handle trouble that matters. Yesterday is history, tomorrow is a mystery, and today — the present — is a gift. You can always guarantee that life will challenge you from time to time.

Of course, the hurt is still there. Talking about this is very difficult. Now, though, it's like I'm watching the whole episode as a third person. Sometimes I wonder how the hell I got through it all. All these years have passed and I've held most of this in. I talked a little with Pete Ortega, who had been close to Frank for many years, and a little with Larry, but that's all. I hope that just getting everything out for the sake of this book will make me feel a little better.

It still crosses my mind: would it have changed things if I had gone with Frank to Puerto Rico? Would this have happened? If Frank's family had been with him, could anybody have done something like this?

Was it premeditated? Because an attacker would have only one chance to disable him, it had to be. I have explored so many possible scenarios. Did the person act alone? Was it a conspiracy, because Frank was doing so much as an independent? Independent wrestlers suffered a huge blow when Frank died.

Now, the only thing I would like to know is *why*.

I hope the person who committed this crime will have to struggle to live with it always. How could anyone lead a normal life with the responsibility for death on his conscience? I believe in karma, both good and bad. There hopefully is punishment, even if it is not legal punishment.

As you get older and you see all the hardships we go through in life, you realize nothing is easy. You think you will never recover, but time has a way. This is especially true when you have a child who depends on you. No matter how you feel, you just have to get on with life.

CHAPTER THREE

THE LEGEND
OF BRODY

Which tale will they tell when they speak of Bruiser Brody, possibly the most ornery, unpredictable, and charismatic professional wrestler anyone ever knew?

Will it be about the bloody brute who made brawling an art before hardcore meant anything? Or will it be about the confrontational businessman who fought for every penny he felt he deserved, no matter who it offended? Will it be about the rebel and independent who backed down for no promoter?

Will the truth of Frank Goodish, the husband and father and complex human being behind Brody, finally emerge?

Bruiser Brody had no peers in professional wrestling when it came to blood and guts, controversy and independence. Most promoters portrayed their talent as exactly that kind of free-spirited, take-no-guff personalities. But those very promoters were also experts at exaggeration and subterfuge.

In reality, of course, Brody's brand of assertiveness was not at all what they wanted and it was why so few would admit to respecting his stance even as they featured him time and again. Why did they book Bruiser Brody when so many did not trust him? Simple. Brody delivered the goods, both in the ring and at the box office. He knew how to get himself over and do it fast.

Brody was an international superstar. His intensity was no act, but bubbled up from an internal source that perhaps no one understood. That sheer ferocity put him into select company among those warriors who made the fans believe — yes, believe — even as they wondered about the shady side of the bizarre business known as professional wrestling.

The spectators believed Brody could snap, that he could destroy an opponent, that he had in fact survived beatings himself only to return the favor. They believed Brody was the incredible athlete who could stand toe-to-toe with any rival for an hour. They believed Brody would tell it as it was without censorship. They believed Brody was truly dangerous, determined, and vicious. They believed he would stop at nothing.

They believed Bruiser Brody would give them a bang for their every buck, not just because he owed it to the fans but because he was driven by some volcanic fury inside.

Anger, rage, hunger, danger — it was all part of Bruiser Brody.

When the bell rang, anything could happen. Remember, this wasn't today's wrestling — a choreographed acrobatic display — this was an improvised art that gave the most expressive individuals the opportunity to show what made them special.

Here was this giant, standing 6'5" and at points in his career tipping the scales at 320 muscular pounds. His chest was huge, his triceps bulged, and his quadriceps resembled massive slabs of concrete atop furry boots. His long, black, curly hair might be pulled into a ponytail or flow freely to his shoulders. His beard was untamed, like the gladiator himself.

He would stalk about the ring, perhaps barking, or, in Japan, swinging a huge chain over his head. Scars were carved into his forehead like the Grand Canyon on the very face of the earth. And his eyes — oh, his eyes — were huge and cold and mean.

Brody could throw a perfect drop kick, his brawny frame heaving six feet into the air, parallel to the mat. He could drop a burly forearm like a hammer onto a foe's chest. Pulling someone's hair, he seemed to yank it right from its very roots. A kick to the chest, or back, or even when demanded the face, was fast and vicious.

His frame was so flexible that from a standing position, he could jerk his huge boot up as high as his own face and then slam it directly into the head of a charging rival. How could anyone that enormous launch himself into the air for the giant flying knee drop, apparently driving his full weight into a rival's chest?

There was a touch, perhaps, of wrestling here and there. A leapfrog over a charging opponent, a headlock, a hammerlock, or even a body scissors as Brody used his mighty legs to squeeze some hapless victim. But this was just preliminary, as everyone accepted and even appreciated. Everyone knew that when Bruiser Brody stepped through the ropes, he was going to war.

Indeed, a winner (quite often Brody) and a loser would usually emerge from the conflict. More often, someone (very, very seldom Brody) would get beat up. And the fans would love it.

Blood? Oh, yes, there was blood. It would often be spilled when that man entered combat. His own blood. His opponents' blood. Gory red, dripping, smeared over bodies and pooling on the mat, touching some primal chord, even a deep need for emotional release, in almost every fan who stood and screamed. If an opponent wasn't bleeding enough, Brody might solve the problem himself with a quick slash or a "hard way" smash.

When Bruiser Brody whipped a chair and whacked it onto some wrestler's head or back, the crack was like a rifle shot and made the audience gasp. There were no gimmicked tables and no flimsy garbage can lids.

Villian or hero? In the end, it didn't much matter. The fans would generally be rooting for Brody. In most places, he began as a heel who tested the mettle of babyfaces — but the adulation would often come anyway. Somehow, the folks sensed an authenticity in what Brody did inside the square, and they sensed the rebel he was against the establishment outside the ropes.

Soon, it was the monster Brody and some other monster, pounding each other into oblivion, often as the blood flowed. Once the crowd decided to pull for Brody, as they usually did, the depth of emotion could be scary. Brody versus Andre the Giant? Brody as the tag team partner of Andre the

Giant? In the end, that too mattered little. The imagination was ignited.

Cheer or jeer? Who cared? The seats were filled with paying customers.

That audience was why promoters would accept Brody's stubborn and often incomprehensible business acts. The audience, in big numbers, came to see him, bought the tickets, slapped down dollars for the programs. One time on television was all it took, maybe two. Shoot an angle, and forget about it! Brody did not need an introduction week after week. The audience knew this man immediately and he was "over."

Wrestling was different in those days, the 1970s and early 1980s. Territorial promotions, many members of the National Wrestling Alliance but still others thriving and independent, dotted North America and Japan. Wrestling needed TV to thrive in each market, but it wasn't the organized national television production World Wrestling Entertainment is in 2007.

Those promotions were small businesses, with no sophisticated marketing, for the most part, save maybe in St. Louis. To stay alive, they needed fans to buy tickets. Each promotion needed the star, or the unique character, who would lure those people and their dollars.

Dallas. Toronto. Tampa. Chicago. Calgary. Vancouver. Cities with a spider web of satellite towns living off the same television program. New York. Kansas City. Montreal. Los Angeles. It was not at all like today, with only one national program on which to "get over." Every market was a different challenge.

The rare ones, like Brody, could capture the imagination of customers quickly and in every location. The majority of other wrestlers lived like gypsies. They'd spend six months or a year in one territory, then move on, try again, and pray for a main event or two and some decent money.

When a major league attraction like Brody was on top, there were more paying customers. Thus, not only did he get paid, but everyone on the lineup benefited and collected more bucks than usual. The majority of the wrestlers wished they could be like Brody. Those few who might criticize him had a grudging respect for the results he delivered. He was proud of being the true independent that others incorrectly claimed they were.

Brody, leaving a trail of big houses and occasionally aggravated promoters, was one of the tiny group able to pick his spots and count his cash for one feature after another. He also benefited from the lucrative Japanese market, which made him even more independent once he had conquered it.

There were promoters who wanted to use wrestlers as pawns. Brody,

This critically ill youngster discovered a different side of the ferocious Brody.

though, was among the few who understood that he was a commodity. He would not be used like a pawn. Not only did he understand the business, but he also recognized his true value in that business.

In this pre-Internet era, communication like magazines, newsletters, result traders, and telephone calls between distant friends spread the word about Bruiser Brody. His legend — his mythology — grew this way. A television appearance — just one, single, lonely outing — could clinch the deal and cement his fame. The camera loved Brody and Brody loved the camera. Imagine all that intensity and energy hurtling through the airwaves! An audience was born: "Gotta see this guy. When do tickets go on sale?"

Even if many promoters hated him — how he fought them for every dinky dime, how he would not blindly follow some code of conduct, how he would close the door on wrestlers who didn't meet some unknown standard in his head, how he could engineer a stinky match to punish the boss who had offended him, and how he was willing to walk out when he felt he had been lied to — those same men knew he could put gold in their pockets. They could not control the beast, but the beast fed them well. So they asked him back, always; they needed Brody to juice gate receipts that had fallen in his absence.

Bruiser Brody had heard the lies most of them told, seen how they shuffled the money so the wrestlers didn't get all they deserved, listened to the promises that were never kept, seen that the "boys" were nothing more than hunks of meat to many of them, and noted their lack of respect for the dangers of the ring. He was not willing to play *that* game. He would play *his* game on *his* terms when it came to promoters. As violent as action could be under the lights, perhaps the nastiest and meanest battles were the business duels happening behind closed doors.

When Brody left a territory or town, no matter the circumstances behind the scenes, the fans wanted him back. Brody plotted, planned, and manipulated so that he always left the customers hungry for more. And when he returned, the crowd was there, even larger than before, eager and anticipating the thrills Brody would give them. He understood exactly what those fans wanted and expected from him. He gave it to them.

The violence. The blood. The fans. The money. The test of wills. Even if some were cautious around him, most wrestlers wanted the chance to do business with him. They found Brody great to work with and loved the excitement they could create together.

Brody was exactly what every promoter wanted — until there was a business conflict. At that point, the dangerous Bruiser they loved in the ring became what they feared and despised most of all . . . a true independent rebel, who was also an intelligent and tough businessman. In other words: Frank Goodish.

CHAPTER FOUR

Barbara Explains . . .
WHY SPEAK TODAY?

After being in the dark and finally deciding to catch up with the 21st century via the purchase of a computer, I was shocked when I typed Bruiser Brody into a search engine. Lo and behold, all of these web sites appeared before my eyes. I was shocked to see how many people were profiting from his image and telling stories about him.

I went into some of the sites and could not believe the information being given out. All the items for sale made me shake my head.

I always respected his image. I knew that he was in a hard, difficult business. I understood that he stirred up controversy because of how he conducted himself in professional wrestling. After all, he was my husband.

I now believe it is time for the true story to be told about who Bruiser

Brody was: not just the wrestler, but also the person. He was also Frank Goodish. The man was so different from his wrestling image. Frank was a father, a husband, a friend, a brother, and a son.

Years ago I decided that our son Geoff should have a normal life. That is certainly not easy when you lose your father at a young age. It's even harder when your father is in the public eye, and you lose him because of a terrible act. The best thing for everyone concerned, I believe, has been for me and Geoff to stay in the background all this time.

Before getting involved in this difficult book, I talked it over with Geoff, who's now a fine young adult. He gave me his blessing to go ahead. This is all so real; nobody could begin to make it up. I almost can't believe that I lived through what I lived through in Puerto Rico, and I can't imagine really being able to talk about it.

Larry Matysik, who has written a book of his own about St. Louis — *Wrestling at the Chase* — was one of Frank's trusted friends. He and his wife Pat have been very kind to me over the years. Larry is co-authoring this project with me. Hopefully, with the help of Frank's friends and associates, we can give some accurate insight into the real person behind Bruiser Brody. Some of his escapades in this crazy business have made people forget who he actually was.

The real person was the fellow who took me and Geoff, who was seven years old, to Six Flags in Texas. He was laughing and joking. Because of all the travel in his profession, he didn't always get to be a dad as much as he wanted. I'm not sure who was happier that day, father or son.

Eventually, Geoff and his dad went on a ride called Tidal Wave. I decided this was a father-son ride, so I watched them wait in line for their turn. Frank was not one to wait in line for anything, but when you are Dad, you end up doing things you normally would not do.

The ride had approximately twenty passengers per car. Along with the others, Geoff and his father got in their seats and I watched as their car was pulled way up high. Once it was at the very top, it was meant to be released so it could come down fast and make a big splash when it hit the water. That splash would soak the riders and, after the ride, you could get wet again standing on a bridge on the way out — hence the name "Tidal Wave." Kids loved it, as they were guaranteed to get soaked.

Just getting Dad into one of those cars was pretty difficult, because he was a very big guy. I knew he would be feeling uncomfortable being as

Building a snowman with Dad.

high as they were, because he had a fear of heights. In addition, other people were packed into the car as well and he was certainly very recognizable. People had been coming up to him from the moment we got to Six Flags Over Texas. He wanted to be just Dad that day, but he always respected his fans so he would give them a kind word.

When their car reached the top, I stood at the bottom waiting for it to zoom down, but nothing happened. It wasn't moving. It was stuck, with Geoff and his father at the very top! I knew Frank was not a happy camper, especially since he had to be Dad and make sure Geoff wouldn't get scared. The other riders were watching him too, since he had the reputation for being big and bad.

Finally, after quite some time, the ride was fixed and their car came down like a rocket and made a huge splash.

They came off the ride and Dad was holding Geoff's hand. He looked relieved, to be sure, but very, very happy to be with his boy.

Dad, of course, was Frank Goodish.

And Frank Goodish was Bruiser Brody.

They were the same man.

CHAPTER FIVE

HE PICKS YOU

The legendary character that Frank Goodish became has lured storytellers. Some have told the truth; others have distorted the facts or, simply, lied. The problem, of course, is this: how do you distinguish between them?

Many gossips are hoping to become part of Brody's history. They want to claim a relationship so they, too, can be included in his cult saga. Frank Goodish was a deeply complicated human being, and the part of him that was Bruiser Brody was inscrutable. There were only a select few he let come close to understanding him.

Pete Ortega might understand best what friendship really was for Frank Goodish. They met while lifting weights in San Antonio. Discovering that they shared interests, they became close. Both men were cautious until a degree of trust began to grow.

Soon, Frank began to confide in Pete. About those days in the gym, during which Frank was struggling with decisions about his future, Pete says, "He was polite, friendly. You could talk to him." But, Pete admits, "There was a line guys didn't cross. Don't cross that line. You could feel it."

Once Frank made up his mind about someone, that was it. "He picked me," declares Ortega. "You didn't pick him. He picked you as a friend. And once you were his friend, that loyalty was a promise. He picked me and I prize that."

Just as Pete Ortega discovered the depth of Frank's character, so did men like Buck Robley, Stan Hansen, and Gary Hart. "He would look you in the eye and look right into your soul," recalls Hart. "If Bruise gave you his word, he kept it. As long as you kept yours!"

"There was never anyone like him," says Robley. "I never had a friendship anywhere close to that after Frank died. I think about him all the time and where he would be today. He associated with everyone, but drew a line over who he'd get involved with. There were very few he'd invite to his home to sit at his table. I can count on one hand how many there were. I feel privileged. Everyone else who claims that kind of friendship is just talking hot air."

When Frank, as "King Kong" Brody, came to St. Louis in 1978, he and I immediately clicked on a comfortable, friendly, professional level. After I decided to stay with the St. Louis Wrestling Club (rather than resign due to growing problems within the promotion) to set up a major championship bout featuring Brody against Ric Flair, Frank promised me, "If you go on your own, I'll be there. You can take it to the bank." Our friendship bloomed even stronger from there.

He never lied to me, not ever. Frank had an energy — a power — that grabbed individuals.

As Hansen notes, "We were close. There were parts I didn't like and sometimes we went different roads. But he was my friend — always. They were good times when we were together and we could count on each other."

Of course, Buck, Gary, Stan, and I were all people Frank met through wrestling or, in the case of Stan, found the friendship strengthened by the hardships and hilarity of wrestling. We all had unique backgrounds and different personalities.

Pete Ortega was not part of the wild and unpredictable wrestling scene;

"Pete was his best friend," acknowledges Hansen. And, of course, Frank's wife Barbara had a special connection to him on yet another level. So did his son, Geoffrey. There were different people, different situations, and different worlds where emotions ran deep.

But those with that wrestling connection . . . oh, what a crew!

For instance, Buck Robley was trained by colorful Al "Spider" Galento, a former AAU wrestling champion and a pro headliner along the Gulf Coast. Buck was a quick learner, picking up the business and booking nuances. After working around Atlanta, he moved to the Carolinas and worked with Jim Crockett, Sr., one of the old line promoters who was a close friend of St. Louis' Sam Muchnick and respected as a solid businessman.

Buck got to work with and learn from the elder Crockett outside the ring and from seasoned performers like Rip Hawk, Johnny Weaver, and J.C. Dykes inside the squared circle. After Crockett died and the promotion went through turmoil under the guidance of John Ringley, Buck bounced to Florida and finally to Amarillo and the Funks. He got to West Texas the very day that Dory Funk, Sr. died. From there, the self-styled "Colonel" made a reputation as a very clever booker, with perhaps a sneaky edge.

Terry Funk, youngest son of Dory Sr. and brother of Dory Jr., laughingly recalls how he'd needle young wrestlers by whispering, "He's out there. He's out there somewhere." When the grappler would ask, "Who is?" Terry would respond with "Colonel Buck Robley is."

And Buck had such a reputation that the worried wrestler would be looking over his shoulder all night. Funk declares, "The Colonel was a crazy ole son-of-a-bitch and I love him!"

Buck was a great ring psychologist, says Stan Hansen, who isn't sure whether that was good or bad where Frank was concerned. Hansen felt that Frank picked up "attitudes" from the cynical Robley. Funk says that Buck kept a lot of "heat" from promoters off Frank, who realized that "The Colonel" was loyal to him.

Gary Hart came out of Chicago, where he had been a lifelong fan of wrestling and had been trained in the ring by Billy Goelz. Hart had a quick mind and loads of imagination. Catching on with shrewd promoter Jim Barnett in Australia in the late 1960s, and later in Atlanta, Hart built a sparkling resume.

He was also in a tragic airplane crash on February 20, 1975, in Tampa. Red-hot newcomer Bobby Shane was killed, while Gary, Mike McCord

(Austin Idol later), and Buddy Colt were all badly injured. Gary became tight with Frank while having great success as the booker (and also a controversial manager) for the World Class Championship Wrestling operation of Fritz Von Erich in Dallas, where he replaced "Red" Bastien as booker in 1976.

In my own case, I was fortunate to be the protégé of famous St. Louis promoter Sam Muchnick, the father of the National Wrestling Alliance. From Muchnick, I learned the ins and outs and tricks of nearly everyone in the business. I also did the television announcing in addition to all the publicity and office management for a promotion that serious observers agreed was head and shoulders above anything else in wrestling when it came to professionalism.

Stan Hansen was first a football friend of Frank from their days at West Texas State. When football slipped away, Stan was brought into the wrestling wars by the Funk family in Amarillo. Having gone in different directions after college, he was surprised to bump into his old buddy Frank in a wrestling dressing room. But they became trusting friends, and were perhaps the most famous foreign tag team ever in the wrestling hotbed of Japan.

Tough and independent, Stan was called "a true red neck" by Buck Robley, who meant it as a compliment. Hansen also has a spot in wrestling annals as the man who allegedly broke the neck of Bruno Sammartino during a New York duel. Stan was such a big star in Japan (just like Brody, Hulk Hogan, and Andre the Giant) that even today he is treated like royalty when he visits in that country — the way a Cooperstown Hall of Famer is hailed at a baseball game in the United States.

The Funk brothers, Terry in particular, had a deep understanding of both wrestling and Frank. Both Terry and Dory Jr. captured the World Heavyweight Championship as recognized by the National Wrestling Alliance. Dory was considered the more serious and "scientific" of the pair while Terry was the rowdy, unpredictable character. That was only the public's perception, though, as the two brothers were both serious students of the game.

Terry Funk complains, "There are a lot of people today who proclaim their friendship and companionship with Frank so it can get them places and give them the rub of his fame." In fact, Frank was friendly and comfortable in all dressing rooms. He had buddies, all of whom could probably relate an entertaining Brody tale. But to how many, or, more accurately, how few, did Frank Goodish ever really give a glimpse of his heart?

Victor Quinones was someone else Frank allowed into his inner circle of friendship. After his mother passed away, Victor left Puerto Rico for the United States and lived with Gorilla Monsoon (Gino Marella) from 1979 to 1984. Monsoon, of course, was the right-hand man for Vince McMahon, Sr., and handled the matches at his television tapings.

Victor got the opportunity to learn more wrestling with the highly detailed World Wide Wrestling Federation run by Vince Sr., whose son, Vince Jr., was the play-by-play announcer. From running messages to being third-man-in-the-ring for a one-hour draw between titleholder Bob Backlund and challenger Don Muraco, Victor did all the little things that matter so much around a wrestling promotion.

When Victor moved back to Puerto Rico, he began to work with the World Wrestling Council organization headed by Carlos Colon and his partner Victor Jovica. The nickname of "Little Victor" was attached to Quinones, who once again did everything from getting the ring set up to making sure the box office worked efficiently to giving ideas for matches.

Frank Goodish latched onto "Little Victor" quickly in the mid 1980s, becoming his buddy and respecting all the tiny intricacies of wrestling that Quinones knew.

"He was a great person," remembered Victor. "I heard the stories and knew he had a hot temper. I heard he beat up a photographer who didn't have permission to take pictures and he fought with promoters who cheated him. But I never saw that side of Frank. We ate together and drank beer together and laughed together. He often stayed with me and we talked about wrestling all the time.

"Frank told me about Japan," said Victor, "telling me how to work and how to make money there. He warned me the Japanese weren't friends, that they were business people. Not that the Japanese were bad — he liked them — but that this was the way they did business. No matter what, you were the foreigner. He told me to always watch out. He told me who to be particularly careful of.

"When I went to Japan and ran promotions for ten years, I remembered all my friend taught me. I was the foreigner, but I was successful." Quinones was involved with legendary groups like W*ings, IWA Japan, and FMW as the key guy making things happen. He was the mastermind behind an IWA card topped by Terry Funk and Cactus Jack (Mick Foley) in the famous King of the Death Match confrontation. It was won by Foley and

Frank measures Pete Ortega's arms.

drew almost 30,000 people to a baseball stadium in Tokyo.

With a background different from any of the wrestling-oriented folks, Pete Ortega connected with Frank in another way. Pete had inherited his father's house in San Antonio. Thus, the only expenses for him were electricity and water.

Having met Frank working out at the gym, Pete became tight with the big guy as both lifted weights, day after day after day. As personal barriers fell and their friendship grew, Pete offered Frank a place to live and said they could split the costs.

To make money, Frank was also working at the loading docks in Dallas. He had just left his first wife and was battling for a place in the football world. "He worked like a dog," says Pete. "He could handle pain, so that was never a deterrent."

To Frank, Pete was always "the kid." To Pete, Frank was always "the big man." Once in a while, because the gym was in a tough area and because the duo liked to get out, there would be some rough times.

"The big man could kick your ass for real!" laughs Pete. "He buried a few guys in barroom fights. Frank would kick the guy or hit him with a beer bottle. He would say, 'I'm not into that Marquess of Queensbury stuff. I'll kick someone before I break my hand.'"

According to Pete, when Frank made the move into wrestling (thanks to Ivan Putski), his work ethic didn't change. "He was very crude at first, but Frank learned from the smart ones around him," notes Pete.

Goodish couldn't watch television or sit and read. "His mind was always racing," says Pete. "Work out, eat, talk. He was a talker and I was a listener, which is a lost art. Wrestling became his business and his life."

And so did weightlifting. Frank wanted to be big and bigger. "He always had that giant Bruiser Brody head," Pete chuckles. "His chest was huge and he was happy with his arms and those powerful thighs and quads. But Frank was upset because his calves were so small," says Pete. "He'd work and work on his calves and they just never got bigger. So I suggested just covering 'em up once he started wrestling."

Goodish and Ortega went to a little shop that sold leather in Houston. They purchased some rabbit fur and glued it on his boots to disguise his (supposedly) skinny calves. "It enhanced his whole physique, made him look even more thick, if that was possible," says Pete. "He liked the look."

Barbara Goodish, of course, has many memories of attaching rabbit fur to her husband's boots as well.

After she and Frank got together and were living in Boerne, Texas, Frank picked another person to get close to. Ronnie Middleton and his wife Dede, along with their three children, were neighbors. Middleton was a highly regarded middle school football coach and taught science. "We met as neighbors, started lifting weights together in Frank's garage, and he'd come over to our place as well," Ronnie says. "I agree with Pete. Frank had to pick you, but once you were in, you were in no matter what.

"He was a very private kind. I gave him his space, though, and he seemed to appreciate it. I let him initiate contact," says Ronnie. "He put on that persona of being gruff, but he wasn't that way at all. He acted like a big, dumb jock, and he was anything but! He was really smart and a shrewd businessman."

The Middletons remember that Frank was terrible at trying to fix or assemble anything. Ronnie recalls Frank coming to his house and asking, "Is my face red?" Ronnie would answer, "Yes. What did you do now?" And Frank would pour out a tale of woe about how he messed up the lawn mower or couldn't get the truck started after he fiddled with the spark plugs. Ronnie would head over to help fix the problem. Frank once told Ronnie, "The only thing I don't like about you is that you make me feel stupid."

Once, both families went out to enjoy a pizza. They anticipated a relaxed, quiet evening. Two teenage girls came up to Frank, who (even with hair neatly back in a ponytail) stood out visually, and asked him for an autograph. Ronnie recalls that Frank told them his name was Frank, and that he wasn't Bruiser Brody. The girls were a bit huffy, but walked away.

When everyone was finished with their meal, Frank went over to the two girls, apologized, and signed autographs. He explained to them he wanted privacy for his family and friends. When all was said and done, Frank was smiling and the girls were laughing and happy.

Another time, both families made a deal to have their houses exterminated. After the job was done, though, both places still had bugs. Frank told Ronnie, "I'm going to go see this guy who runs the company." He arrived at 7 a.m., talked his way into the owner's office, and was waiting there when he arrived. Frank was sitting cross-legged on top of the owner's desk. "All I know," laughs Ronnie, "is that the guy who did the job was fired and we had both houses treated for free." The owner had probably seen more Bruiser Brody than Frank Goodish!

Ronnie remembers Frank coming to an occasional football practice; he didn't interfere or bother anyone, but was such a celebrity at the little school that everyone loved the attention and got a kick out of Brody's presence.

"Sometimes we would pick each other's brains," Ronnie says. "We didn't offer advice to each other, just talked about why he took dates to wrestle in Puerto Rico and why I didn't take a college coaching job."

Perhaps the best times, Ronnie recalls, were after a hard workout in Frank's garage, just having a beer to relax and trying to "philosophize" (as Frank called it). One day they were talking about the problems kids have at school. Frank really liked kids and was planning unique ways to give them an anti-drug message along with a push to take advantage of education. Frank said, "If everybody would take care of their own business, it would be fine."

Ronnie was so impressed with the thinking that he made that statement one of his class rules. Even today, two decades after their "philosophizing," Ronnie has that as classroom rule number one: "Take care of your own business." It's printed and prominently displayed in the classroom. He tells the story of Bruiser Brody to the students whenever he explains the maxim.

Remembering Goodish, Pete Ortega laughs, "Frank was protective of me and a bit jealous of our time together when he first moved into my dad's house. This was well before he met Barbara. When I started dating the gal who became my wife, and she would call the house for me, Frank would be gruff and tell her I wasn't home when I was."

Ortega goes on, "Eventually, though, Frank and Rowe became good friends. In fact, when we got married and moved, Frank moved too! He

John Studd, Stan Hansen, and Pete Ortega with Frank's nephew Mark.

lived in an extra room in our house before he met Barbara."

By then, Goodish had become close with another he had chosen, "Big John" Studd (John Minton when he played college basketball and before wrestling). Frank arranged for John to get the same deal he had made for himself, and "Big John" moved into Pete's father's old house for only the cost of utilities.

Frank and John were also extremely close. John came to understand the Brody perception of wrestling and said of their friendship, "The hardest battles in wrestling aren't in the ring. The hardest battles are behind closed doors, in offices. Frank was one of the very few who had the courage and confidence to make those fights. Other guys talked big, but then they ran when it came time to stand up. Frank stood up!" Sadly, Studd passed away on March 20, 1995.

Pete got the chance to hear about Frank's business philosophy. "He was a hard businessman," he says. "Lots of times Frank just wanted more than they would give. But he was a student of his business. I didn't know the background, but Frank would tell me about situations and ask, 'What do you think?'" Ortega recalls. "It was his business and his life. Frank just wanted to leave a town in good shape, and him strong, so he could come back to it again. He enjoyed that power game. He was smart and that was his nature.

"It wasn't all dollars and cents. We'd laugh together when he would tell me about a match he had with Abdullah the Butcher where both of them were trying to see who could bleed the most!" laughs Pete. In fact, Frank was also tight with the controversial Abdullah and respected what he had learned from The Butcher.

Once, in the mid 1980s, after his marriage to Barbara and after Geoffrey had been born, Frank and Pete were lifting weights in the gym Frank had put into his garage. Frank told Pete, "I have something to ask you, kid."

Surprised at his tone, Pete said, "Sure."

"If something happened to me, would you be willing to take care of Barbara and Geoff, look out for them?" It was clearly not an easy thing for Frank to ask.

Pete said he laughed and told Frank to stop it. "You'll live longer than any of us," he told Frank. They were both monsters, still young and tough and hungry. Pete thought, what could happen? It was ridiculous. "We were going to grow old together lifting weights," Pete says.

But Frank persisted and, naturally, Pete agreed he would do whatever he had to, under those circumstances, to aid Frank's wife and son. Pete almost forgot about it, until one day Frank invited him to meet at a lawyer's office and Pete saw that Frank was serious.

"I always wonder," says Pete, "if Frank knew something. If he had a premonition? I think of it a lot even now."

Pete, just like Hansen or any other close associate of Goodish, knew about the big man's dark side. Yet friendship is like any intimate relationship in that knowing someone's bad habits, his or her dark side, can make it even easier to like and respect that person. Everyone is a mixture of emotions, desires, faults, and strengths. It all creates a depth of personality with many facets.

According to Gary Hart, Frank was "like a beautiful rose surrounded by thorns. You had to take him with all the barbs."

Terry Funk was once asked to describe what he really thought of Frank Goodish. After long consideration, Terry had one word: "Complex." That term almost always arises when discussing Goodish with anyone who knew him well.

"Frank always had a reason for everything he did," says Funk. "He had a different heart than I did. Not cold hearted, but just different." He laughs fondly. "When I saw him come into a dressing room," said Terry, "what I saw were dollar signs!"

Stan Hansen explains, "Frank's attitude was a combination of how wrestling was run and his own independent nature. I developed the same philosophy, except that I realized sometimes you have to get along to get along. Usually I was able to give the benefit of the doubt. I wanted to achieve certain goals, but I could come home and forget about it.

"With Frank, he went the hard way. He was business 24/7. He was completely defensive and on the alert all the time. If we went different directions sometimes," maintains Stan, "that was just the way it was. We were so together in some ways, and so apart in some ways. But I guess that's what friendship is."

Sam Muchnick, the wise St. Louis promoter for whom Frank seemed to have more respect than almost anyone, had a realistic attitude about friendships in wrestling. "Just because a wrestler or promoter asks about your family or sends you a Christmas card doesn't mean he's your friend," said Sam, who died on December 30, 1998.

"I had many wrestlers who worked for me and made big money. They'd send cards and say thanks all the time, but once they moved on I never heard from them. Were they really friends or just business acquaintances?" asked Muchnick. "A great promoter has to work with everyone. Nobody says you have to be buddies and go out eating together. You just have to do business together."

Muchnick knew it was rare for real, deep friendships to form in wrestling, even though it happened for him with Gene Kiniski and Dick "The Bruiser." Sam explained, "It's got something to do with trust and honesty, but everybody should always be cautious because of the politics in this business. Don't be fooled."

Wrestling, indeed, has always been a strange discipline. While the performers must rely on and trust each other in order to avoid injury while doing battle, they are also competing for that lucrative spot at the top of the program. In the end, the promoter or booker makes that decision. Keeping a bit of distance is a wise choice, even if it is convenient, and actually enjoyable, to travel and hang around together. A true friendship, devoid of jealousy and personal ambition, is rare.

Gary Hart points out, "A lot of people in wrestling, especially some promoters and bookers, were Frank's friends in front of him. Bruise knew that. When the door was closed, they weren't friends anymore. Usually they were figuring out how to take money from him, not pay what the gate was worth, he figured!"

Ric Flair, the colorful performer who eventually held the NWA title, seemed to expose a similar vigilance during a KMOX radio interview in St. Louis during the mid-1980s. Relaxing and talking openly, Flair was asked about who his friends were in wrestling. "Real friends are very hard to find, in wrestling especially. This is a tough business," said Flair. "Most of my friends are really business acquaintances."

For young Randy Curry in St. Louis in the late 1970s, friendship was a different animal entirely. Randy was a teenager and a big wrestling fan. He had, perhaps, more problems than most — life was difficult — so wrestling was a terrific release for Randy. After seeing Brody in action, Randy picked this ferocious brute as his number one favorite.

Curry made sure he was around to walk with Brody when he left the building after a card. They weren't actually friends, but young Randy could fantasize about that when the giant grappler took time to acknowledge and talk to the kid. Randy's spirits got a boost, though it was in fact just the amicable contact between a fan and a wrestler.

Curry looks back and, of course, understands all of that. But for a youngster who had more than his share of troubles and worries in those days, the walks and chats after a show with this superstar he idolized meant everything. Did Frank, a father-to-be, somehow sense what he meant to this kid? Did he perhaps give the youngster a little extra attention, knowing how much it meant to the boy?

Randy saw the hint of a smile, the brief humanization of a character, the relaxation of someone who liked him. Now Randy considers it all and grins. "I was just a sad kid who could believe I was friends with the baddest man on the planet! He'll never know how much it meant to me, what he did for me personally, every time Brody said, 'See you next month!'"

CHAPTER SIX

Barbara Remembers . . .
HOME IN NEW ZEALAND

I was born in New Zealand — a lovely place to grow up. The weather has four distinct seasons, but even in summer you always have to carry a jacket with you. The temperature was seldom below freezing in the winter or above 80 in the summer. The land is rugged, but just marvelously beautiful. It reminds me of the coast of northern California, which I love to visit.

It also rains a lot, so New Zealand has very green, lush vegetation. Everything loves to grow. I remember as a child always going out in the garden to pick vegetables for our meals. Nothing like fresh veggies from the garden.

Actually, we were glad it rained so much because that was the only water supply in those days. You even did your cooking by a coal stove that was also a heating device in the winter. The milk was delivered to the door in bottles by a milkman. You put out the empty ones and they replaced them with full ones.

Boy, times certainly have changed in the last fifty years. Back then, even washing clothes was a challenge. There were no electric washing machines or dryers. To dry the clothes, you would hang them outside on the clothesline and hope they would dry before it started raining again. Then, after all that, you had to iron everything.

I really appreciate New Zealand now that I am older. When you are young, you sometimes don't appreciate the simple things that are right in front of you. The Internet and cable television have really opened up New Zealand. I have even heard my native country called "the adventure capital of the world."

One of my memories was the Beatles coming to town in the 1960s. This was before they set foot in America. They had to drive by my house to get to the hotel and I remember standing outside for hours in hopes of getting a glimpse. Finally they went by — and what a thrill! To me, the Beatles were royalty. In fact, I also saw a lot of the British Royal Family driving by over the years.

My parents would not let me go to the concert that night, even though I begged. I regret not seeing the Beatles live in concert, but parents were very strict in those days. All they saw were long-haired musicians. Look back and you'll realize how times have changed.

I know now that I am the person I am today because of my parents and the way they raised me. Parents are right when they say, "Wait until you have your own children — then you'll understand." You do. You realize so much. Unfortunately, both of my parents are deceased.

It was so isolated living there, though, back in the 1950s and 1960s. New Zealand was almost like two countries. At that time, and even today, the North Island was populated and modernized, while the South Island was not as developed and had fewer people. I grew up in the South Island.

It certainly was thousands of miles and very different from where Frank Goodish was a youngster, in Michigan. It's funny how different paths lead us to change who we are as people and to find each other over time.

In New Zealand, back then, if you did not want to be married young and have kids, you dreamed about escaping into the big cities. I would go to the movies on Saturday afternoons and watch news clips from around the globe. It was a chance to see things I could only imagine.

Television at that time had barely been introduced. It wasn't until 1960 that it had its official national transmission. Even then, it was only one channel, two hours per night, two nights per week. Really, it did not have any impact on me as a person. I grew up reading books and playing outdoors with friends.

By 1968, as a young lass of 19, I was living in Wellington and making plans with a girlfriend to take off for Sydney, Australia. The plan was to get a job, earn some money, and end up in London, England.

At the time, my friend Cheryl was boarding with my parents in the South Island, so I made plans to visit them, say goodbye, and meet up with her. Then we were going to get the train to catch the inter-island ferry *Wahine* back to Wellington on April 10, 1968. That would lead us to taking another ship, *The Southern Cross*, from Wellington to Sydney. My friend was having her 21st birthday party on the night of April 7.

As I came to realize about life, things happen beyond our control. As Cheryl was cutting her cake, the trestle table with the food collapsed and landed on her foot. We ended up spending a good part of the night in the emergency room, where they proceeded to put plaster up to her knee.

When we finally got back to the house, we looked at each other and realized we did not want to cancel our trip that we had dreamed about for so long. Truthfully, our escape was against everyone's advice. Our families wanted us to postpone the trip. But it was something we had been planning for so long.

With my friend hobbling and not supposed to get her plaster wet (this was a long time ago!), we rearranged things, canceling the train and then the ferry trip on the *Wahine* from Lyttleton to Wellington across the Cook Strait. We were lucky enough at such short notice to find a flight to Wellington on the 10th, the same day we were meant to get the ferry across. This meant we would be in Wellington on the afternoon of the 10th instead of the 11th. Arriving a day early gave us a chance to visit with my roommates and stay at my old flat for the night.

Lo and behold, that night cyclone Giselle came ashore. It was the worst single recorded storm in New Zealand's history. Giselle, heading south, hit Wellington at the same time as another storm was driving up the coast from Antarctica.

There were no weather alerts in those days, and, luckily, we were already in Wellington when it hit. The winds in Wellington were the strongest ever recorded at approximately 170 miles per hour. In one Wellington suburb, wind ripped the roofs off 98 houses. Three ambulances and even a truck were blown over as they tried to get to injured people.

We had to get our luggage down to the ship we would be sailing on the next day. I can still remember being blown against the side of the house where we were staying. It was hard enough that I got bruises from the impact. Windows in the house were being broken by the wind. I have been reminded of that day in New Zealand now that I have lived in Florida and been through hurricanes. It was very scary.

The *Wahine*, which we were supposed to be on, got caught in the horrible storm. It was battered and trapped on Barretts Reef. Even though a Wellington harbor tug managed to reach the vessel, when a tow rope was attached, it broke away in the storm. They attempted to abandon ship, but only four lifeboats could be launched and they were swamped.

Finally the *Wahine* rolled onto her side. Though many survivors managed to reach other rescue boats, over 200 were washed across to the rocky, unpopulated eastern side of the harbor. In all, 51 were killed by drowning, exposure, or from being slammed into the rocks.

It was a life-changing moment for me, suddenly realizing that I could have been on the *Wahine* — that I could have been one of those 51 lost souls. The next day, the *Southern Cross* kept on schedule and we had to sail past the *Wahine*, with part of her side out of the water. It gave me chills up my back. The crossing to Sydney was extremely rough, with most of the passengers seasick and none allowed outside on the decks as the waves were so heavy they crashed over the rails.

Neither my friend nor I knew what would be waiting for us in Sydney, especially with one of us on crutches. The events at her party saved us from a terrible ordeal — maybe even death. I have to admit: I do believe in fate. It did not enter our young heads that the storm was still bad out in the Tasman Sea, and we were out in the ocean. Now I look back and realize that when you are young, you "just do it." There is no thought involved as there is when you get older.

We finally arrived to start a new life in Sydney, Australia. Frank Goodish was trying to start a new life as well with newspaper writing, football, and weight lifting in Texas, half a world away. Who would have ever guessed we would find each other?

Bruiser Brody applies pressure to Antonio Inoki.

Frank Goodish at age 8 in third grade.

Graduation from eighth grade.

Aspiring young sportswriter Frank Goodish at the San Antonio *Express*.

OPPOSITE, BOTTOM: Geoff (far left) and his dad visit the San Antonio Zoo with the Ortega family (Travis, Tanya, Rowe and Pete in the background).

TOP: In snowy Japan, even in civilian clothes, Brody was always the center of attention.

BOTTOM: Frank Goodish, the captain of his own ship, studies the sea with Jimmy Snuka.

Brody uses a wicked piledriver to record another victory.

OPPOSI
Japanese star Tenryu gets
eat Brody's kn

Landing a picture-perfect drop
kick on Jumbo Tsuruta.

Brody polishes off the late John Tenta,
who would go on to become Earthquake
in the WWF.

With referee Joe Higuchi watching, Brody blasts Giant Baba with the big boot.

OPPOSITE: There was a good reason that Brody was nicknamed "The Intelligent Monster."

When Brody stalked the ring, fans knew excitement was just a moment away.

OPPOSITE TO
Pandemonium! Bedlam! Chaos! Here com
Bruiser Bro

OPPOSITE BOTTO
A bloody Brody scores with the knee to fini
Ba

Brody was always willing – and able – to take the donnybrook anywhere.

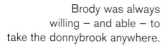

Another victim at the big man's mercy.

Brody prepares to rattle the ring with a body slam on Inoki.

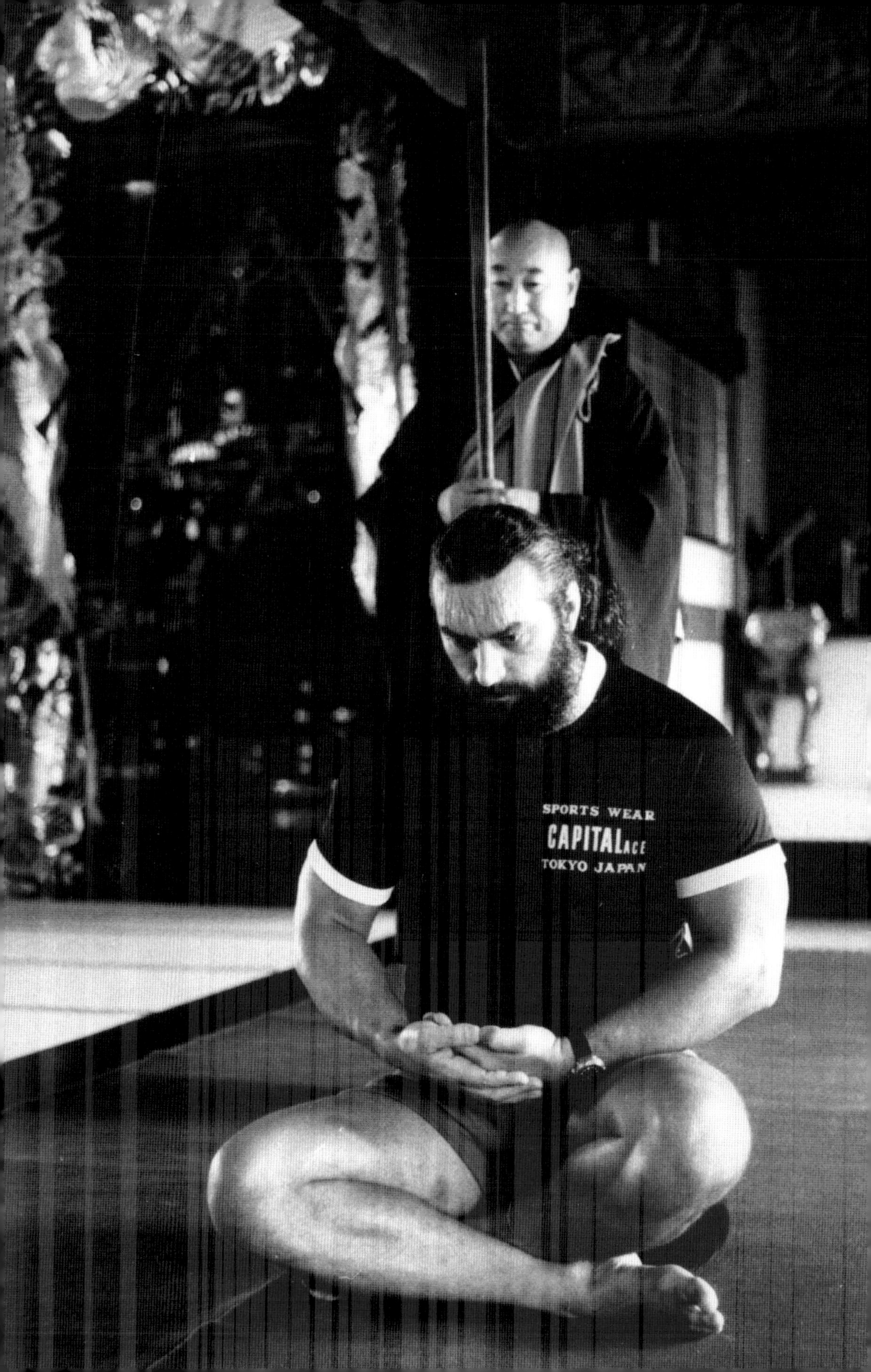
SPORTS WEAR
CAPITALACE
TOKYO JAPAN

GOODBYE GRIDIRON,
HELLO GRAPPLING

When someone asked the boy what he wanted to be, the answer was always the same: professional football player.

Wrestling really wasn't on the radar for the young Frank Goodish. Born June 18, 1946, in Pennsylvania, he was raised in Warren, Michigan, a suburb of Detroit, along with three sisters — Gayle, Gloria, and Kathy. Gayle, Frank's older sister, recalled that her brother wanted to play football more than anything. His pursuit of the gridiron lasted quite awhile.

"We never spoke of wrestling at home or otherwise," Gayle says. "My mom says they never spoke of wrestling until after he entered that arena. That was not a sport we watched at home. I have to assume that one of his acquaintances turned him on to that."

Gayle has fond recollections of growing up in Warren in the 1950s. "It was a simple life," she remembers. "My dad worked hard to provide for his family. He taught us so many important things: to do the best we could in school, to save money for a rainy day, to be responsible."

Their mother was devoted to her husband and the kids. "Everyone loved her and she was so pretty," says Gayle. "Mom was, and still is, the greatest mom in the world. I tell everyone that and I think they are a little envious."

For a long time they were a family of four: two parents with Gayle and "Little Frankie," as Gayle called him. Then it became Big Frank and Little Frank. Frank was ten when Gloria was born and 12 when Kathy arrived. He was four years younger than Gayle. "Frank loved to have pillow fights with my younger sisters and they loved it, too," Gayle recalls. "He hated liver, which we ate once a month because it was healthy. Frank could smell it when he walked in the house. He would ask, 'Are we having liver?' My parents said it was steak, but he never believed them."

Family vacations were spent with relatives in Pennsylvania, a long drive for kids, especially with Frank asking, over and over, when they would get to Grandma's. His father would point out the window and say, "It's just over that hill."

According to Gayle, Christmas Day brought a house full of relatives, friends, and neighbors. "I miss the holidays with family. It was Dad's favorite holiday," Gayle remembers. "He would come into our bedroom at 6 a.m. and tell us to get up. He didn't leave until we were on our feet. He liked to see his family open their gifts.

"Dad died on Christmas Day in 1988," Gayle notes sadly. "Most people are stunned when they hear that. I choose to remember how much he loved Christmas."

Little Frank was "a charmer and sometimes very devilish," says Gayle. "Everyone loved him. We both had lots of friends. Eventually, I got married and Frank went away to school. When he came home for visits, he and my mom would talk for hours."

Eventually, though, that youngster became the explosive Bruiser Brody, after the football dream had passed away and wrestling had become his profession. Gayle still remembers all the trips her little brother made to Japan. "Sometimes Frank would spend a night with my husband, my son, and me on his return from Japan. My son, Mark, worshipped his uncle.

He would invite all his friends to the house. The boys would wait hours until Frank woke up, to see the big man."

Today Gayle reflects that "it all seems so long ago and in a different world." But in that different world, so many years in the past, football was good to Frank — for the most part. He was big even in high school: at that time, Goodish packed 215 pounds on his 6'4" frame. He played tight end on offense, the line on defense, and also served as the kicker.

Teammates recall that the opposition didn't even try to run against his side of the field since he was next to impossible to take out. As well, he had "good hands" and could catch anything near him. When Warren High School went to the ground game, they had their biggest success running off-tackle with Frank Goodish doing the blocking. He was such a devastating player that he even got prep All-America notice.

Frank also starred in basketball at Warren High School. He once said that he really enjoyed playing with that team because they "had a great guard who could handle the ball and shoot. I could hit the boards hard and get those cute little passes for lay-ups."

Pete Ortega was used to "pushing iron" with Frank, but remembers many times going to play basketball together. "He didn't dunk, and he really didn't jump much," Pete says. "But Frank knew how to play the game, how to use his body, and how to get position."

It was football, though, that led Goodish to college. He got a scholarship to Iowa State, where he became a tackle. But he only lasted a year — the young man was wild and untamed. He bounced to Wayne State for a year before moving on to legendary West Texas State, where he was redshirted for one season. That was the school that produced "Mercury" Morris of Miami Dolphins fame, along with plenty of athletes who would become wrestlers. Morris was on the roster with Frank in 1967. West Texas State had an "outlaw" reputation; it was a home for those who just didn't fit in anywhere else.

Tales of Goodish on campus are legendary. Many have heard the one about a bunch of football players cutting down a campus tree. When the football coach angrily questioned who had done it, Frank stepped up and said he had. This, along with a few other incidents, got him removed from the roster. Terry Funk, who is two years older, says it's all true: "And, it was a cherry tree — just like George Washington!"

Goodish was a presence, both a giant and a character. Stan Hansen was another one of those West Texas State football studs. His gridiron career overlapped with Frank's for a year. They developed a friendship that would be rekindled in professional wrestling.

Still, at West Texas State, his sights were set on football. "Going pro was the dream," Hansen stresses. "Getting to the National Football League, playing in the Super Bowl. That's what we talked about. Frank was a hell of an athlete."

Those aspirations would die hard. Both Hansen and Goodish, along with the likes of Bobby Duncum and Ted DiBiase, at different times, chased that goal rigorously. For different reasons, though, it wasn't to be.

Terry Funk was part of the famous Funk wrestling family who were legitimate celebrities in the area during that era. Terry also played football for West Texas at the same time as Frank and claims that football "was just a lark" to Goodish.

Funk jokes that Frank "majored in good times" before he was booted from the school for disciplinary reasons. Goodish never graduated, says Terry, because "he was nuts back then!"

Did Funk sense that Goodish did not take football seriously enough because it came easily to him? Terry is blunt about it. "If he had liked football enough, Frank would have played it. Maturity was probably part of it. He was a great football player, hardnosed and tough. But he didn't give a shit. He didn't need it and it didn't have meaning for him.

"Frank hadn't found his place in life. I'm not criticizing him, because I had a helluva time myself, but I was more focused," explains Terry. "Frank loved being physical, loved being part of the camaraderie, and liked the attention football brought. But no matter what he said, he didn't love football like he came to love wrestling."

Funk also recalls Goodish visiting the matches (usually headlined by the Funk patriarch, Dory Sr.), though not on a regular basis. "He was drawn to it even then," says Terry. "Frank liked that we had respect as athletes. Wrestlers were somebody and it was fun to watch."

Goodish enjoyed being around what Terry calls "the Bolsheviks." Funk considered himself a radical, a "Bolshevik" too, but he had different responsibilities, with a family that ran the office.

At that time, many professional football players wrestled during the off season. Pro football was just barely becoming lucrative enough for players not to need other income. For Alex Karras in the early 1960s, or Dick Afflis, who became Dick "The Bruiser" in the 1950s, wrestling was a common way to earn bucks during time away from the gridiron. The NFL hadn't become the giant revenue producing entity that it is today. Some, like Ernie Ladd and Wahoo McDaniel, made the move to wrestling full time as their football careers wound down. Many who just missed making the grade in football often diverted their energies toward professional wrestling. Football provided a breeding ground for grappling during that period.

Stan Hansen explains, "It was a fine line to cross and accept. To be a borderline player at that level is difficult to accept. You have to do it, though," Stan admits. "I accepted it and never looked back. Wrestling became a real option, in my case, thanks to the Funk family.

"When I finally ran into Frank again, it was through wrestling and I didn't even know he was doing it," Hansen recalls. Their reunion came late in 1974 in the Louisiana-Oklahoma territory run by "Cowboy" Bill Watts and Leroy McGuirk. "Wrestling gave us a chance to make money and still feel that physical thrill.

"And we became good friends. The business moved you around, but when we were together, it was always good," Hansen says. "We trusted each other."

Accepting the end of his football career had not come without headaches for Goodish. In fact, he may have been more interested in playing *after* college than during. Or was it just that he wasn't desperate enough, as Terry Funk suggests? We can't know for sure: Frank Goodish was even then a highly complex personality.

His enrollment at West Texas State, where he majored in journalism, ended in the fall of 1967. Earning a living became job one. In 1968, Frank landed with the now-defunct San Antonio Toros, a semi-pro squad. At the same time, Frank was also working for the sports department of the *San Antonio Express*.

The Toros' owner, Henry Hight, called Goodish a good offensive lineman. And like so many others, he describes Frank as "quite a character." Apparently, in what was perhaps a foreshadowing of what was to come in wrestling, Hight and Frank engaged in a few salary battles. Hight said of Goodish in the *San Antonio Express*, "He certainly did say what he thought." He went on to explain that he believed Frank had the determination to become successful, and that's what led him to wrestling, which Hight called a "crazy" business.

Journalism was also something Goodish dabbled in. When he became a member of the sports department for the *San Antonio Express*, Dan Cook was the editor. Cook hired Frank after hearing that he was loading concrete for $100 a week, and offered him the same pay. He describes Frank as "A good guy who did a decent job for what he was paid." Goodish revisited his newspaper days years later, saying, "Dan Cook used to laugh at me. I'd be trying to type some story . . . But look at these hands!" Frank then raised his huge paws into the air, fingers as thick as Polish sausages. "I'd be hitting two keys at once and cussing to beat the band. And Cook would just laugh harder the more aggravated I got."

In the summer of 1969, the Toros sold his contract to the Mexico Golden Aztecs in Monterrey. Frank made plans for the move, even giving two weeks' notice to Cook at the newspaper, but in the end decided against heading to Mexico. His decision might have been prompted by being unable to explain, thanks to the language difference, who he was and when he was coming when he telephoned the team. He couldn't even get through to tell anyone he'd decided not to report.

In 1970, Frank finally landed his break: a chance with the Washington Redskins of the National Football League. To top it all off, the legendary Vince Lombardi was in his second year as coach of the Redskins. Pete Ortega explained that getting his release from the Toros was a major headache for Goodish. Many harsh words were spoken before the Redskins agreed to purchase Frank from the Toros.

Goodish developed all sorts of respect for Lombardi, even in the short time they got to spend together as player and coach. "After working with Lombardi, I realized that I really did have the ability to do something in football. Until then, though, I'd never paid attention to drills and mechanics. I got serious. It was an education I got too late," Goodish told Buck Robley.

Unfortunately, Lombardi soon contracted cancer, and passed away in September 1970. Bill Austin stepped in to replace Lombardi as head coach and, according to Frank, "it just wasn't the same." Frank hovered right on the edge of making the squad before he was cut at the end of camp. When football ended with the Redskins, though, Goodish had no excuses.

At the time, he told Ortega, "I wasn't coachable." A few wrestling promoters down the road would have vouched for that evaluation.

A long time later, Goodish said, "I always got by just being a great athlete and tough as hell. I could beat people up, so I never bothered to learn the fundamentals. When I got to the Redskins, I was as tough as everyone else, but they knew the fundamentals."

Frank was just as blunt with his wife Barbara years later. "I got lazy when they took me," he told her. He mentioned, though, that Lombardi presented a quality he was just finding within himself. He wondered about what he could have done in football if he'd met someone like the legendary coach years earlier.

"I was just as fast and as strong as all of them," Goodish lamented. "But they had all these basics down cold, and I fought trying to learn them at that point. I always wondered, though, what might have happened if Lombardi hadn't gotten sick."

Down deep, Frank had reached that moment of recognition Hansen talked about. And even though he signed with the Edmonton Eskimos of the Canadian Football League in 1971, the gridiron was going, going, gone.

Frank was married, too, briefly, at the end of college. A relationship of which he spoke little to friends and family, it ended and Goodish returned to San Antonio and lived with his buddy Pete Ortega. The duo got into serious lifting and body building. Goodish spent hours on the loading docks in Dallas for a while, but would always return to pop up at Pete's house, saying, "I'm here, kid."

Eventually Ortega and Goodish would spend Wednesdays unloading meat at the PX in San Antonio. That earned just enough money for them to eat all week and lift weights at the San Antonio Health Club — a place which belonged to a motorcycle cop who loved Goodish. The club also drew many of what Ortega called "the nasties." San Antonio had rough sections, but the pair had connections and friends everywhere through the gym. They ate at the Tip Top almost every day, and many times at Luby's Cafeteria.

This was the early 1970s. Frank and Pete had read about steroids, but mostly they just lifted and lifted. Another smart athlete who was doing the same was Joe Bednarski, who had just gotten into the wacky world of professional wrestling. Of course, Bednarski became famous as Ivan Putski to mat fans around the globe and was on his way to that level in the early 1970s.

But, like Frank, Joe B's background was football. Frank loved football. Joe B loved football. Joe B had been a fullback in college and, like Goodish, couldn't quite get over the hump to the next level. He was cut from the Toros, but he wanted to be part of the team and feel the atmosphere of the gridiron so much that he begged to practice without a uniform. Other players made fun of him, according to Ortega.

Joe B didn't care. He wanted football passionately, and that led to a strong connection between him and Frank. Pete recalls that they worked like dogs with the iron and, finally, Joe B suggested wrestling to Goodish. Frank was open to the idea and, through Bednarski, was put in contact with the biggest name in Texas wrestling — Fritz Von Erich. He was the man who got Bednarski/Putski started.

Wrestling worked for Bednarski. As his fame grew, the same football players who once taunted him now needed jobs and begged him to help them into the mat game. Pete Ortega laughingly recalls that "Joe B just ignored them." But Joe put Frank with Fritz, as well as Joe Blanchard, who was involved in promotion with Fritz at the time in San Antonio.

Von Erich, the "master of the Iron Claw," was really Jack Adkisson, a former rough-and-tumble football player at Southern Methodist in the days of running back Doak Walker. Just as Joe B had, Adkisson clicked with Goodish. Blanchard had played college football himself and was later with Edmonton. Fritz agreed to help Goodish break into wrestling, and later would tell his own sons that he considered Frank "family." Perhaps it was the common thread of football that started it all.

It's possible that, deep down, Frank was unsure. Despite the bravado he showed Stan Hansen, when it came to making the NFL, maybe Frank Goodish himself never really believed he could succeed.

Keep in mind that Goodish had bounced through three colleges and had not, by any stretch, made any All-America teams. At West Texas, Funk saw that "I don't care" attitude and knew Frank's belief in himself was no longer there. Yet the little boy buried somewhere within led to the talks about the NFL with Hansen.

When the opportunity with the Redskins came, Frank wanted it. He had fought to get it. He wanted it more than anything. He wanted it bad. And he failed. He knew why; he took the blame squarely on his own shoulders, and it hurt.

Then, Frank Goodish found professional wrestling. Terry Funk remembers, "Frank fell in love with it. He loved it from the start."

Destiny and reality had collided. Bruiser Brody was about to be born.

CHAPTER EIGHT

Barbara Remembers . . .
AUSTRALIA

You have to experience everything, and I experienced a lot in Australia. My girlfriend and I ended up with a flat in Glebe. I did several months' work for a temporary agency in Sydney. It's a good way to meet people and not get locked into a job that you may not like. I ended up in a big department store as a personal secretary to the gentleman in charge of furniture.

But after several years of the nine-to-five routine, I was looking for something else. I thought of the hotel industry, as it definitely would not be a nine-to-five position and it would offer a chance to meet interesting people. I went to several interviews, but because I had not worked in that area I did not know the machines involved. I had no luck.

I knew I could learn the machines and not have any problem. The question was how could I get some instruction on what I needed to know. So I called up the manufacturer and said I was in town looking to buy equipment for a motel we were opening in Queensland. Of course, they welcomed me with open arms and proceeded to show me all the workings of all the machines involved in hotel/motel management.

The file system was actually quite complicated — this was before everything was computerized. We had to enter all the daily charges — for the room, laundry, food, and so on — into the machine, manually. Then cash payments had to be deducted. In those days many guests did not have credit cards, so they'd pay cash to cover their room charge and other expenses. At the end of each day, everything had to be manually balanced.

At the next interview, I had all the knowledge I needed and ended up getting the job. It was a start to a whole new life. I didn't know at that time where it was going to lead me. Frank thought it was a great story when I told him after we met. He was very surprised to learn that I could be so inventive to go after something I really wanted. Of course, he was never afraid to go after anything.

The hotel was across the road from where I lived at the time, so it was great to get up in the morning and just walk across the street to work. It had advantages, but disadvantages too. Being that close meant you got called in for everything. Someone didn't show up? Guess who got called? It meant working a lot. They were, however, good people to work with and I met a wonderful Maori lady I still keep in touch with.

I decided to leave the job and go traveling. I still wanted to experience it all. When I returned, my friend said she had a job for me if I wanted it. She was now working at a place called the Texas Tavern, which was also a popular hotel. I was a bit doubtful because it was in Kings Cross, which is the place where anything goes in Sydney. Just about everyone who goes to Sydney will visit Kings Cross. I guess it's kind of like a red light district.

She said to come for an interview and wondered if I was like everyone else who prejudged the place without knowing the real Kings Cross. So I went for the interview and found that the people were absolutely great. The owner of the establishment was a Texas gentleman from Big Spring. Even though those interviewing me didn't know me, they met me like I was a long lost friend, so I took the job.

What an experience that was! I learned more about life than any book could ever teach me. People are people no matter what they do for a living. It taught me to look inside people and see their personal struggles. It didn't

BRUNO BEKKER
BRUISER BRODIE
BUTCHER BRANNIGAN

"Brodie" was billed on top of the card in Australia.

matter what side of the social ladder they came from or what color they were. We all breathe the same air and see the same moon and sun.

I also met a truly nice gentleman and we had a wonderful relationship that ended up in marriage. Unfortunately, it didn't work out. Maybe it was for a reason. We should never have been married, because friendship was what we shared, not love. We were such good friends that even after the marriage ended we shared a house with another woman friend. It is hard to find good friends and it was certainly cheaper sharing the rent among the three of us.

When I lived in Sydney, I used to go to Bali, Indonesia, to unwind from the hectic city lifestyle. It was so pristine in the 1970s. I stayed at Kuta Beach in a pension, which was a hut with two cots, a shower that depended on rain to function, and a squat-down loo. It was very primitive.

There was no television, newspapers, radios, or clocks, so you could totally relax and enjoy the Indonesian lifestyle. When you visit a country and stay in the tourist sector, you never see how the real people live.

Staying on Kuta Beach, I learned to tell what time of day it was by the position of the sun. At sunset everyone would meet on the beach and watch the sun disappear on the horizon of the ocean. It was spectacular on a good night.

I know that today it would not be like it was in the 1970s. Progress has reached all the pristine spots in the world. I was very saddened when I heard about the terrorist's bomb that went off at Kuta Beach, especially since I had been there a few times.

Bali touched my soul and left me so much richer for the experience.

A lot of different people from all over the world stayed in the hotel where I worked in Sydney. Many American tourists would stay there, and so would all of the wrestlers who toured Australia. I didn't know anything about wrestling, but the performers were all nice and polite.

The wrestlers became my friends, because a kind word means a lot when you are away from home. They would share their letters from home. They would show me the photographs of their wives and their kids. Actually, most of them were just lonely when they were away from the arena. I was no threat, just someone they could trust and talk with.

As it is with anyone in the public eye, there were always groupies hanging around. The guys called them "arena rats." Most of the time, though, they were really nice ladies who just wanted more than some of the guys were willing to give.

It was a sight seeing everyone from Andre the Giant to the midgets coming into our lobby. One of the midgets had a crush on me, I guess, because he always brought me flowers. I can still remember turning around to see the very top of his head at the level of the counter and he was holding up a red rose.

One day started as simply ordinary, but it turned into the day that would change my life forever. I was working the front desk when I felt this presence. I turned around and here was this gentle giant of a man. He was huge across the chest and shoulders. He had a beard and black curly hair pulled back into a ponytail.

He was very humble, as a stranger is when coming to a new country. I checked him in, gave him a better-than-average room because he was very polite, and sent him on his way.

Hotel policy demanded no fraternizing with the guests on the premises. This man told me later that he liked my calves — he was a "leg man." He said he really believed he was somebody special, but I brought him down to earth because I had treated him like an ordinary person.

His name was Frank Goodish.

CHAPTER NINE

FRITZ, VINCE SR., AND MORE

Frank Goodish wasn't Bruiser Brody right away. He didn't jump into the ring and suddenly become Superman. Most who remember his early days note the fact that he was "green." Pete Ortega explains that Frank was "very crude, even wearing bib overalls!"

But his potential and his look, even with his black, curly hair much shorter, was so evident that it would smack observers right in the face. Something was there.

Fritz Von Erich began working with Goodish immediately and recognized that Frank really had little background in what wrestling was. Luckily, Fritz made the effort to give him some training in the fundamentals he needed to know inside the ring. Bob Roop, an amateur champion from Southern Illinois University, and Bob Orton, Jr., a second generation professional and himself a nationally ranked amateur grappler, were both active with Fritz at the time. Fritz had Orton and Roop show Frank the mechanics.

"We worked with Frank," says Orton, who came to be known as "Cowboy" Bob Orton and is the father of current WWE star Randy Orton. "I really liked Frank. He was a good guy and a great athlete. In the ring, he picked it up very fast."

Thus, on April 22, 1974, in Fort Worth, Texas, Goodish was this giant guy who "bought" a ticket and made a challenge from the audience to test Roop. The challenge was accepted and one week later, on April 29, Frank Goodish butted heads with the highly skilled Roop.

Although it was Roop who emerged victorious, Goodish showed enough determination and raw ability to earn everyone's respect. It allowed Fritz through his "front men" to announce to fans that Goodish had certainly earned the chance to become a professional wrestler and would be training toward that goal. For once in the notoriously deceptive world of wrestling, fans were being told the truth.

Fritz sent Frank to the Oklahoma territory owned by Bill Watts and Leroy McGuirk. It was there that Frank met the wily, inventive Buck Robley, who was booking the territory. Robley picked Loranger, Louisiana, for Frank to make his debut by duplicating the challenge from the crowd angle.

"We didn't let him do anything right away, because he had so much to learn. Plus, he had a lot of back problems. But you know Frank — he was always worried about being sick and always seeing a doctor!" Buck Robley recalls.

Buck notes that Frank was "quiet, actually shy at first in the dressing room. I urged him to come out of his shell, to be who you are. And he did pretty quickly. He was laughing, joking, always getting along with the guys. But he did a few things different — that's when I first saw him eating those beans or peas or whatever they were out of the cans!"

For a while, Robley thought Frank was no more coachable in the ring than he'd been on the gridiron. "We just couldn't get him to relax; he was so intense," explains Buck. "I was loose and light, but not Frank. He was stiff." Frank was also getting input from two experienced "big men" in the business, Grizzly Smith and Luke Brown.

"But he learned, man. Oh, he learned so well," Robley continues. "The facials came easy to him. When we saw how Frank could get into the air at his size, the drop kick became a natural. Nobody could get up there and extend his legs like Frank could. He'd just cut an opponent in half, chop him right off! Frank's legs were the key. They were soooo big. They made him look huge."

Over a decade later, Goodish discussed what a difficult adjustment professional wrestling was for "a real competitor. I was trained to win, to hurt the other guy, to take every advantage," he said. "When I was starting in wrestling, I had to learn how to use my athletic ability to work with someone else and protect them. It went against the grain for a real athlete and competitor."

In that territory, Frank bumped into his old college chum, Stan Hansen. "I didn't even know Frank was wrestling. The last I had heard, he was trying to be a newspaper writer," Stan remembers.

Hansen and Goodish were quickly put together as a tag team and won what was billed as the United States tag team title from Terry Latham and Johnny Eagles on October 10, 1974, in Shreveport, Louisiana.

Goodish definitely learned one lesson about the art of "working" a wrestling match from Dan Hodge. Pound for pound, Hodge might have been the greatest wrestler ever in the amateur ranks. Hodge never lost during his career at Oklahoma University and was accepted as the best on the face of the globe. If he were in his prime today, Hodge might have been untouchable when it came to the newly popularized style of shoot or ultimate fighting.

In 1974, Hodge was the junior heavyweight champion and one of the greatest all-time "shooters" in the pro business. He was in a tag team bout across from Goodish, who had little knowledge about wrestling's history or characters at the time. What Goodish saw was something that made no sense to a "green" 300-pounder — putting over this little guy even if he was the junior heavyweight champion. Frank apparently thought the fans would not buy it.

Jim Ross, then a television announcer and assistant to Watts in the office, recalled that the conflict was extremely short-lived, not a mean-spirited attack or a lack of respect. Ross says, "Hodge was such a gentle soul that he did not take Frank personally and the matter was quickly resolved. I think a few takedowns and one well-applied wristlock convinced Frank that doing show biz was easier than trying to out-horse Hodge. Frank was a fast learner."

Ross recalls a young, tough Dick Murdoch getting into the same situation with Hodge. Dick irritated Hodge so much that Hodge applied one nasty chicken wing which, Ross describes, "was going to cause Murdoch to wet himself."

Goodish was indeed a fast learner, and Murdoch was too. Years later, Goodish praised the likes of the real ring "assassins, the hookers," such as Hodge and Lou Thesz. The respect Goodish had for Thesz in particular was second to none. Additionally, Frank discovered that "working" was, in fact, an art, and the ability to back it up with legitimate toughness was also vital.

Jim Ross, who in time would come to national prominence as announcer and office operative for both World Wrestling Entertainment and World Championship Wrestling, was starting his career about the time Frank was in the same territory for Watts. "He was a real beaut!" says Ross. "Frank was a complex yet simple man."

Ross was often the third man in the ring as a referee for many of Frank's early matches. Jim recalls, "Frank was so *stiff* in the early days."

Even at that time, though, Frank Goodish had a plan and he had opinions. Jim says, "I remember Frank encouraging me to set my sights higher than being 'just a ref.'"

Says Ross, "Goodish was probably the original 'Cerebral Assassin.' I met Frank for the first time in the early 1970s when he was just starting his career and got booked in Mid South Wrestling, which was operated by another ex-football player and intelligent individual, 'Cowboy' Bill Watts.

"Watts and Goodish had a great deal in common as a result of their backgrounds and intellect, not to mention that they were both hard-headed, stubborn son of guns who more often than not did not openly or freely trust those they worked with. I don't know why and it certainly did not make either man a bad guy in my book as I got along with both Frank and 'Cowboy' well."

Ross continues, "Frank and I always had great conversations back in the day and rarely about wrestling. Frank was well read and with his sports writing background was intellectually light years ahead of many of the older, uneducated fellow wrestlers with whom he shared a locker room."

Ross and Goodish, both "rookies" in wrestling (so to speak) bonded quickly. "I don't remember ever having a cross word with him — which probably puts me in the minority especially with some wrestler-promoters around the globe," declares Ross.

The teaming of Goodish with Hansen definitely caught the eye of Ross, who was a superb judge of talent. "One could almost sense that they would be a special entity if they chose to stay together for any substantial length of time. They were two big, rugged stallions who played in the trenches in college football and were both really bright men. They had a nice run in Mid South before leaving to obtain more experience in other areas of the country when wrestling territories actually existed.

"I know that Goodish and Hansen had a blow up or two with Watts, which was not unusual in those days, for talent to disagree with the promoters or bookers," says Ross. "In this case, Watts was both, plus the top hero in the territory. Was there a conflict of interest here as far as the wrestlers were concerned? Absolutely. Frank had no problem expressing himself, even to an intimidating boss like Watts, but as the years went on, apparently, Frank got even better at verbal confrontation with promoters he thought were out to screw him."

Clearly, issues with authority, power, and control popped up early — and were likely always part of the Goodish make-up.

"I am sure that many times Frank was in the right on these issues, but I would equally speculate that at times Frank created a personally induced mindset that motivated him to make bad business decisions," asserts Ross. "As the years went by, I would hear 'horror stories' about Frank's controversial behavior and found it hard to believe because that was not the guy I knew his rookie year in the business."

Robley relates an incident that might have helped form or reaffirm Frank's perception of promoters. After a show in Greenwood, Mississippi, Goodish came out to his old Datsun and found someone had sugared the gas tank. His transportation home was not going to work.

Goodish found Watts and asked for some help by catching a ride. Robley remembers clearly, "Watts said, 'Fuck you. No way.' I guess Watts thought some fan seeing a heel and a babyface in the same car might kill a town that couldn't even draw twelve hundred dollars. Frank got hot and they had a nose-to-nose confrontation." Buck adds, "The message that Frank got was the big-shot star and promoter didn't give a shit about the boys."

Watts and Goodish obviously did not see eye to eye. According to Buck

Robley, Watts saw Goodish getting a big reputation and, as a rugged giant, figured Goodish would be someone he could beat up. "We saw it coming, though, and got Frank out of there before Watts could take advantage of him," Buck declares.

Terry Funk pointed out that Frank learned a lot early in his career from Buck. "Ole Buck could really aggravate you," he comments. "But I loved Buck Robley. He was so smart and he saw that Frank could make money. Robley did a great job at the time running that territory for Bill Watts."

Robley pointed out that Frank also learned a few things that had nothing to do with wrestling but affected his perception of how to handle finances from Boyd Pierce, a ring announcer in the territory. "Boyd was into investing. He was a smart man," Robley says. "He and Frank talked about managing money all the time. Frank learned the money game from Boyd."

Robley adds, "Good thing, too, because Frank also learned that the promoter gets first count on the money in the box office."

Over the years, his acumen at investing the big bucks he earned helped make Frank Goodish even more independent because he wasn't living hand-to-mouth like so many wrestlers who could not or would not manage the cash they were paid.

In late 1974, Goodish spent a few months with the Funks in western Texas, where he picked up more knowledge and experience. Working with the Funks, Dick Murdoch, and "Killer" Karl Kox helped hone what was becoming more and more a unique ring personality. Frank added the nickname "The Hammer," so his billing was Frank "The Hammer" Goodish.

Terry Funk says of Frank's early wrestling days, "It's a learning curve and part of maturing. You could see it coming with Frank. He was going to be the man and, for him, wrestling was a vehicle for what he wanted."

While in west Texas, Frank became buddies with Bobby Jaggers. Two hot and eager young guys trying to make their mark, Goodish and Jaggers bonded at a Waffle House in Odessa, Texas, at two in the morning after a show. "We were half drunk and talked for three or four hours," Bobby laughs. "We were going to change the business!

"Frank was going to weigh over 300 pounds and be in the main event at Madison Square Garden. I was going to be the National Wrestling Alliance champion," recalls Bobby wistfully. "We were going to be fair with the boys and not cheat everyone. We became buddies. He picked me."

Jaggers, though, always accepted one thing. "Frank could be an asshole.

He stuck up for nobody else but himself. You had to understand that. That's the way the business was and Frank knew that."

Frank learned how to work "like a Funk" as well. Jaggers described how over the years, he'd often hear the phrase, "work like a feather or work like a Funk." "Funk" referred to someone who had broken in around Amarillo, Lubbock, El Paso, Odessa, or Albuquerque, or another demanding small town. It referred to someone who worked stiff and hard, laying in punches and kicks. Goodish liked that. "Frank could do it either way — like a feather or like a Funk," Jaggers recalls. "He learned what to sell, when and how, and what *not* to sell too."

Frank headed for Florida and clever promoter Eddie Graham. Soon after he arrived, on December 31, 1974, Goodish became the Florida champion by knocking off high-flying Rocky Johnson (father of Dwayne Johnson, a.k.a. The Rock) in Tampa. The location served the fast-improving Goodish well, as his in-ring persona continued to develop and his natural charisma and athleticism drew crowds.

Frank also had the opportunity to work with, and learn from, the likes of "Thunderbolt" Patterson, Jerry Brisco, Abe Jacobs, Dino Bravo, and even Billy Robinson. Imagine what a battle of wills could have transpired between the proud Robinson and the free-spirited Goodish! But, apparently, all was well, as Robinson did jobs for Frank and Frank did jobs for Robinson. Frank also met "King Curtis" Iaukea for the first time in Florida.

Frank revived his relationship with Jim Ross here as well. Ross was attending the major league baseball umpire school in Tampa at the same time Frank was headlining in Florida for Graham. Ross got word to Frank, who provided Jim and three of his umpire buddies with tickets to a show at the Armory in Tampa.

Afterward, Frank went out with Ross and his pals. "We went to a Denny's for a bite to eat. Frank loved to hear our stories of going to baseball umpiring camp and we loved to hear his stories of his evolution in the wrestling business," Jim recalls fondly.

"Did Frank buy the meal? Heck no!" laughs Ross. "Frank was known for being wise with his money, which on this occasion included *not* buying a meal for five!"

Adds Ross, "I still wish he had bought the meal. Because then I would *really* have a story to brag about."

At that point, one of the pipelines to big money with Vince McMahon, Sr. in New York went through Eddie Graham. Fritz Von Erich could also get a wrestler there. Goodish's size and aggressiveness made him a logical "monster" heel to put against McMahon's World Wide Wrestling Federation champion, Bruno Sammartino.

The territorial system was serving Frank Goodish well. In only two years, he had had the chance to perform in four different areas. Each had slightly different ring philosophies and each had many seasoned grapplers from whom the big man could learn. He observed and discovered what worked, and, just as importantly, what didn't. An entire shadowy culture of professional wrestling was absorbed by Goodish. It all helped hone a strong personality who was ready for Madison Square Garden much more quickly than he or Bobby Jaggers could have imagined over coffee in Odessa, Texas.

As was often the case in wrestling at the time, Goodish picked up a new name — "Bruiser" Frank Brody. He also was fed a series of "jobbers" to destroy on television in the far-flung network wwwf had in the Northeast. Vince Sr. told Goodish/Brody that he was "the monster who's going to challenge Bruno. Don't sell anything for anybody until you are in the ring with Bruno."

Of course, Goodish had received a different set of instructions the first time he got into a cab at the airport in Allentown, Pa. "The driver stuck a gun in my face, robbed me, and tossed me out. That woke me up!" Frank exclaimed.

Where was Vince McMahon, Jr., today the ruler of the mat world as owner of World Wrestling Entertainment, back then? He was the slender play-by-play announcer for those television programs. Years later Frank would recount how much Vince Jr. wanted to become a wrestler, but his father would hear none of it.

"Think the business would be different now if Senior had let the kid wrestle?" he once asked. Frank also remembered Vince Jr. often being late and delaying interview taping sessions with his tardiness while all the boys sat around and waited.

Vince Jr., though, called the action as Brody made his mark. Senior also had Frank take a picture next to a giant poster of the original "King Kong" movie character crawling up the Empire State Building. That photo caught the eye of Gary Hart, then booking in Texas for Fritz. It also got my attention and later was the inspiration to use "King Kong" as Brody's title in St. Louis.

Inside the ring, Brody moved quickly into the top spot against Sammartino, whom Frank described as "strong as a bear and a class guy." Frank and Bruno battled from New York to Boston to Baltimore to Philadelphia. A Texas "death match" at the Garden reputedly drew a capacity crowd of 19,418 on October 4, 1976. There were lumberjack matches and cage matches. While there were plenty of disqualifications and double DQS, in the end it was Sammartino who got his hand raised, and Frank understood that.

During that same run in the WWWF, Frank got to tangle with his old mentor, Ivan Putski, and usually it was Frank who got the win. He also bumped heads with a wrestler named Jose Gonzales, though those bouts were one-sided squashes in favor of Brody.

According to voluminous records compiled by Matt Farmer, a huge Brody fan and independent worker himself, Frank also got to be a tag team partner of none other than Stan Hansen. Of course, Hansen had his own feud with Sammartino. Hansen and Brody had some good scraps against Chief Jay Strongbow and Billy White Wolf, plus a dandy loss via disqualification against Bruno and Putski. Additionally, Frank got to "buddy-up" with John Studd, who was one of the masked Executioners during that period in the WWWF.

By the end of Brody's time with the McMahons, Fritz Von Erich and Gary Hart were eager to have him back in Texas. Stories have always abounded that there was ill will, especially between Frank and Vince's right-hand man, Gorilla Monsoon, when Frank left New York. Today no one can verify the rumor, but Robley remembers Frank saying, "they lied to me." Barbara, however, remembers friendly telephone calls between Frank and Vince Sr. after she had come to Texas.

The rapport between Frank and Gary Hart really blossomed, beginning in February 1977, when Brody (not Goodish anymore in the ring) returned to the wrestling hotbed of Texas.

Hart saw the enormous talent and potential of Brody, and the two clicked on a personal level. In addition, the Von Erich boys were now athletic teenagers who really got close to Goodish.

Kevin Von Erich says emphatically, "Frank was family. My dad treated Frank like a son. He was like a big brother to me, David, Kerry and all of us. We all loved him. He was a big part of my life."

He remembers, "Frank was the real deal. He'd work out so hard. Man, he'd hit that heavy bag and just pound away until the sweat was flying off his body."

Once, when Kevin was feeling full of himself, having worked out hard and being a terrific athlete himself, he began flexing in front of Brody. Frank started laughing, Kevin recalls. "Kevin," Frank told the eldest Von Erich boy, "there's only one thing better than a good little man. And that's a good big man!"

By this point in his career, Brody was very careful about the opponent he would sell for. He worked stiff and snug. Hart explains, "Bruise had the gimmick of being a wild and crazy guy. He hurt opponents, made people believe and get scared. He had a persona."

Kevin recalls, "Working that way, I'd catch a potato [a legitimate and hard punch or kick] now and then from him when I got in the ring a little later. But I could never complain, because I know I did it to him a lot. And he never complained or griped. So I knew I couldn't either — just part of the business. 'If it didn't knock you out, keep going.' He had to have his respect. If someone was a problem in the ring, Frank would kick their ass."

Kevin, who was himself a top attraction by 1980, benefited from Brody's success. "I learned how to work in front of big crowds from Frank. So did David. We'd be nervous, but if Frank was there, it was like a night off. Just relax, he'd tell me. He was real easy to work with."

So comfortable was Fritz with Brody that the "master of the Iron Claw" put Frank over right in Dallas on April 13, 1977. The victory gave Brody the North American title that Fritz had held and was, next to the NWA World Championship itself, the territory's biggest prize,

But Texas was not without its bumps, most notably in Houston. Paul Boesch was the promoter there, and he had a working agreement with the Dallas office. At the time, Boesch and his booker Joe Blanchard put together their own lineups but with ample use of the talent from Fritz's office in Dallas.

Boesch was enamored with Bull Curry, who had been a major star during the 1950s throughout Texas. With curly, dark, black hair and huge eyebrows, Curry was a tough guy and made a ferocious appearance. By 1977, however, Bull was almost in his seventies.

After a special referee appearance, Blanchard and Boesch wanted to put

Curry against Brody in a Houston main event. They figured it would be a guaranteed box office with the two tough guys from different eras. Hart begged Blanchard not to do it. "You know how Bruise is. You can't do this. Brody won't sell for him because of his age," warned Hart. "Bruise will be in a bad, bad mood and he'll just do the walk back to the dressing room and wave good bye."

Unfortunately, Boesch ignored Hart's plea and made the match. As Hart had predicted, it was a fiasco that ended with Brody smacking Curry around and walking out of the ring.

Boesch and Blanchard were furious and called in Hart.

"Why did you let that happen?" they asked him, even though he had forecast the problems. But the heat was put on Hart, especially when Boesch told him that Brody had intentionally hurt Curry with hard punches.

Hart contacted Frank, who looked Gary right in the eye and said, "I'm not proud of what I had to do. But trust me, Gary, the old son of a bitch tried to sucker punch me and I won't take that from anyone."

Amazingly, Houston wanted to do a rematch! The first bout had drawn well, relations between Houston and Dallas were tense anyway, and Hart had been stuck in a tricky spot. He was always clever and a true diplomat, trying to placate all concerned, so again he went back to Brody.

"Bruise, I'm in the middle here," Hart told Brody. "I understand personal pride and I understand wanting it to make sense. But please, please, as a personal favor to me, don't hurt Bull this time."

Brody just shook his head and looked at his friend. But he kept his word in the match, working "like a feather" with the aging Curry, getting disqualified, and storming out of the ring, all within two and a half minutes.

Over that sizzling spring and summer, it was far easier for Brody to have slam-bang donnybrooks with the likes of Fritz, Wahoo McDaniel, Jimmy Snuka, Rocky Johnson, Harley Race, "Big John" Studd, and even Andre the Giant. He was drawing big money. Says Hart, speaking not only of that run in Texas but of other controversies later in Frank's career, "If he was in a bad mood, someone gave him a damn good reason to be in that bad mood."

"There are a lot of mid-card guys who put in quality time and get main events in the right context," explains Hart. "But there are not many real show-stoppers. Brody was a show-stopper."

The big man was also learning about the business. In those days, Frank always pestered Hart about getting a copy of the National Wrestling Alliance directory that was given to members only at their annual late summer convention. "I can't do that, Bruise," Hart would say. "It's got everybody's home phone numbers too. It's the Holy Grail of the business, brother!"

Brody, though, kept bugging Hart for a booklet. When a new one came out, Frank suggested Gary rip off the cover or even black out certain items; Frank said he would figure out the rest. So Hart tore off the cover and gave Frank an old booklet. It was what gave Frank Goodish the chance to start booking himself, as he made his own contacts to set up a tour of Australia and New Zealand. Before he left, Frank did "the right thing for business," as they say, and dropped the North American laurels to old friend Studd on July 25, 1977.

Two very important things happened to Goodish, one personal and one professional, as he headlined throughout Australia and New Zealand. First, he met Barbara, the lady who would become his wife and the mother of his child.

Second, he became much closer with "King Curtis" Iaukea and Mark Lewin. Both were strong-willed free thinkers who had great success outside the mainstream of wrestling in the United States. Lewin, however, had earned a good reputation in his early days as a tag team partner with Don Curtis in the Northeast. "King Curtis" and Lewin were very independent, and this probably appealed to Goodish.

According to Gary Hart, Curtis deeply influenced Frank to the point that he almost became, in Hart's words, "a disciple." Already full of fight, fire, and self-reliance, Frank Goodish picked up even more as he learned about the mental game of wrestling from "King Curtis."

According to Hart, Curtis strengthened the belief Frank had in himself that said, "I can do anything I want in wrestling because I am who I am."

Buck Robley notes that Curtis, and later Abdullah the Butcher, taught Brody how to "get color" and make the blood mean something. "The way Frank worked," says Robley, "he needed to do it." Most importantly, according to Buck, Brody knew *when* to bleed and he learned much of that from both Curtis and Abdullah.

Buck said that Frank always got the razor blade he carried as sharp as he could, to a very point. "He liked to carry the damn blade in his mouth!" Buck recalls. "Most guys taped it to a finger or something. Lots of times Frank had the damn thing in his mouth."

"I'm a blade freak," Frank admitted once, discussing the method of using a tiny, sharp piece of razor blade to gash one's own head and get color. "Must be something weird somewhere, but I like it. I like the reaction I get when I fight through the blood and the crowd is with me.

"I can tell when I'm going to bleed good," said Goodish, describing the subtle noise when he sliced his own forehead. "If it sounds like a scratch, that's a scrape and it won't be much color. If it sounds like paper tearing, it's going to bleed buckets. I did it a few times, and then it was what most promoters expected from me. So I did it again."

Terry Funk explains that everyone in wrestling takes things from someone else. "I grew up watching Johnny Valentine, Pat O'Connor, Jose Lothario, and Eddie Graham. You incorporate things you see great workers do into your own style, maybe tweak it a little bit, put your own twist on it.

"That's what Frank did with 'King Curtis.' He saw things that worked, added a little or took away a bit, and made it his own. Everyone emulates someone. Mick Foley, when he was Cactus Jack, took little pieces of Bruiser Brody. That's how this business evolves in the ring," says Funk.

Hart says that Mark Lewin, a very clever character but not trusted by many promoters, taught Frank subtle psychological tricks of wrestling. "You don't have to kick someone twenty times to make an impact with the fans," he explains. "Mark got through to Frank that two or three really hard kicks at the right time were what counted."

When he was booking Texas, Hart put Lewin and Brody together hundreds of times over a year and a half. "Every match was different. It never got old; it never got stale. Brody and Lewin could bring down the house," he declares.

Once, when Robley was booking San Antonio after the town had split away from Von Erich, Brody discovered that the promotion was paying another wrestler more, even though Brody was in the main event. "Frank was working with Lewin and they just killed the town," Robley says. "They did 28 minutes that seemed like two hours of nothing." In other words, Brody and Lewin rested in a headlock for nearly half an hour. The attendance went down for cards following that boring main event.

"If they weren't getting paid what they thought was right, that way they made sure there was no money for anybody, especially the promoter!" explains Buck.

"King Curtis" in particular really made Brody understand the impor-

As a booker, Buck Robley was like a clever colonel manipulating his soldiers.

tance of the interview and the television camera, which have been a life-or-death combination for wrestling since the late 1950s. The ability to "get over," to project a unique character, is crucial to any wrestler who wants to draw money in main events. Iaukea was known as great "on the stick [microphone]" in many territories. Brody rapidly became one of the finest at that demanding art as well.

Robley notes that when Frank returned from Australia, he knew exactly how to move during an interview, "Forward, back. Hands moving. That giant face pushed forward. Keep looking into the camera with those eyes. He was so big and intimidating. He got your attention and made his point. The image was frightening."

On one occasion, Brody dropped to his knees during an interview for *Wrestling at the Chase*, the St. Louis television show. He was so strong visually and verbally that the camera found him in a second. When it did, Brody was just staring and driving home the key points of an upcoming match.

Hart adds, "He always had that big Brody head and piercing eyes. He kept his forehead looking that way with all the scars because of the impact it made on television. His energy just jumped out at you, especially after Curtis got into his mind."

When Frank got back in action in Texas early in 1978, all the pieces were really coming together. Says Hart, "Frank really understood his character. It was so clear he was one of those few who could really draw money, and he knew it."

Robley landed in Kansas City as the booker, opening the door for

Brody to hit that area. "He knew by then you usually didn't want to work for a place doing good. Go to the bottom, build it up, and call your own shots," he explains. "We both learned together.

"It always came down to the pay day, always the pay day!" Robley says. "The promoter got the first count, and we learned that the wrestlers didn't always get the right count. How much got skimmed? Frank had the heart. He was willing to fight for his. He was usually two steps ahead. 'They're gonna get their money because they get first count, but then I'm going to get mine,' was Frank's theory."

Both Hart and Robley admit to having had "little bumps" with Brody. "He caused a few little problems," recalls Gary, "but nothing major."

"Frank learned how to call his own shots," Buck noted. "He stiffed me a time or two. It was a power trip for him. He just wanted to remind me that you can't draw without Brody."

But Hart insists that if "he was upset, there was a damn good reason. As long as everyone kept their word, he was like the rest of us. He wanted to make money. We all did. Because of the character he was, Bruise was going to be a *big* part of drawing money anywhere."

J.J. Dillon met Frank when both were wrestling in Australia. After working in many territories, Dillon later came to national notice as the manager of Ric Flair's "Four Horsemen" before doing a tenure working in the office for Vince Jr. in the early 1990s. He also chronicled his career in the book *Wrestlers Are Like Seagulls*. While J.J. didn't cross paths all that often with Brody, he had great respect for the big man.

"We got along great. He was enjoyable to be around. He had simple needs, a frugal lifestyle, and knew what he was," Dillon says. "Frank was a free spirit, even rebellious. Lots of guys talked big about standing up to promoters, but then shut their mouths when the time came. Frank was not intimidated. He stood up."

J.J. was aware of all the stories about Brody. "Despite [the stories], he definitely never wanted for work. Something Frank had came through to the people. One time on television and he was over. He always got hired because he always drew money."

After St. Louis was added to the mix, the door to Indianapolis opened. There might be a side trip to west Texas and Amarillo, maybe a shot or two in the mid-South. It always came back to Texas. Definitely on top of the card.

His fury in the ring was captivating; everything clicked whenever that camera locked onto Brody's magnetic face and personality.

The week before he took on Harley Race in St. Louis for the National Wrestling Alliance title, Brody did a memorable interview with me, as I was the television commentator for St. Louis' legendary *Wrestling at the Chase* show. I'll tell you what was said, what was *not* said, and *how* what was said was said . . .

During my first question, Brody was pacing relentlessly and puffing, a bundle of energy close to the announcer and grabbing the viewer's attention both by sight and sound. Then . . .

"I've waited one long stinking year to get my chance at Harley Race. I've proved myself in this ring time and time again. Right here in St. Louis, I beat every active former world champion." He drew out each word with a growl.

"I beat Jack Brisco. [Pause] I beat Terry Funk. [Pause] I beat Pat O'Connor. [Pause] I beat Dory Funk."

Moving his face into the camera head-on, he continued: "It's about damn time 'King Kong' Brody collected some dues from your World Champion, Harley Race."

I pointed out that Race would have to be crippled before he'd lose the gold belt. Brody was intent, and then he barked, "Harley Race has had an easy street, let me tell you. He's been in the ring with Dick 'The Bruiser,' who I personally almost crippled." He pointed his thick fingers right into the viewer's face. "He's been in the ring with Teddy DiBiase, who I personally ran head face-first into this wall over here."

More movement, back and forth, drawing the camera.

"He's been in there with 'Nature Boy' Ric Flair, who's just a little too pretty to be winning any titles at all." There was disdain in that gravelly snarl.

"Well, finally, he's gonna get into the ring with somebody who, if he wants to get crippled, can cripple him!

"If he wants to come out there and take a beating like he should, he can come out there and get beat fair and square . . . Or he can get beat *up* fair and square."

Hands moving, big paws, threatening, pointing.

I asked a question that referred back to a Race interview, in which the champ claimed Brody was not quick enough, mentally, to beat him for the title.

Brody's voice lowered, became serious: "I don't claim to be the smartest man that stepped inside this ring, but I'm smart enough to know that when

I get in with Race or any other man in professional wrestling . . ."

Suddenly, it was as if the volume had been turned up: "I'll stick one of these" — he raised his huge boot to the camera — "you know where!

"And one of these" — a big fist threatened the camera — "you know where!

"Harley Race has made the claim that he's better than anybody else in the world at what he does — professional wrestling. He's beaten everyone else."

Brody leaned into the camera, wild hair falling over his scarred forehead: "But Race, your best is not good enough for the king. You just be there and I'll show you what the best is."

Something Frank truly believed was that you should never promise something in an interview that wasn't going to happen — doing so would devalue every future promise. So, please note: he never promised to win the title. Obviously, he realized that wasn't going to happen. But he did say that he would physically pound the champion — and, of course, he did. But ultimately, it was Brody's movement — the intensity, the eyes — that made his interviews unique.

More than four years later, in 1983, when I was running opposition in St. Louis and Brody was set to clash with Professor Toru Tanaka, Frank did a great psychological interview. Tanaka was near the end of his career, physically imposing with a terrific look, but not nearly the soldier he'd once been. Injuries, age, and illness had robbed him of his mobility, though he was still deeply respected by those in the dressing room.

With the interview, Brody managed to make Tanaka more dangerous than anyone thought he was. Telling a story about Tanaka using his vicious chops to bust bricks out of a wall, making clear how impressive it was, pulling his eyelid back when he talked about keeping an eye on the Professor's dangerous hands, making clear he would take punishment and letting everyone see his forehead which, by then, was a road map of scars, Bruiser Brody sold tickets for the event with the sheer force of personality and charisma.

In the bout itself, Brody was a fabulous "worker." He put himself into position for Tanaka's ruthless chops, sold them perfectly, and made Tanaka look ever-so-dangerous. Brody's triumph was made that much more important by the simple fact that he had become a tremendous worker by any definition, both in the ring and on the microphone.

Terry Funk maintains that the key to success for Brody or any superstar is "the ability to work with a broomstick, and Frank learned how do it. Working isn't choreographing forty bumps in a row that have to follow in that exact sequence. A great worker has to know how to lead and control a match. Frank had that talent naturally.

"Eventually Frank reached the point of knowing he was better than great. He was able to understand and to dominate when he had to."

Mark Nulty, who was handling the play-by-play on television in San Antonio, was in awe of an interview Brody did for an upcoming "street-fight" match. "He was just brilliant," remembers Nulty. "Brody wore combat boots, sweat pants, and an army helmet over that long curly hair. It was right out of the movie *Patton*. You couldn't take your eyes off of him."

Robley, wanting to do something different to help Brody get over in Atlanta, gave Frank an idea for an interview and the big man ran with it. The show came from a small television studio where the room was set up for a few folks in wheelchairs to watch the action. "Colonel" Buck Robley suggested Brody grab one of the wheelchairs to put his fallen victim in during the interview.

"The young guy Frank beat was terrific, really sold and took a pounding. Frank grabbed a wheelchair and put this fellow in it," Robley laughs. "Then he started to push him over to where Gordon Solie was for the interview. By accident — it wasn't intentional — Frank ran the damn wheelchair into the ring post and the poor guy jerked forward and cracked his head on the post.

"Man, the blood was flowing while Frank did the interview and the kid just laid half-conscious in the wheelchair," says Buck. "When Frank finished the interview, he knocked that guy right out of the wheelchair. He was over big time then!"

All of those qualities were coming together in such an incredible package in 1978 that Bruiser Brody, or "King Kong" Brody in St. Louis, was becoming one of the hottest commodities in wrestling. Though his dark side rattled some promoters, the fact that this man could draw a house — a big house — gave Frank Goodish the opportunity to cash in.

CHAPTER TEN

Barbara Remembers . . .
THE ROMANCE

After my first encounter with this huge, rugged wrestler who had such a gentle side, we had many other conversations. I had really been the first person he had talked to when he arrived in Sydney. Our friendship started to grow.

About six weeks later I was working a three-to-eleven shift on a Friday evening, which was the night of the wrestling matches in Sydney. I was getting ready to go home at the end of my day. My boss also had a restaurant and bar called the Bourbon and Beef just up the street from the hotel. Occasionally, we would go there to unwind after work. It was like our second home — we couldn't eat or drink at the Tavern because we worked there. Going to the Bourbon and Beef, though, was fine.

As I was leaving, all the boys came back from the card and asked if I would like to have a drink up the road with them. One of them was "Killer" Karl Krupp, whose real name was George Momberg. Sadly, Karl passed away on August 24, 1995, after contracting hepatitis while in Japan. He was a very nice fellow.

At any rate, Karl had been staying at the hotel for some time and we had become good friends. When he asked me to join everyone, I didn't think anything of it. There were about six of them, including the midgets, who went to the Bourbon and Beef.

We got a big table at the restaurant and simply had a wonderful time and great conversations. They were talking about the matches for that night: how they went, about working with each other, what the crowd was like. They knew me and trusted me, so everyone was talking honestly and openly.

After a while, I noticed that one by one the boys were disappearing until finally there was only me, Frank, and Karl left. Then Karl excused himself from the table, which left just Frank and me alone. Karl never came back, and I found out later that Frank had asked Karl to help get an opportunity to talk with me alone.

We stayed and chatted about everything under the sun until the place closed down. Then we just walked the streets and I remember finding this park bench where we sat down and talked some more. It was the wee hours of the morning. Finally, Frank put me in a taxi to go home and he walked back to the hotel.

That was the beginning of our relationship. Over a period of a couple months, we became very good friends, going out on a Friday after work and getting to know each other. There were many hours of conversation without being romantic at that point. It may sound silly, but it really was an old-fashioned romance.

I sensed a lot of private things about Frank. He was so different from the others in wrestling. For instance, I liked Karl, but there was no spark. With Frank, there was definitely a spark. We had so much in common. The relationship built very slowly, though. He sent flowers and little telegrams when he was on the road.

We became friends before becoming lovers. It made falling in love more intense, I think. We gradually became so comfortable with each other and

Frank and Barbara enjoy a Las Vegas vacation with friends George and Margaret.

then we realized — my goodness — we were in love!

As things evolved, Frank began staying with me and we kept our relationship away from the hotel. When the folks at the hotel found out, they were very surprised. They warned me, because they had seen many people hurt and left behind. Don't be fooled, they would tell me. Don't take this seriously.

Frank and I always talked. He told me about his life in wrestling. I learned how hard and demanding it was. We talked about us and what we felt. Finally he asked me, "Where do you want this to go?"

My mom passed away two days before Christmas, on the 23rd of December, 1977. I had been scheduled to arrive home on the 24th for the holiday season. Sadly, I was too late. I had been excited, as I was going to tell my mom about Frank Goodish, the wonderful man I had met.

Frank had gone home to the States to wrestle over the holiday season and then he was scheduled to come back to Australia. I remember calling him at Pete and Rowe's, where he was staying, and informing him about my mother's passing. He talked to me and comforted me in my time of grief.

One Friday night after he'd returned, he came back from the matches around 11 p.m. He had had a slight disagreement with the promoter, which I had learned was nothing unusual. Most promoters promised the earth and delivered nothing. When it was promoters against wrestlers, the wrestlers were always the ones losing.

Frank said he was going back to the United States on Sunday. "I want you to come, Barbara," he told me. He was so serious. Frank invited me to join him in the States when I could. Then he put money down on the table, lots of hundred dollar bills. This would pay for my way to the States — and back, if I didn't like it there.

By then I knew he was tight with a dollar and the money on the table was all the conversation that was needed. No promises, just an open invitation to be part of his life. Frank showed he trusted me, because he had no guarantee I would come. I could have just kept the money, but our whole relationship was a trusting, honest one.

I believe you have to make the most of opportunities when they're presented. It was my chance to visit a country I had never expected to go to but had heard so much about. It was a chance to be with Frank. I guess if it hadn't worked out, I'd have gone to London like I'd thought about years before instead of back to Australia.

Ten days later, I followed Frank, with no real idea what to expect.

CHAPTER ELEVEN

KING KONG
IN ST. LOUIS

Mix together the naturally independent, rambunctious personality of Frank Goodish with the hard education of cut-throat professional wrestling learned by Bruiser Brody. No wonder Frank Goodish found St. Louis and the St. Louis Wrestling Club, under the stable hand of promoter Sam Muchnick, to be something of a paradise island surrounded by a huge sea of backstabbing sharks.

This, of course, was prior to Vince McMahon, Jr.'s changing the landscape of the business, until it was essentially just one organization, whether any performer liked it or not.

The St. Louis promotion was organized and detailed. The money was good, with no attempt to hide the actual gate receipts from the talent.

Best of all, Frank found that he could trust Muchnick to keep his word, perhaps even more reliably than Fritz Von Erich himself, as far as Goodish was concerned.

Fritz had coached Frank about how important St. Louis and what happened there were to the wrestling world. Thus, Frank was primed and pleasantly surprised to find the town to be everything Fritz, and others, had told him over the early part of his career.

Needless to say, Frank "got over" immediately. Huge, charismatic, very athletic, able to talk with deep emotion. The explosive violence was always right there, on the very edge, easily recognizable. Plus, Frank was a massive, muscular 300-pounder who could throw a nasty drop kick!

The only drawback was the influence of the Kansas City operation (owned by Bob Geigel, Pat O'Connor, and Harley Race), which had a portion of the stock in St. Louis. O'Connor was the booker for Sam, who laid out ground rules and frameworks inside which O'Connor (and any booker in St. Louis) had to work. Still, Frank's rapport with Kansas City was always rocky. The key question was usually whether or not Buck Robley was booking there.

In St. Louis, Frank became a close and trusted friend of mine. I was Sam's right-hand man and contributing more and more to the booking as time went on. Frank told Pete Ortega that "you can't trust anybody in this business, but I know I can count on Larry. He gets it done." Once again, Frank had picked me — just as he had picked Pete Ortega — and let me inside a tight, select circle.

I was the television commentator for *Wrestling at the Chase* on July 29, 1978, when "King Kong" Brody made his St. Louis debut by whipping Ed Schaeffer. And yes, it was "King Kong." I had suggested to Muchnick that having another "Bruiser" when St. Louis was already headlined by Dick "The Bruiser" would be confusing, and both Sam and Frank agreed. I had been impressed by a publicity photo of Brody standing next to a giant poster from the original "King Kong" movie that was taken when Frank worked for Vince McMahon, Sr.

Brody delivered the goods for Muchnick and St. Louis. His matches were intense and exciting. On television, he had a draw with Terry Funk and a double disqualification with Ted DiBiase. At the hallowed Kiel Auditorium, he pinned Jack Brisco on September 16 and whipped O'Connor on October 6.

Schaeffer would again be Brody's foe for television on October 28, 1978, when the nondescript but very strong performer made the mistake of barking in Frank's face during the introductions. Barking upon his ring entrance was a Brody trademark, and he was irritated at the disrespect Schaeffer had displayed.

Buck Robley, watching the monitor in the dressing room, saw that Schaeffer tried to muscle Frank into the corner. Referee Lee Warren recalls, "Frank told me to stay out of the way unless I wanted to get hurt real bad." Warren did. And Schaeffer was — hurt real bad.

Brody split Schaeffer's eye open and pounded on him with sledge-hammer forearms and kicks that a football punter would unleash. Nothing was held back; everything was meant to hurt. It was a shoot. Schaeffer was destroyed. In the commentary, I picked up on the fury of Brody's assault and added a fervor that let every viewer know they were seeing something totally unexpected and unique.

Ed Warren, Lee's brother and the other referee, was in the dressing room when Brody stormed in after annihilating Schaeffer. "Frank found the two guys Schaeffer had driven in with and challenged them since their partner was so unprofessional," Ed recalls. "They wanted nothing to do with it. Then Frank grabbed Schaeffer's clothes and threw them out in the hall."

But that was a rare kind of moment in St. Louis. Muchnick actually understood that Schaeffer had tried to embarrass Brody and thus had paid a price for his mistake. He was not angry. In addition, the Warrens loved working with "King Kong."

"Frank was a good guy," Ed Warren explains. "He never put you in the middle and always respected us."

Ed's brother Lee, who later officiated independent St. Louis area shows with bloody battles between Brody and Abdullah the Butcher, adds, "I don't know how he was other places, but Frank was a real professional and a lot of fun to work with here."

One young fan at that time found a small crack in the ferocious façade of Brody. Randy Curry, who later became an independent wrestler himself, was perhaps 15 at the time of the Brody destruction of Schaeffer. "I went to the shows with my dad and two of my brothers," Curry explains. "I just became a big Brody fan right away, even though everybody booed him. He was almost in a gray area, though, because it seemed as though fans liked him even when they booed him.

"I started walking with Brody when he left Kiel after the shows. He was very careful not to break character, and I was respectful. Eventually he started to loosen up and finally I got him to smile one night. That was tough, to get Brody to smile," Randy recalls. "I had a T-shirt made with his picture on it, so he knew I idolized him.

"I was just a kid, but I started to realize there were two sides of him," says Randy. "He was so big, massive and scary, but I knew he liked us." In those days at the KPLR-TV studio, Brody often tossed his furry ring jacket to the youngster as a way of acknowledging him.

The explosion with Schaeffer sticks out in Curry's mind even today. "The studio got so quiet. All we could hear was Larry all excited and calling the match. The sound of Brody hitting Schaeffer was like bombs exploding! People's eyes were bugging out; their mouths were just hanging open. We almost felt compassion for Schaeffer," Randy explains.

"Brody was obviously in a rage. When he jumped out of the ring, everybody just scattered. They were scared. I was a kid, though, so I sort of reached out to touch his elbow — to maybe say it was okay — when he went past. My dad grabbed me, nearly tore my arm out of the socket he was so terrified that Brody might do something to me," Curry recounts.

Randy turned to his father then, and said, "Dad, he won't hurt me. Brody *likes* me!"

And, after the taping finished, Brody made sure he took a moment to chat with Randy in the KPLR parking lot. Perhaps he had cooled off by that time, and maybe Buck Robley knew the reason. According to Buck, the battered Schaeffer approached Brody in the hallway — and apologized.

Early on, Frank grasped the importance of St. Louis. "This is pressure," he said. "St. Louis *always* draws. So a new guy has to bring in the crowd or it's definitely *his* fault. But if you get over big in St. Louis, everybody everywhere wants you. Made it in the big time!

"Go to a place like Kansas City, where their crowds are lousy," explained Frank. "If you don't draw, it's the promotion's fault. You don't get blamed. But when you draw money there, everybody notices because they know it has to be the performer. So you get more bookings because you brought alive a dead territory."

Muchnick, older and wiser, became comfortable with Brody when many thought he would not. They forgot that Sam had become close friends with Dick "The Bruiser," a rebel from an earlier era. Sam and

Frank were not close friends; time and their age difference prevented that.

But Sam sensed the fire in Frank Goodish and he respected it immensely. Muchnick followed his own credo of going with what he knew personally about someone, not what rumors and stories said. Obviously, Frank also sensed something in Sam Muchnick, perhaps a level of professionalism that was rare in wrestling. There was no drama, no controversy, in what Goodish did in St. Louis.

Well, there was some minor controversy. At one point, Frank became embroiled in an argument with Muchnick's friend Dick "The Bruiser." Dick owned the promotion in Indianapolis, where Brody worked in main events. Always sensitive about money, Brody felt "The Bruiser" had shorted him. Talking — well, arguing — about it didn't solve the problem.

Things came to a boil at a "spot" show in Peoria, Illinois. At the end of the evening, Brody stormed back to the locker room and first spotted Dick's son-in-law, wrestler "Spike" Huber. "You want part of this?" snarled the irate Brody. "Spike" said it wasn't his battle.

It took only a few angry words before the two "Bruisers" were battering each other. Frank cracked Dick's head open, knocking him goofy, and a row of lockers was demolished before the situation could be defused. Word of the altercation spread fast, and O'Connor tried to get Muchnick to pull Brody off a card in St. Louis on February 6, 1981. Geigel called Hart to complain that Frank had knocked out "The Bruiser."

In Sam's own effective and quiet fashion, though, he did not change a thing and made a few phone calls to inquire into what had happened and, more importantly, why.

That evening, it was odd for "The Bruiser" (usually a late arrival) to be in the building so early, and the atmosphere was unusually tense for the normally relaxed St. Louis dressing room. Eventually, Brody stomped up the steps. At that moment, Dick came around a corner. He held out his hand, with thumb cocked and forefinger and middle finger extended like a gun pointed at Brody.

Between the fingers was a check. "Here!" snapped Dick. Brody examined the check and said, "That's fine. Thanks." Dick nodded. "We're square then." And life went on smoothly for St. Louis wrestling. The simple fact that Dick "The Bruiser" had coughed up money after the scuffle would seem to indicate that Brody had, in fact, had a reason for his outburst.

A few years later, Brody recounted the entire story. "I'll fight for what I got coming. Dick was the same way. He had to be 50 years old when we had that fight! Brother, did he battle. He must have been something when he was thirty. We had an argument, we settled it, and that was that."

On November 7, 1980, Brody was booked for a preliminary "squash" against Takachiho (later to be "The Great Kabuki" in Texas) at Kiel. Early that morning, while Frank was on the road from a Kansas City booking, his wife Barbara had been rushed to the hospital to give birth to their son Geoffrey.

Arriving in the morning, I got the message from the hotel operator in the Lennox Hotel (where the office was at the time) downtown in St. Louis. I left word for Brody to come right to the office. By then, Frank knew Barbara had delivered Geoffrey. When he walked into the office, the first thing Sam said was, "Why are you here? Go to the airport and get home."

Frank smiled, for he knew that Sam normally frowned on no-shows and substitutions. While Frank intended to head back to San Antonio, Muchnick's response earned him a ton of respect from Frank, a free spirit who already liked the promoter.

Perhaps more than a few observers were waiting for what they felt would be an inevitable blowup in St. Louis when the time came for Muchnick to ask a "favor" from Brody. That never happened, though, not even close. Brody did three main event "jobs" in the town, losing twice to Harley Race, when Race held the National Wrestling Alliance title, and once to Ted DiBiase.

On March 23, 1979, Brody dropped two out of three rugged falls to Race. "King Kong" dominated the opening fall, finally winning with an atomic knee drop to Race's tailbone after 9:02. Race battled back and actually was able to use his suplex to gain the second stanza in 7:14. Since part of Brody's gimmick was how difficult it was to hoist him into the air, allowing Race to do that was a clear sign of respect for Muchnick, St. Louis, and the title itself.

In the third fall, Brody took command but sidestepped a charge from Race, and referee Joe Tangaro was knocked down. The champion turned around just in time to catch a big boot to the jaw from Brody. Then Brody lifted Race high overhead for a big slam. Tangaro, however, was on his hands and knees behind the challenger, and Brody fell backwards over the referee. Thus, Tangaro was in the right spot to count three as Race landed on top of Brody.

It was a perfectly executed finish that kept the challenger strong and required no histrionics in the dressing room beforehand.

On September, 14, 1979, Brody lost by disqualification to Andre the Giant when he came off the top rope with a knee drop on The Giant (illegal in Missouri at the time) after putting Andre on the canvas. A 16-man Battle Royal followed, and it was Brody who engineered pitching Andre over the top rope to eliminate him. When Brody went on to take the decision as the lone survivor in the ring, it earned him another crack at the crown.

Thus, it was Race and Brody again on October 5. The rumor mills must have been frustrated, because once more there was no problem whatsoever putting the package together in St. Louis. Race was manhandled in the first fall, but surprised Brody with a sunset flip (jackknife and cradle) at 11:20. The champion did a superb job selling and Brody, pounding as the challenger, used his flying knee drop to capture the second fall after 5:41.

Brody came out firing in the decisive round. Finally, he slammed Race to the mat and unleashed another flying knee drop. Referee Charles Venator counted "one . . . two . . ." and just as he came down for "three," Race draped his leg over the bottom rope. Brody jumped high into the air, thinking like many in the crowd that "King Kong" had indeed won the World Heavyweight Championship. But Venator caught Brody's arm, and said, "No," pointing to the rope Harley had gotten his leg on.

Brody screamed in agony, but turned quickly as Race staggered toward him. Brody went behind the champion, lifting him for an atomic knee drop on Race's tailbone. Race's legs stiffened as he was dropped down; he blocked the move, turned quickly enough to hook the challenger with a small package (front rolling cradle), and held Brody just long enough to get the count of three.

Clearly, Brody was a complete professional in the way he approached finishes with the champion.

Over the years, the question has been asked: was Frank Goodish ever offered a reign as the National Wrestling Alliance champion? To the best of my knowledge, the answer is: no. At least, not by anyone who really meant it. . . .

Keep in mind that probably half of the men who ever pulled on the tights had promises of the title dangled in front of them like doggie biscuits in front of a hungry pup by less than scrupulous promoters. Their goal was always control: over a finish; over work in a specific territory; or to get someone to do something for a bit less money.

"Do this for me, and I'll put a word in for you. I've got pull. What a terrific champion you would make…" is how the manipulation would go.

Frank believed you should never refuse an offer outright, no matter how ridiculous it was, until the moment of truth. If someone had promised him the belt, he would have said, "Great, I'd love that." And then he would have demanded the same money or refused the same finish: he would have kept trying to play the player. Privately, he'd snicker at the folly. Frank knew no crown awaited Brody.

One moment in particular sticks out vividly for me. In the mid 1980s, Frank and I were driving from St. Louis to an Illinois show, on Route 255 just north of the 17A exit for Belleville. (Isn't it funny how an isolated second can stay in your mind?) We were discussing something going on with the NWA championship and Jim Crockett, Jr.

I asked him, "Did you ever really want the belt? Did you want to be the champion?"

Even now, I can see his face turn sour, as though he had swallowed pure vinegar. "Get serious!" he said. He understood that the title was being devalued, that essentially it had been ever since Sam Muchnick lost control of it in the late 1970s. And he also recognized the political hassles and the loss of freedom that came with being champion. Besides, once he was established as a money player in Japan, he was likely earning close to what the titleholder was, without the headaches.

The final job in St. Louis was for Ted DiBiase on October 24, 1980. It was asking Brody to return a favor, as "King Kong" had flattened Ted on July 13, 1979, when Brody destroyed DiBiase with the flying knee drop after a truly red hot 17:04 of action.

Before the 1980 rematch, Brody went to DiBiase and said the only reasons he was doing this was for him and because it was St. Louis. "Brody was strictly business and would never put his shoulders down for just anyone," says DiBiase. "He was a tremendous athlete and great performer."

On the other side, Brody had huge respect for DiBiase as a worker. Frank did claim, though, that DiBiase "had a soft ear" — DiBiase could be talked into doing things that were not in his own best interest.

In 1980, however, Brody was superb as he and DiBiase executed a brilliant Japanese style battle that ended with DiBiase catching Brody in the small package after 14:28. It was the start of a run for DiBiase that would culminate in his winning the Missouri State crown and getting a couple of shots at the NWA prize. Clearly, it would be wrong to say that Brody failed to do what was right for business in St. Louis.

Frank Goodish gave the wrestling world something else to consider. Under Muchnick, during a period of more than 30 years, the main event grapplers always split 16% of the net gate receipts after tax. This might as well have been written in stone for Sam. If it were a double feature, each performer received 4%. If it were a championship tussle, each wrestler got 8%.

Since the tax statement as calculated by the state Office of Athletics was always included with the pay, each man could clearly see that he got every penny coming to him. There was no finagling as there so often was in other spots. Pay was not subjective, but rather totally pragmatic. In addition, each wrestler's transportation expenses were reimbursed separately.

To be in the same spot as Brody meant a good hunk of money. And even though there was always a battle (involving the Kansas City office and me, with Sam making the final decision) about how to use him, Brody knew that Sam would do a smart booking sequence that never devalued a main event talent.

As Jack Brisco once said, "In St. Louis, everybody did jobs. If you didn't do jobs, you couldn't work for Sam." Because of the way Sam had his outline sketched, like a baseball pennant race, a loss here and there never hurt. It only made the victories more meaningful. Plus, I was a friend and getting more booking influence every day.

St. Louis was a regular stop, but on an irregular basis. Muchnick was phasing out of the wrestling business, especially after the death of his wife, and I was not on the same wavelength as the partners (O'Connor, Geigel, Race, and Verne Gagne) who were buying out Sam's stock.

Because Brody habitually aggravated Geigel and the others from Kansas City, they would have liked to have prevented him from becoming even more popular in St. Louis. But putting him in main events lured large crowds, which meant lucrative paydays for Frank and, as partners in the promotion, for them, too.

Still, O'Connor knew the occasional disqualification, against the likes of Dick "The Bruiser" or the Von Erichs, was easy enough to sell to Frank. And it kept him from becoming any bigger than he already was — at least in their minds.

One time, O'Connor and Geigel complained to Gary Hart, who was booking for Dallas and had inked Brody into Kansas City. Frank had been

A dapper Gary Hart is interviewed by Gordon Solie.

creating chaos for KC, balking on finishes and challenging them on gate receipts.

Gary knew what to expect, because Frank had already blown off steam to him. Apparently, there had been a couple of shows where Geigel claimed either that they were lacking cash or that the checking balance was too low, and KC had shorted Brody on the money he was due.

Hart just laughed and told O'Connor, "Pay the man what you promised and he's owed. Then there won't be a problem."

Brody was also not above no-showing a Geigel program because the big man felt Geigel had shorted him on a payoff or had broken a promise. In fact, Buck Robley (who was booking for KC at the time) recalls that on one occasion, Brody simply did not come to a KC production in Des Moines, Iowa, but made the big money date the next night in Kansas City just to make his point.

The night Frank blew off Des Moines, his wife Barbara had to politely take the frustrated calls from Geigel. He even had Terry Funk contact Brody, who did take Terry's call. Frank laughed about Terry moaning, as only Terry could, "Bruise . . . Bruuuuise . . . Bruuuuuuise . . . what are you doing to poor ol' Geigel?"

Geigel and crew had to swallow and take it, for it was Brody in a cage with Kimala that had drawn what was, for them, a huge gate in Kansas City.

Likewise, Brody was making more and more trips to collect big bucks in Japan. Still, Brody's gate magic and our friendship played a role in getting "King Kong" several large paydays in St. Louis.

Most notable was February 11, 1983, when Brody and National Wrestling Alliance king Ric Flair staged an incredible one-hour stalemate before

16,695 fans at The Checkerdome. Muchnick, though a careful observer, was retired and no longer had any influence on final decisions. I had been prepared to leave the promotion as well prior to the Flair match, but Frank convinced me to stay until that date. "I need you here to engineer the whole thing," Frank said.

One aspect of the success of that evening is forgotten. So strong was the World Heavyweight Championship in St. Louis, so strong was Ric Flair as the titleholder, so strong was "King Kong" Brody as the challenger, that absolutely no angle for the match was shot in advance.

Neither ran in to attack the other on television. Neither came to help an injured friend. Neither smacked the other during a contract signing ceremony. They did not go head-to-head in a tag match engineered to create a bloodbath the week before the showdown.

Brody simply had a series of victories on both *Wrestling at the Chase* and at Kiel Auditorium to establish himself as the leading contender at the time. Flair and Brody both did get television smashes for the two weeks prior to The Checkerdome confrontation. The champion did a fiery interview. The next week Brody tried to top Flair's work with an equally explosive interview.

The tremendous audience, so full of energy itself, was drawn strictly on the strength of the athletes and their personalities. Those fans came knowing they would see something special, because Ric Flair and "King Kong" Brody made them believe it.

Making that night even more important was the fact that Shohei "Giant" Baba, the owner of the All Japan promotion, which was the keystone of Brody's independence at the time, was having the card taped for airing in Japan. Baba, of course, wanted to show what would be his victory over Race and also the battle between Flair and Brody. The National Wrestling Alliance crown that Flair was defending carried enormous weight with Japanese fans.

Obviously, the evening had huge implications for Brody. And it all came together perfectly. I set Baba up to get the production expertise from KPLR-TV. To top it all off, everyone was shocked when Baba's representative paid KPLR several thousand dollars — in advance, in cash!

The match itself did everything it was supposed to do. Some have called a one-hour "broadway" a nothing situation, only an athletic display. Done properly in the correct context, however, it can be extremely valuable in making both combatants even stronger personalities. The St. Louis classic between Flair and Brody did just that.

In this case, it proved Brody was not just a wild man — a brawler with limited tools — who would get disqualified. It proved Flair, even giving away size, could stand up and survive against a monster challenger. It proved Brody was in fact a talented, athletic wrestler, using leapfrogs and even takedowns and head scissors. He did things that not everyone realized he was capable of pulling off. Flair displayed the moxie and strategy of a wily titleholder who would be hard to dethrone.

Though there were portions of both, this was not a "Flair match," nor was it a "Brody match." It was an epic confrontation that indeed told a story.

Every move, hold, grimace, bump, or near fall meant something. Credit for this success was due to a superb promotion and an intelligent, believable television show that both educated and engaged its fans. It was also recognition for a pair of consummate performers, spectacular workers and unique characters, who understood both themselves and their audience.

Most importantly, in the end, it left every fan hungry for more. Flair himself has called it his favorite one-hour match, simply because of the amazing crowd reaction. No fireworks. No music. No confetti. Not even a spotlight. No audience manipulation of any kind. The fans simply wanted to enjoy themselves, to believe and to care. They had an emotional investment, one rarely, if ever, seen today.

Flair came out first to a deafening roar — a cliché, except it's true. The noise literally shook the foundation. Then a moment . . . another moment . . . and another moment passed. The St. Louis crowd began to chant, "Brody! Brody! Brody!" Brody waited, tensing, out of sight as the fans built to a climax.

And then Frank Goodish, now embodying Bruiser Brody, stomped into view, and the roof blew off The Checkerdome. Even as the pandemonium calmed, it never ended. For one solid hour, even at its most quiet, there was a steady hubbub that was only broken — repeatedly — by vocal explosions of booming thunder.

The action was almost constant from the opening bell. Even when Brody latched onto a head scissors or a bearhug, the selling by both combatants was visible and engrossing for the fans. Both teased taking the warfare onto the floor just enough to foreshadow the rest of the duel.

Flair finally took control of the grueling action, but even then he was unable to get the leverage to lift Brody for a suplex. Brody stormed back to overwhelm Flair with flying tackles and vicious body slams. When Brody scored with his flying knee drop, the big man earned the first fall after 21:04.

As the second fall got even more heated, it was clear that every maneuver did indeed grab the spectators. The crowd, completely enthralled with the savage ballet of professional wrestling at its best, reacted with roars. Finally Flair was able to rocket Brody into the air for a suplex. When Brody tried his flying knee drop again, he missed and Flair narrowly avoided disaster.

Punches and chops that sizzled had the 16,695 spectators screaming and on their feet. Battling on the apron as referee Lee Warren counted on both warriors, Brody ducked a punch and back dropped the champion high into the air over the top rope and into the ring.

His balance gone, Brody stumbled and rolled off the apron to the floor as Warren finished his count. Flair was in the ring, Brody was out, and therefore the second fall went to Flair as Brody was counted out outside the ring after 22:40. In typical St. Louis fashion, with me as ring announcer, the finish of the fall was explained concisely and accurately. The execution by Brody and Flair had been so flawless, however, that everyone already understood and accepted it.

Now it was time for the champion and the challenger to go for all the marbles. It was stiff, tight, and the fans were willingly mesmerized. Finally Flair was able to clamp on his figure four leglock, but Brody was too powerful and reversed the grip after a struggle. Brody scored with a piledriver, missed an elbow drop, hit the big boot to Flair's jaw, and delivered his own ring-rattling suplex. Yet the one-hour time limit expired with Flair still in control of the gold belt, despite the awesome attack by Brody.

That was the story the battle told thanks to two masters of action and psychology.

In 2006, when he saw a tape of the duel on *St. Louis Wreslting Classics, Volume XII*, Dave Meltzer of the authoritative *Wrestling Observer* newsletter, raved about the match. Michael Holmes, my editor at ECW Press, had the same reaction when he watched the classic Brody and Flair had created.

And there was pride involved as well. Brody's wife Barbara had never been to St. Louis, but Frank flew her in to see this historic duel. Frank's sister Gloria, who was living in St. Louis at the time, finally came to watch her brother in action. The crowd was fabulous and the action the two masters provided was equal to that fervor. It was a moment of triumph that Frank Goodish wanted to share with those who mattered to him.

But another tale was unfolding behind the scenes.

The gross for that card was comfortably over $100,000, leaving a net after tax of above $90,000. By St. Louis standards under Muchnick, the payoff would have been 8% for Flair and 8% for Brody — at least $7200 each. Remember, though, that Muchnick no longer had any say.

In fact, the actual show statement verifies that the gross was $113,014. With just over 17% tax in St. Louis, that should have left a net of approximately $93,000. Apparently, a couple of unexplained "expenses" were added and the net displayed was $91,294.82. By traditional St. Louis guidelines, this still should have produced a pay off for Flair and Brody of $7303.59 each.

When I sat down with Geigel, who wrote the checks when paying talent, he told me he gave Brody and Flair each $5958. I brought up the established rate of pay St. Louis had under Muchnick.

Geigel laughed. "No wrestler is worth more than $6000 for a match." A few hundred of that extra couple grand went to talent, which was almost all from Kansas City, in the early preliminaries. Most, by far, became profit, which went to the four owners, and I admit a small part ended up with me as part of my own existing deal with the company.

Nonetheless, I was unhappy that a change had been made from a successful formula. In the deteriorating situation of St. Louis, it was not the first time. If the predicament continued, the short-term gain of a few bucks would not be worth the long-term harm as big names figured out that the money was being split differently than it had been for decades under Muchnick.

Frustrated, I told Brody about what had happened. Surprisingly, though Brody's eyes got big, he did not erupt. "It's okay. I'll get it back in other ways," said Frank.

Was that stealing from the talent? Not really. Was there a contract signed between everyone involved? No, wrestling was not conducted that way in 1983. Had anyone even negotiated? Of course not.

Yet was it in some way unethical? Was it the type of conduct, maybe to a lesser degree than at other times, which helped make Frank Goodish into the Bruiser Brody who did not trust promoters and looked for every ounce of leverage he could find?

Yes. Certainly. A change had been made and nobody knew. But it was all in the context of what wrestling was and actually still is now, this very moment, on a different level. There was no union waiting for a grievance to be filed. There were only individuals, willing to argue, or "negotiate," as best they could.

Even in St. Louis. Muchnick was gone and it would never be the same, for Brody or anyone.

Why did Sam Muchnick leave? Age was part of it, as was the sudden death of his beloved wife. Important, also, were the changes Sam saw in his business. In his role as National Wrestling Alliance president, he got tired of putting out brush fires when promoters fought each other.

When he resigned as the NWA boss, Muchnick became equally unhappy as he saw changes in the philosophy of how the champion was used. Thus, the man who built the National Wrestling Alliance bowed out. Sam had been the balance point in keeping this bizarre and often nasty industry on somewhat even turf for more than three decades. The NWA began to crumble, as did St. Louis itself, when Sam bid adieu.

Once I decided to leave the St. Louis Wrestling Club, Frank had no hesitation, actually encouraging me to make the split and go out on my own against big odds.

Sam Muchnick himself was equally supportive, behind the scene.

Brody had also promised me, back when I agreed to continue through the Flair versus Brody showdown, "If you go on your own, I'll be there. You can take it to the bank." Indeed, Frank had picked me as one of those few friends and it was a promise.

When I announced that I would open a new promotion, it was Frank and Barbara who called to explain to both me and my wife Pat the type of threats and tricks that could be expected if I put myself into the position I did.

Nobody expected a promotional war in St. Louis, the home of the NWA, and certainly not a skirmish ignited by Larry Matysik, Muchnick's loyal protégé. The times, though, were changing. I saw that the ideas being pushed from the KC faction would bring the high-level operation in St. Louis down, as, unfortunately, the Kansas City office was always considered minor league.

As Sam had drawn away from the booking and, more importantly, the dollars-and-cents business in St. Louis, the headaches and confusion had grown. Since I was from the area, and everyone figured I was in charge, I had no intention of letting things fall apart when I had no final say in what was being done.

Perceptive as always, Goodish understood my frustration and motivation in striking out on my own. If the NWA had truly been a solid organization, odds are the St. Louis battle would never have started. Instead, I found all sorts of talent and unexpected allies. In particular, I discovered help from none other than Fritz Von Erich and — of all people — Vince McMahon, Jr.

Even without their assistance, I had Brody as a start for my talent base and was surprised to easily connect for dates with Dick Murdoch, Tully Blanchard, Adrian Adonis, "Macho Man" Randy Savage, "Spike" Huber, Jerry Oates, Scott Casey, Bobby Jaggers, Dominic DeNucci, and a future governor of Minnesota — Jesse Ventura.

Brody was impressed with my spunk and helped put me in touch with Nikolai Volkoff and Professor Toru Tanaka. Later, Brody volunteered to talk to another stubborn independent superstar — none other than Stan Hansen — about taking dates.

All-time great and St. Louis native Lou Thesz eagerly agreed to be involved as a special referee and sounding board for ideas and problems. Local celebrity and ring announcer Mickey Garagiola jumped ship with me, and the media was open and available. Sam was regularly in private, personal contact.

I traveled to Denton, Texas, to talk face-to-face with Fritz. Although I was close with Fritz's sons and David Von Erich in particular, I hesitated (in retrospect, mistakenly) to ask for bookings on the boys for fear of the position in which that would put Fritz, a former NWA president.

Fritz, however, asked me for a promise. Assuming I won the war and got the prime KPLR outlet, would I then make peace with the former partners (Gagne, Race, Geigel, and O'Connor) for the good of the wrestling business? Von Erich explained that he had been involved in a similar dispute in Dallas in the 1960s, and Sam Muchnick himself had quietly swung his weight behind Von Erich when he made the same promise regarding his own former partners.

I was comfortable making that agreement. Fritz, then, opened the door for me to book Terry Gordy, one of the red-hot "Fabulous Freebirds," and vowed to let his sons be added to the lineup in 1984. To keep Fritz from

getting any heat, the deal was that I would book Gordy through Terry's partner, Michael Hayes, on what were "off" days from the Dallas office.

Brody, who talked with me almost every day during the spring of 1983, was originally skeptical of the connection with Fritz. "Hell, David wants to work for you," Frank scoffed. "Don't worry about Fritz." But Brody liked the look of what was happening and was particularly thrilled about the addition of Gordy, an incredible young worker who knew Frank from both Texas and Japan.

Brody and I sketched out plans that would have eventually ended up with Gordy and Brody butting heads. The big man growled, "Even in St. Louis, this will make them yell. Wait until they see a pair of 300-pounders like us up in the air the way we're going to be!"

Frank was non-committal, but a little suspicious, about my relation with McMahon. At that point, nobody (despite what some may claim today) really knew what McMahon was planning to do that would turn the entire wrestling world topsy-turvy. McMahon did lead me to booking "Black Jack" Mulligan for the main event against Brody on my first card on June 18, 1983.

Wrestling was and still is a gossip-fuelled business. And on cue, stories about Frank no-showing my event began to spread. These rumors were clearly started by my rivals, and even through our friendship was getting stronger, the worry I felt was human. Frank, however, laughed it off as "typical wrestling bullshit."

And it was Mulligan who no-showed. McMahon was surprised, and I had no reason to doubt him, as time would show he wanted me to have short-term success, especially as it affected the valuable KPLR slot. Mulligan reputedly was bought either for money or the promise that his son, Barry Windham, would be made the NWA champion if Mulligan were a no-show.

Only a few dollars had to be refunded. Understanding the importance of his outing, Brody destroyed — absolutely destroyed — two foes in a handicap match. Only days later, I scored with a television slot on UHF station KDNL, the same outlet which aired Fritz's blazing *World Class* wrestling program. Mulligan's absence had meant nothing.

In fact, Frank had come to St. Louis early for promotional work and was with me the evening of June 17 when we ran into Pat O'Connor. Amazingly, all of us were eating at the same time in the Tenderloin Room of the Chase–Park Plaza Hotel.

Since rumors were all over that Brody would not be at my card, the room was loaded with tension. But not for Frank Goodish. He winked at me and said, "This will be fun."

Frank ordered a drink sent over to O'Connor. Pat nodded his acknowledgement. Then Frank and I went right over to O'Connor's table and engaged him (or forced him) into a friendly, animated conversation. Most of the customers in the Tenderloin Room probably had no clue what was happening in the wrestling world, but Brody's physical appearance made sure every eye was on the pleasant chat with O'Connor.

Frank and I laughed about that evening for a few years.

Goodish also got a good chuckle at my expense. One Sunday afternoon in July, Frank called my house to find that I was outside cutting grass and having a small conniption fit because the mower wouldn't work right. I was fuming, cursing the miserable lawn mower, as I came to the phone. Goodish broke up laughing. "I've never known a wrestling promoter who cut his own grass," the big man chortled.

On September 17, there was another chuckle. I had a show featuring Brody against Nikolai Volkoff at The Checkerdome (as The Arena was known in 1983), and the television was on air at 5 o'clock that afternoon. The Geigel-O'Connor-Race crew had run the evening before at Kiel Auditorium and some were still in town the afternoon of the 17th because of a "spot" show that evening.

This included Buck Robley, who was booking for Kansas City — in other words, in opposition to me and Brody. I stopped at the Drury Hotel by the airport so I could go over Frank's finish with Volkoff. The television program, headlined by a tag bout pitting Brody and Jerry Oates against Volkoff and Adrian Adonis, was just starting.

Frank had found out Robley was staying at the Drury, so Brody called him and told him to come to his room. Even Buck, as crotchety and independent as he was, may have balked a moment about being in the same room with the opposition, especially with me, who had started the promotional skirmish, at a hotel where many of his so-called guys were staying. "Don't worry about it," growled Frank.

Everybody relaxed quickly, of course, and had plenty of laughs as we watched the show and traded gossip about the St. Louis war. At one point as the television card progressed, Buck suddenly barked, "You're really serious about this!" to Brody.

Frank nodded and said, "I certainly am. Why'd you bring that up?"

Robley pointed to the television screen and said, "Look. You're selling.

You're actually selling on TV!" At that point in the tag match, Brody was on one knee and taking forearm smashes and kicks from Volkoff. Since Buck was well aware of Frank's theories on selling, that moment drove home the fact that Frank Goodish was, indeed, serious.

Frank had already proven to me how committed he was when a potential problem cropped up about the finish of a two-ring battle royal on July 22. My new group had a number of heels (Murdoch, Volkoff, Adonis, Blanchard, Savage, plus Ventura and Gordy on the way), but only one truly established babyface in Brody. Jerry Oates was close, but "Spike" Huber was the next best bet until David Von Erich could be sprung free.

The finish for the Royal was therefore going to be Huber getting the best of Tully Blanchard. But Tully whined and griped when I told him. Truthfully, by normal standards, it made some sense to give Tully the win and have the good guy ("Spike") chasing revenge. But at that point, the triumph in a huge donnybrook was more important for Huber. In addition, it set the stage for a main event between Huber and Blanchard.

But Tully groused so much that I was worried he would double cross "Spike" on the finish.

Frank always touched base with me during the evening and picked up on the vibe of worry. I explained Tully's attitude. Frank was irate. "Bullshit!" he snapped. "That's his job! If he goes off the finish you guys worked out, give me the look and I'll hit the ring and beat the hell out of everybody. See how much he likes working with me."

Of course, Blanchard was completely professional and executed a letter-perfect finish putting Huber over big. Brody had been standing ten feet from me in the dressing room entry while it happened. When "Spike's" hand was raised, Frank ambled over to me. "That's just Tully and most guys," Brody said. "Bitch and moan, but then they do it."

"But if he hadn't . . ." Frank's eyes got big. Probably my eyes were just as big, for it was shocking to find Brody of all people on the side of a promoter. But the vow was loyalty to a friend.

It was more light-hearted, but every bit as effective, when Brody scaled to the nose-bleed top of The Checkerdome marquee to imitate the movie King Kong crawling up the Empire State Building. Traffic on the nearby highway was snarled as the cameras rolled and Frank swung blonde Angie Werner, one of the building's secretaries, while he barked out a promo for an upcoming card.

For another spot, with brave Angie off-camera and catching her breath after being manhandled a few stories above the asphalt parking lot, Frank also ripped a "T" out of the lettering that said wrestling before howling another eye-catching promo for television consumption. It was the end of July and 100 degrees while Brody paced, yelled, and performed on top of the huge building that day. The whole town was talking after that unusual scenario.

The new promotion did well and the old St. Louis Wrestling Club floundered badly. The real hit came on the television ratings, as my show zoomed and *Wrestling at the Chase* went into the dumper. Ted Koplar, the owner of KPLR and the first director for me when I became the play-by-play announcer in 1972, knew something had to be done.

Unfortunately, I did not have my legal ducks in a row. And I loaded so much on myself that the burden was overwhelming. When my financial angels, a company fronted by Charlie Mancuso, the manager of The Checkerdome, wanted to change the deal to 80-20 in their favor from 50-50 as verbally agreed upon, I was shaken and angry.

There had been significant losses in starting up, as both Muchnick and I had warned Mancuso. But that was the primary reason given for trying to change a deal that was based on a verbal agreement. I found out that not everyone operated like Sam Muchnick — on his word and a handshake. Brody had been in Japan for most of October, and thus out of contact with me. All Frank knew was that the 24-hour days were eating me alive.

But a bigger shock was awaiting when Koplar told me that the St. Louis Wrestling Club would be cancelled at the end of 1983. Ted felt a partnership between me and Vince McMahon, Jr. would be in the best interests of St. Louis to begin the new year.

While Koplar was impressed with what I had done, he was even more impressed with the stable of talent McMahon controlled — wrestlers with names that had more starpower than the independents I was relying upon.

Okay, I was shocked. I had no idea that Vince Jr. was in the St. Louis picture. Now we were thrown together in a shotgun marriage. Vince Jr. laid out his plans to conquer the wrestling world and create a single dominant national promotion. St. Louis would be his springboard.

Before a climactic meeting with both Koplar and McMahon on October 23, I called Von Erich and tried to convince him to combine with me, melding *World Class* with the St. Louis style I knew so well, in the hopes of holding off McMahon's plans.

The idea was one program for KPLR based out of St. Louis with Fritz as a silent partner with me, while the *World Class* show continued in its current slot on KDNL. Fritz, however, would not accept and could not understand that Vince intended to eventually have it all.

Fritz told me that I would win; I was doing great and should stay the course with different financing. I tried to explain the box that had been built, as well as the incredible threat of what McMahon would do. But Fritz said that it would not happen and simply wouldn't budge.

The die was cast. McMahon wanted me involved, but the personal deal became an up-and-down promise and betrayal that left me bitter, angry, and, eventually, a WWF employee. Vince ended up with the prime spot in St. Louis, the home of the National Wrestling Alliance, from which to launch his dream.

Nobody knew this, not even Frank Goodish, until my last program at Kiel Auditorium on October 29. Before I told any other talent, I wanted — needed — to explain what had happened to Brody. I had even discussed adding Brody to McMahon's roster with Vince, although it is likely Frank himself would have resented anyone speaking for him in a situation like that.

Sitting in a room at the Drury Inn (now a Pear Tree Inn) across from the St. Louis airport, I quietly laid out the entire story for Frank Goodish. There was no explosion, no anger. Frank tried to convince me that I shouldn't give in to the power, that I should fight and find other financing, that the talent was obviously there.

But I still remember it clearly. Frank looked away at the airport runways across the highway, then turned back to me. The big man's eyes were sad, something I had never really seen before. "Don't worry about me with Vince. I'll be fine," Frank Goodish said. "Will everybody know about this tonight?"

I said they would know I was folding the promotion, but probably wouldn't know about the McMahon connection for a few weeks.

"Good," said Frank Goodish, and offered his hand. "I'm still your friend. I think you could have won, but you have to do what you have to do. I'm still your friend."

By the next day, Brody, through his buddy Buck Robley, who was booking for Geigel and company, had engineered what appeared to be a jump from me for guaranteed money. Inadvertently, however, what happened at that moment also caused a major disaster for Randy Savage and left Frank with an enemy.

Along with his father Angelo Poffo, Randy had been running a so-called "outlaw" promotion in opposition to the established NWA companies in Tennessee, Kentucky, and surrounding areas. The competition had been fierce and, occasionally, violent on a personal, behind-the-scenes level.

When Frank and Randy met on my shows in St. Louis, they got along and Randy booked Brody to appear at Cape Girardeau, Missouri, on October 30. In fact, Savage had decided to clash with Brody and lose, thus giving Brody what Randy's promotion billed as the World Heavyweight Championship.

But Frank, moving fast, had convinced the Geigel faction that he would jump from me in St. Louis if they were willing to meet his price. That side had no idea they were going to be booted off KPLR, nor did they have any inkling that Vince Jr. was about to steamroll all of us. Having secured the arrangement with Geigel, Frank decided that making the Cape Girardeau date for Randy was not a wise choice since at that time Geigel was with the crumbling NWA group.

So Brody didn't show up. I had no idea what Frank was doing until Randy called me. He was in anguish when he asked, "Where's Brody? Why is he doing this to me?" There was no good answer, no reasonable explanation that would satisfy Randy. Frank did what he did because he thought it was in his own best interest to do so. He apparently felt there was more money to be had in picking the bones of the NWA in the upheaval to come.

Although the old promotion in St. Louis was unceremoniously ousted from KPLR, they landed a spot on KDNL for their tapes from Kansas City and managed to stay alive for another year or so. They even drew a couple of big houses, putting Brody against Flair before going out of business. Before the first one, on January 6, 1984, at Kiel, Frank needled me until I agreed to walk through the building.

"The fans don't even understand what is happening yet," Frank declared. "This sellout belongs to you and me, not people like Geigel. Go in there and be proud. Let the fans know you're alive and strong." It was pure Frank Goodish/"King Kong" Brody. And I went, walking in the stage door with Brody and then circulating through the spectators.

Frank's brain was always clicking and he kept in constant contact with me through a stressful time that ended when none other than Vince McMahon and his then-World Wrestling Federation began smashing the foundations of the sport.

There's one more vintage Brody story to come out of the St. Louis of that era. On March 10, 1984, Brody was once more booked to tackle Flair at Kiel. The KC office, trying to gain favor with Baba's All Japan promotion, made arrangements to tape the match and send it to Baba for use in Japan.

The finish they planned was to have Brody disqualified against Flair before 450-pound "Crusher" Blackwell, another Brody buddy, jumped into the ring. Together, Flair and Blackwell would beat down Frank and leave him for dead. Hopefully this would set up bouts for Brody against both men. (Flair and Brody, again! Truthfully, it was the only way they could draw a significant house at that point.)

I knew, of course, since I was already getting regular midnight telephone calls from Frank, who was also eager to hear what news I had about the McMahon organization for which I now worked. I told Brody, "You know how much Sam would hate that finish in a title match in St. Louis! Are you sure it's good for you?"

Goodish laughed and laughed. "Wait until you find out what happens," he chuckled.

On March 10, when Flair thought he was going to get the better of Brody after the final bell, he was met by a very stiff boot to the face. Blackwell got into the ring and was immediately pounded — hard — by Brody. Flair, smart as always, read the situation and began taking bumps as Brody knocked the champion all over the place. Blackwell had no problem with that and he too took the easy path rather than the hard as Brody battered him.

Another "horror" story, another "double cross" by Brody?

It all depends on perspective. The tape was going to Japan, where Frank had no intention of looking weak or anything less than a monster. Ric Flair still had the title. "Crusher" Blackwell still was an amazing character and heel who knew he could trust Frank to involve him in future plans.

And then St. Louis was lost. The wrestling world changed as nobody ever believed it could. Vince McMahon had begun his march. And Frank Goodish, aka "King Kong" Brody or Bruiser Brody, was a giant figure of independence and controversy.

CHAPTER TWELVE

Barbara Remembers . . .
COMING TO AMERICA

What a plane ride it was. I didn't have a clue about what to expect. I was taking such a big chance. I didn't know whether I would be met at the airport or not. After living ten years of my life in Australia, I had tied up all the loose ends in a few days. Talk about a life change! I was changing countries too.

I remember looking out the window and seeing all the lights of Los Angeles as the aircraft made its final descent. This was it, no turning back. The first people that approached me after I came out of customs were the Hare Krishnas, of course. I made my way to the terminal where I was to get the San Antonio connection.

That feeling of the complete unknown came to reality as I started the final leg of a journey that included 36 hours of travel. Once again I saw lights twinkling as we landed in San Antonio. As I walked from the plane down the hallway to the arrival lounge, it felt like the longest walk I had ever taken.

Then, all of a sudden, towering above the crowd was this gentle giant with a huge smile on his face. This incredible man had picked me as his friend and partner. That smile was all the welcome I needed to dispel any fears I might have had. I knew at that very moment this was the start of a new life — a new adventure — wherever it would lead.

Frank greeted me with such warmth. We left the airport and headed off to the home of his best friends, the people he lived with. He said I would be welcome there for the next few months until we could get an apartment of our own. Pete Ortega and his lovely wife Rowe had their firstborn, Travis, who was just a baby, at the door to greet me and make me feel right at home.

It must have been a change for Pete and Rowe to have me around after Frank. He lived like a wrestler in a hotel, popping in once every week or ten days or so. I was there 24/7. Luckily, Frank was working out of Texas, or he could have been gone even more. I made the best of the time I had. I joined a gym, helped out around the house, and served as a babysitter for Travis so once in a while Pete and Rowe could do things together, just the two of them. It made me feel good to be able to repay at least a little of their hospitality.

Even today I classify Pete and Rowe as people I really care about and trust. Pete was a man's man, just like Frank, and Rowe was just terrific. Pete wasn't in the wrestling business, although I know Frank liked to talk with him about it. The friendship was just different, but it was very strong.

True friendships are hard to find. Years might go by and then you talk to or see them again. With real friends, it's like no time has gone by at all. You just take up right where you left off.

I have to admit it was hard to get used to Frank's schedule. In our first year together, I'd conservatively say that Frank was gone for nine months. When he went to Japan for weeks at a time, we would schedule maybe one or two telephone calls and that was it. Even if he was within driving range during those other three months, he still had to leave early and get home well after midnight.

I made many meals at 2 and 3 a.m. when he'd get home from a show. When Frank worked in Houston, there was a late flight he could catch to

Across the generations – Barbara's father with his son-in-law and grandson.

San Antonio and be home before the sun was up. Sometimes he'd bring another wrestler with him, somebody who was on the road and lonely and had nowhere to eat. I recall Stan Hansen joining us several times.

At least Frank had warned me exactly how it was going to be. "This is who I am," he had told me. I knew, going in, basically what to expect, but it was an adjustment. I wonder now if that was part of the reason he picked me to be his partner.

Frank must have seen that I was adventurous, having left my home at 18 and then changing countries by the time I was 20. I was not high-maintenance and I didn't need constant reassurance. I could take care of myself. Frank was careful with the dollar, and he knew he could leave me with a certain amount of money and I would budget it to make everything work.

I guess it came down to trust. It was not a walk in the park, to be sure, but I could be content to be by myself and handle things. Then, when we were together, it was even better.

One of my happiest memories with Frank came when he took me to visit his family in Warren, Michigan, during Christmas. Being from New Zealand, Christmas to me was about bathing suits and beaches. December was summer in New Zealand. I had heard the stories about "white Christmas" but obviously never experienced anything like that.

Here we were at his family home, with his sisters there too. The whole family. It was snowing! We walked around his streets and saw the carolers singing as the snowflakes fell. And all those colored lights! It was great being there with him.

Of course, Christmas morning we had to fly out because Frank was wrestling that night in Dallas. But the experience still sticks in my mind as such a happy time.

One other Christmas we went together on an early morning flight into Atlanta. He had to work Christmas Day and was gone early to drive somewhere. My Christmas Day was spent alone in an Atlanta hotel room. I watched television and read. He got back with the boys around 1 a.m. and we wanted to have Christmas "dinner." Of course, everything was closed, but we finally found a Denny's open and had our "dinner" around 3 a.m.

The next morning we were both on planes, me back to San Antonio and him off somewhere else to wrestle. Unfortunately, he had left the lights on in the car and the battery was dead. There I was, outside, in an open parking lot. It was rather scary. Someone did eventually help, but that was how it went with your husband on the road. If your battery is dead, or a light bulb explodes, or you're locked out of your house, or your son is sick, you're on your own. Anyone who has a husband or wife who travels understands what this is like.

I also learned even more about the business as I answered many of the calls and heard his version of the problems in wrestling. In San Antonio, he was a local celebrity. We became friends with some of the players on the San Antonio Spurs basketball team and other athletes in town.

When we ate at Luby's, people would come up constantly, and he always treated them with respect. It didn't matter if they looked bizarre or not. You can't judge by appearance. Everybody has a story, whether a midget or giant. Frank knew this.

As his popularity and workload increased, he wanted to maintain his ordinary identification as Frank Goodish. That is no easy feat for someone in the public eye. You're always going to get calls from people trying to make trouble. Sometimes it happened after a promoter became upset with Frank.

If you allow them to make problems like that, they win. So we'd turn it back on them. If a lady called asking for Frank, I'd say, "Let me get him for you. He's in the shower." Then they would hang up. It was just part of the deal. You accepted it and carried on.

Eventually we purchased a five-acre ranch outside of San Antonio in Boerne. It was just 30 minutes from the airport. That way he could get off the plane, go to his property, and be himself. Inside the garage, he made a weight room where he could lift. He thought our home would be a place where his child could grow up normal. Our home was Frank's pride and joy.

He never did anything without a lot of thought. His habit of planning everything rubbed off on me. Even when we got officially married, it was typical Frank thinking and planning. And, yes, Frank was thinking about a child just like I was.

In the late 1970s, lots of wrestlers and weightlifters were starting to take steroids to get bigger. Frank was no different. Nobody at the time knew all the horrible things that steroids could do to you. The athletes just knew that they helped make bigger muscles and more power.

Frank came back from one of his first trips to Japan and he was just so sick. Larry said Frank had had a match in St. Louis before he came home and that he looked just terrible, physically. He'd been sick on the flight all the way back from Japan.

When he got home, he put himself in the hospital and that was a big step. He hated hospitals, so I knew he was concerned. At first, it looked like he had a parasite that he'd picked up in Japan. The doctors ran all sorts of tests. Frank said that as long as he was in there, he wanted to know what was wrong.

He was always in tune with his body. He wanted to be healthy and, in addition to constantly working out, took all the things that people of the time thought would make you bigger and stronger. I remember making him these shakes with raw eggs. Today, nobody would feel safe doing that.

Nobody really knew about the dangers of steroids at the time. Naturally, he tried them as well. Even though they may have helped him in some ways, Frank could tell other things in his body just weren't right.

When he got sick, it scared the devil out of him. The doctors found some unusual things. Frank felt like something was eating away at his insides, and he wanted all of that crap out of his system. He stopped using steroids — just like that. In fact, he got off steroids before we even started talking about having a child. Most people probably didn't even realize that something had changed. He was such a big man — he still weighed 280 pounds.

The funny thing is that he thought his calves were too small, just like he always had. Pete and Frank got me started putting the rabbit fur on his boots that he wrestled in. I don't know how many pairs of boots I glued rabbit fur to! What was even worse was finding two furs that matched for two boots. Some were brownish, some were grayish. It was always a major shopping trip to get the fur for Frank's boots.

And then I got pregnant.

CHAPTER THIRTEEN

JAPAN
AND INDEPENDENCE

By the start of 1979, Bruiser Brody had landed what was in fact *the* big one. The Funks, Dory Jr. and Terry, booked Frank to work for Shohei "Giant" Baba and All Japan Wrestling. It would open a giant door and make Frank Goodish even more independent.

On January 2, 1979, at Korakuen Hall in Tokyo, Brody won a handicap match and was part of a Battle Royal won by the legendary Destroyer (Dick Beyer under a mask) — another wrestler so popular in Japan it was as if he were Japanese. The next night, in the same building, Brody whipped Kim Duk and won another battle royal.

On January 5 in Kawasaki, Brody joined forces with his old pal "King Curtis" to win a tag team battle against The Destroyer and "Giant" Baba himself. Right there was the headline. For that verdict to be rendered, Baba had made the decision to give Brody the big push.

Even though he and Curtis would eventually lose to The Destroyer and Baba, as well as to both "Jumbo" Tsuruta (All Japan's other shining superstar) and Baba, and to Tsuruta and The Destroyer, Brody was protected. His partner dropped the fall.

Bruiser Brody was the monster. Coming to the ring swinging a huge chain over his head, Brody scattered fans and caught every single eye. His first two singles outings with "Jumbo" ended in double count-outs. His first collision with Baba ended with Brody disqualified. Within one month, Bruiser Brody had been established as a main-eventer for All Japan.

"We pushed him hard," notes Terry Funk, talking about the booking plans he and brother Dory laid out. "If there was a business problem [i.e. money], that was Baba's headache." Apparently, though, Baba and Brody got along fine. Of course, Frank quickly earned top dollar.

Brody was clearly part of a change inside Japanese rings. For decades, with the exception of Lou Thesz and maybe one or two others, the hometown wrestlers ate up the foreigners, stretching them and pounding them — for real. The Funks started changing that. Brody and Hansen blew it right out of the water.

Brody nonchalantly remarked, "We beat up those guys. You had to show them that you deserved respect and wouldn't be pushed around. The Funks did it, Hansen did it, Jimmy Snuka did it some, and I sure as hell wasn't going to let one of them pop me. We beat the hell of out of them."

Terry Funk echoes Brody's comment: "You could *not* let them eat you up. If it became physical, it became physical. And if you take care of yourself, you better dominate. I think I sometimes had more compassion for my opponent, but Frank had none. And that was true in the United States too.

"Once he realized he could do that, though, he moved past great to phenomenal. To produce like he could, to be at that point, to be able to lead — and I don't mean to brag, but Junior and I were there too — the matches you could create were absolutely phenomenal," raves Funk.

A comparison would be Michael Jordan in the National Basketball Association. Before the Chicago Bulls ever won a championship, he undoubtedly believed he could take over a game by himself. He would make a difference in any competition because he was the best. When the Bulls won those championships, Jordan knew how great he was. According to

Funk, the same was true of Brody inside a wrestling ring.

Hansen is adamant that he and Frank "could not let them [other wrestlers] push us around. I'm not saying we were the toughest ever," he explains, "but we could just go. Nobody could stay with us. We wouldn't stop. We'd take over and we'd keep going until they blew up and then we'd take over. For most of them, it was easier just to let us beat them up."

Hansen notes, "Some guys were and are so naïve about it. They'd get all excited about how Frank and I wouldn't sell. They were happy if they could plan some spots for themselves. That's not how to work a bout or to get yourself over.

"What nobody understands is that we knew we were going to get to a certain point in the match [the finish]. What we didn't know was how we were going to get there," Stan says emphatically. "Hell, we didn't know ourselves. It just happened."

Lou Thesz once described working a wrestling match as "an art form." All artists, of course, are different. Just as Thesz worked one way, Brody and Hansen worked another. Success came when they took into account the abilities and strengths of the warriors involved. Often, for that "art form" to work best, the dominant party had to take control.

It wasn't that Frank suddenly discovered, in Japan, the need and ability to assert himself in the ring; that was always there from the start. More than a few opponents had the wounds to prove it. Now, however, he fully understood why doing that was so crucial and how it led to an unrivaled level of excitement with the right foes. He recognized how great he was at that tricky and hard-to-define science.

The lesson about taking care of yourself was universal. Frank mentored a young Kevin Von Erich after a bout in Dallas. Gino Hernandez, talented but cocky, gave Kevin a hard time during a match, even splitting Kevin's lip and essentially stealing the show in a duel that was designed for Kevin to shine.

Frank watched the match and was waiting for Kevin afterward. "That's bullshit!" Brody snapped at Kevin. "He made you look like crap. He didn't sell for you and he disrespected you." Kevin got so fired up as Frank angrily scolded him that he went after Hernandez in the dressing room and smacked him around.

"I learned the lesson," Kevin stresses.

A few years later, Brody was booked in what was then the shaky

Northwest territory — shaky from a business standpoint, because Vince McMahon, Jr. and the World Wrestling Federation were putting most territorial promotions out of business. The promotion was desperate to get houses, so they booked Frank for a few dates. He tackled Bobby Jaggers on September 26, 1985, in Boise, Idaho.

"All of those so-called tough guys were scared of him. With some guys, that had been true for a long time," claims Bobby. "Jesse Barr, Buddy Rose, even Roddy Piper were all pussies. Dusty Rhodes didn't like to be hit when we were in Florida. I remember one so-called star who complained about Frank. Told the promoter, 'Why . . . he *hit* me!' Can you believe that stuff?

"They didn't want to be touched. I told the promoters in [the Northwest territory] to book me with Frank," says Bobby.

Jaggers remembers that before the card, the promoter told all of the wrestlers to stay inside the ring and not battle on the floor. Frank caught Bobby's eye and smiled. "Now why would anyone book Bruiser Brody in 1985 and say that?" Bobby asks. "That's why you booked Frank! There was no reason not to have that stuff if you had the right guy doing it.

"We had a great match. He could work like a feather or work like a Funk. Frank was great. He worked like a real man and earned his money. He was the right guy to do it," Jaggers declares.

Nick Bockwinkel, the articulate former American Wrestling Association champion, was not a fan of Brody on a professional level. He remembers a match in San Antonio in which Brody was hot about something and just blew off the finish, even though Nick was offering himself to be hit, punched, and slammed. Yet Nick had barn burners with Brody too.

In Japan, Bockwinkel and Jim Brunzell were once up against Brody and Hansen. Knowing how zealously Brody and Hansen guarded their positions in the country, Bockwinkel warned Brunzell beforehand to expect "a semi-shoot." He cautioned, "They will show no respect for your body, especially not here in Japan. If they pull your hair, they'll try to yank it out of your head. If they kick you, it will be to break you."

Brunzell wasn't sure if Bockwinkel was putting him on or not. Nick went on, "At some point, I know enough wrestling I may take one of them down and tie him up to slow things down. But that will bring the other into the ring and you better do something. Throw a drop kick, use a flying tackle, fall down in front of him!"

The match, leaving Bockwinkel and Brunzell both bruised and battered,

Roger Deem believes this may be the best picture he ever snapped: the Brody knee drop.

went just as Bockwinkel had anticipated. But, despite his displeasure with Brody, Bockwinkel tempered it with telling praise. Naturally, everybody has his own taste and preferred style. But Bockwinkel admits, "When he wanted to be, Brody was one of the three best workers I was in there with. I'd put him close to the level of Ray Stevens, and that's the highest praise I can give. Brody was, when he decided to be, a great worker."

Terry Funk maintains, "It's necessary to make the fans believe in you. Frank could certainly do that. He understood how to mesmerize. He picked up stuff he saw from me and others and made it his own. Brody became the man."

During one tour of Japan, Baba's office set up interviews with wrestlers, including Terry and Frank, on a major television news and interview program. It was, by all accounts, a big deal. But the host began making fun of wrestling, knocking the business and degrading the talent.

Frank and Terry stood up and stormed out in the middle of the show.

"We walked out of respect for the business," says Terry. "We knew the price we paid with our bodies and minds whether it was a work or not. Frank and I were very similar in the respect we wanted for our business."

Bockwinkel feels that the only Japanese stars Brody would sell for were Baba and Tsuruta. Of course, he adds, "This never bothered Baba. Since Brody beat up everyone else, it just made Baba a bigger star when Brody sold for him."

Funk laughs. "Well, Baba and 'Jumbo' were the office. Frank understood how to make money."

Landing hot dates after that first tour of Japan was simple. Dick "The Bruiser" in Indianapolis and Chicago, even "The Crusher" in Chicago, Mark Lewin or Nick Bockwinkel in Houston, The Spoiler (Don Jardine) in Dallas, teaming with the Von Erich boys and feuding with manager Gary Hart's talent all over the Lone Star state, a hot trip to Charlotte, Harley Race or Andre the Giant in St. Louis, Ted DiBiase in Kansas City.

Big bucks. Big matches.

Hart still marvels, though, because Frank was always careful with the money no matter how much he made. "Bruise wasn't cheap, but he understood how spending bucks on the road could hurt you in the end," he says. "He'd travel and pick up cans of tuna and pork and beans to eat in the hotel room after a match!"

Says Robley, "Tuna, beans, and the cheapest beer he could buy!"

My wife Pat remembers the first time she met Brody after a bout in St. Louis. She and I were going to the office at the Warwick Hotel, where Frank was staying. "We asked if he wanted to grab a bite somewhere, but he said that he was fine and showed us the tuna he was going to eat," Pat recalls. "He was so happy and I was afraid the poor guy was going to starve."

No matter how much money he made, Frank was always careful on the road. He knew hard-earned income could be devoured by living too high. The tuna and even cans of cold green beans were regular menu items. Too many steaks could eat up most every penny earned.

"The road is tough enough," Goodish would say. "If you have any weakness at all, whether it's booze or drugs or women, traveling all the time will find it. The road will break anybody."

Frank often stayed with Robley when the travel allowed, not only because Buck was a friend but also because it saved money. Buck remembers Frank chowing down on the tuna as well. "He was always worried

Brody celebrates a victory with Tommy Rich and Austin Idol.

about being healthy, so he'd eat that damn tuna!"

The Brody business was more than healthy; it was on fire in the early 1980s. Each tour to Japan brought more recognition and more money. He was able to add lucrative dates in the U.S. Plus, World Class Championship Wrestling was red hot, and Frank was one of the main reasons.

Fritz Von Erich had raised the bar on television production for a wrestling show, which ended up syndicated to a large number of markets regardless of whether they were in Fritz's territory or not. The lighting was brilliant. More cameras were used. Pulsing rock music greeted the entry of most wrestlers. The Sportatorium, where the show was taped in Dallas, was changed from an old tin shed into a dazzling home for wrestling, at least as far as television was concerned.

Nonetheless, it still would have flopped without the right talent. "The Fabulous Freebirds," a trio composed of Terry Gordy, Michael Hayes, and Buddy Roberts, were charismatic heels. So were Jimmy Garvin and his lovely valet, Precious. Gino Hernandez represented the smart-aleck, handsome, arrogant "bad guy." Kabuki was the mysterious and dangerous Oriental threat.

Of course, Gary Hart was right in the middle of most of the mayhem as a manager always at odds with Fritz himself. Behind the scenes, he also was the wily booker for Fritz's operation. "I understood what was in Bruise's heart; he wanted to do the right thing and make money for everyone," says Gary. "But I knew nobody could control Bruiser Brody. The type of relationship we had, though, we could work together and I could direct him a bit."

And it all worked, according to Hart, because of the babyfaces. "It was a great combination. The high-flying, handsome, All-American kids: Kevin, David, and Kerry Von Erich. The big ruffian enforcer, the butt kicker: Bruiser Brody. Brody was every bit as important as the Von Erichs themselves were in how hot World Class became," Hart explains.

Hart is also quick to credit Frank for helping Gary get Kabuki, who was red hot at the time, rolling. First of all, Hart had told Frank of his idea for this new character, so Frank was keeping an eye open during his travels for the right wrestler to fill the slot. When he spotted Takachiho, underrated and underpaid working in Kansas City, Brody told Hart to take a look. Hart made the next trip with Brody to Kansas City and immediately signed up Takachiho.

The Japanese grappler became The Great Kabuki, painted, vicious, and managed by "Playboy" Gary Hart. Most controversial was when Kabuki would spit green mist into the eyes of a foe, thus blinding the opponent. "Frank was the first to take the green mist," says Hart.

In other words, Brody had Kabuki blow the perilous green stuff into his face and, right on *World Class* television, for all the fans to see, sold the act as though he had been destroyed. Why would Brody do this? First, he trusted Hart. Second, he trusted Fritz Von Erich.

Frank believed that doing it correctly would create an opponent for Brody, who would seek revenge in a series of battles that would draw serious money at the box office. An added bonus was that when the run between Brody and Kabuki was over, Kabuki would be established as a meaningful headliner in the territory and Brody's feud with Hart would continue as the wily manager sought another fiendish monster to take out arch-rival Brody.

"Frank made sure Kabuki got over. He did the right thing for business. The Brody character was so powerful and established that when he was in trouble, it made his opponent real," explains Gary. "Frank was the key piece of the puzzle in getting Kabuki over."

Fritz was so high on Frank personally that he wanted to set up Goodish in a business outside of wrestling, Kevin remembers. The details never came together, but the attempt flattered Frank. "Dad really did think of Frank as another son and believed that Frank was smart with money," Kevin says.

Frank Goodish was at the top of his game. "It didn't matter who was in the ring. It could be Andre the Giant or Ric Flair. When Bruise kicked open that dressing room door and stormed to the ring, every eye — and I mean every single eye — in the place was on Bruiser Brody," proclaims Hart. "What a sight he was. There was bedlam and pandemonium!"

Terry Funk says, "Frank had a passion for working and it had all come together for him."

"He could produce and deliver the crowd," Buck Robley adds. "And he could produce in the ring. You could build around him."

Much of the Goodish booking in the early 1980s went through the Dallas office and Hart. Of course, he also booked himself in some dates and had the Japanese deal with Baba. "Frank knew how to pick the televisions that mattered," says Hart. "He would always make sure I had him on the *World Class* tapings and available for St. Louis.

"Even though there was not one national program like wrestling today," adds Hart, "Frank got over nationally by the way he used the regional television shows. He even was on Atlanta a few times when cable was starting. He really was ahead of his time in using television for his benefit."

Robley says that Frank "had learned how to call his own shots. He knew you had to be able to call your own shots to make money. Plus, Frank understood the power of television and what he could do on it. He knew the inside of the game."

Hart notes that Brody was always booked or booking himself, often with help from Robley. Hart recalls Frank telling him, "there is a promoter somewhere out there who has $300 with my name on it and I want it." He understood his power.

Robley did too. "Lots of guys wanted to do what Frank did, but he could intimidate like nobody else could. Promoters cater to someone who can sell tickets, and Brody could."

Buck was in the middle of one dispute in Atlanta. He admits he often served as Frank's fall guy, "to get him in the door and throw out some ideas about him." That was Buck's role in Atlanta in the spring of 1981. Robley snorts at "the masterminds like Jim Barnett, Bill Watts, and Eddie Graham who didn't know what they had or they were just too afraid of losing control."

On one occasion Frank was supposed to be on camera for an Atlanta TV interview. But, as Frank himself later explained, "Everybody talked on that show. Lots of talk, talk, talk." And because other wrestlers would be involved, talking, in the scene, he decided to do something different, something unique to make the viewers watch him.

He prowled around the studio and found a giant globe-shaped light bulb.

"When I came on, I just stuck that light bulb in my mouth and stood there while everyone yacked. Didn't say a word, just opened my eyes wide and stood there staring with that big ol' bulb in my mouth," chuckled Goodish. When it was over, which personality was likely to be the one that viewers were talking about?

A program between Brody and Abdullah was built, but it was violent and bloody. Robley made a few enemies in the office and was fired by the time Abdullah and Brody tangled at the Omni. "They gave the fans a blood bath," says Robley. "Frank gave 'em a show and then he got the money."

Once, when Frank was returning from Japan, he was booked into Little Rock, Arkansas. His old Waffle House partner Jaggers was working in the territory and picked Frank up at the airport. Japan always paid cash at the time, so Frank was flush with thousands of dollars in his bag.

Knowing how Japan operated, Bobby made Frank aware that there had been a thief in the dressing room for a few weeks. Money had been missing, maybe a wallet or a watch or a ring. Jaggers told Frank who most of the wrestlers thought was the thief. Jaggers offered to lock Frank's luggage and money in the trunk, but Frank was skeptical.

They went into the dressing room, with its usual mixture of noise, whispering, laughing, politics, and cursing. Suddenly Frank yelled, loudly enough to dominate the room, "Hey, Jags! I hear you got a thief in the dressing room."

Sudden silence. Bobby answered, "Well, Bruise, yeah, that's true."

Goodish stood up, grabbing his bag with all the money inside, and walked right over to the grappler Jagger had fingered as the culprit. "Here, brother. The best place to keep this safe is to have you hold this," growled Brody as he handed the bag to the startled wrestler.

Jaggers said Brody finished his match and went into the dressing room to find the fellow to whom he'd handed his goods waiting right by the door and with the bag still in hand. He gave it to Frank and promised, "There's not one damn dime missing!" And there wasn't.

"That took care of the thief problem in the dressing room," laughs Jaggers. "Any wrestler who was in Little Rock will remember that forever!" Frank later said the thing to do was go directly to the one who was suspected. What could any crook do under those circumstances?

According to Jaggers, and many others, Frank Goodish had respect in the room. "All of the guys wished they had the balls to do what Frank did," says Jaggers, speaking not only of the thief incident but also of Frank's ability to stand up and demand his share. "Frank could pop a territory like nobody else. He'd hug you when he came and he'd hug you when he left. But Frank would make clear he was going to make his money. You had to accept that."

Robley explains, "There was no friction in any dressing room about Frank. He had harmony with everyone. If he got moody, it was always about the promoter, or maybe the booker. And it was almost always about money."

Not only was Frank hitting Texas as much as always, he also turned the

Atlanta television showings into outings from Columbus, Ohio, to Roanoke, Virginia, and back to Atlanta. He had a great run again in Florida, where he often formed a tag team with buddy "Big John" Studd to tackle "Butch" Reed and old West Texas acquaintance Dusty Rhodes. As Hart says, there was money with Frank's name on it ready and waiting all over the country.

"Guys could ride that gravy train," Robley says. When a house was full because of Brody, all the wrestlers on the card made more. And, Buck adds, "Frank had the heart and he was willing to fight. He was always two steps ahead of everybody."

In those days, promotions weren't major corporate entities like the current WWE, with diversified revenues and modern accounting practices. Many territorial promotions took profits after every week, or even after every so-called major program. The money flowed quickly from box office to owners. In reality, a high percentage of these promotions (unlike today's WWE, or a town like St. Louis back then) were living hand to mouth.

If the promoter or booker had become angry about something Brody did, they didn't schedule him. Perhaps more often, Brody would refuse to accept a date because he was irritated with the promoter. A show would run, but there would be no profit to split or the proceeds would be significantly lower. Maybe there would even be a loss, requiring the promoters of that particular territory to throw a few bucks into the kitty. Ouch.

Thus, they had to find another top attraction. But top attractions, especially on short notice, were always difficult to obtain. So, they had to book Brody again. He drew money. It's not that they didn't like him personally — they did. But his stubborn, no-backward-step business philosophy made them angry.

Maybe perturbing them even more was the fact that they needed Brody or someone like him. And the hard fact was that there were very, very few — maybe none who were as independent — close to him as an attraction. Since he drew money, the promoters made a profit. They had cash to count whether or not they liked the philosophy of the star who got them into that position.

Japan was rapidly becoming a major part of the business foundation for Frank Goodish as well. Every trip to the Orient added to Brody's reputation for exciting matches and drawing crowds. Soon his salary was in the stratosphere for foreign wrestlers, at approximately $10,000 per week plus expenses. "Japan was the key to the whole thing for Frank," says Robley. "From 16 to 22 weeks a year for huge money gave Frank room to operate." Brody had arrived at the position where he didn't need to work for someone that he didn't want to work for.

The booking at that time in Japan was very precise. Many main events were tag team matches, featuring perhaps two or three established stars and one or two on the cusp. That allowed the big name, like Brody or the Funks, to tease what a one-on-one duel might be like with Baba or Tsuruta while still getting a decision in the particular bout. While foreigners were usually kept together on one side, different combinations were often put together. When all four were solid headliners, it was at a large facility for capacity crowds.

Sprinkled throughout a three or four week tour would be a few head-to-head battles, foreigner versus Japanese. The philosophy in that era was that those tussles usually ended in disqualifications, double DQs, or double count-outs except on truly major shows. The evolution of the business eventually changed that thinking to decisions and pins every time out by the 1990s, but a glance at Brody's slate in the 1980s showed how highly he was regarded and marketed.

For instance, Brody did "do a job" for Baba in the finals of the Championship Carnival April 23, 1981, in Osaka. Baba, though, returned the favor as he was beaten by Brody on April 27 in Gifu. Otherwise, as Matt Farmer's detailed research shows, the slate is jammed with DQs and double count-outs involving Brody with either Baba or Tsuruta (and even a rare win or two over "Jumbo").

Occasionally foreigners would clash, giving Frank a chance to tangle with the likes of the Funks. "Junior just loved to work with him," Terry says. And it's no wonder, reviewing a tape of one of the collisions between Brody and Dory Jr. from Japan in 1982. The donnybrook was stiff, athletic, beautifully paced — the match showcased the strengths of both performers as they hooked the crowd deeper and deeper into the story of the bout. Finally Brody exploded with a vicious attack on Dory Jr. outside the ring, going rows deep into the spectators to batter Dory Jr. By the time Funk struggled back to the ring, Dory was gushing blood.

But then Funk got his revenge with a sizzling comeback that left Brody bleeding badly as well. What an image to see Dory Jr. nailing Brody with wicked forearm uppercuts that bounced the big man into the turnbuckles and back out again, with Brody's gory head conveniently landing against Funk's chest and smearing even more of the blood for all to see.

False finish, false finish — near pins for each combatant. The audience stood and roared, totally immersed in the brutal, bloody ballet. Then Funk moved behind Brody for the classic Greco-Roman back body drop — shades of the famous Lou Thesz. Dory Jr. hoisted the 300-pounder on top of his shoulder, freezing for an instant before driving the big man backwards onto his head and neck.

Suddenly, Brody lashed out with his powerful legs and kicked off the top turnbuckle! Funk, thrown off balance, crashed backward beneath his burly opponent and was trapped long enough for Brody to get the pin. The clever Japanese announcers and media were left with a superb story to tell of a razor-thin margin in one match for Brody, who had demonstrated he was much more than just a wildman by the method he used to snatch victory.

One other element was also at play in Japan during that period. Baba had once been allies with Antonio Inoki, who later came to fame for a mixed wrestler-versus-boxer match with Muhammad Ali, in the dominant promotion operated by the famous Rikidozan. After Rikidozan's death, the parting between Inoki and Baba was extremely bitter. Both wanted power and control.

When the smoke finally cleared, there were two major Japanese promotions — Baba led All Japan; Inoki, New Japan. Ironically, Frank's friend Stan Hansen became a top foreign name for Inoki. So did Andre the Giant and Hulk Hogan.

On December 13, 1981, at the Sumo Hall in Tokyo, it all came together for All Japan in one of the most famous events in Japanese wrestling history. At the end of the evening, what happened in the main event guaranteed everyone involved legendary status. Terry Funk claims, "We knew we had a good thing going with Baba even before that bout took place. But this was a turning point, a monumental moment."

At stake was the championship of the prestigious annual All Japan tag team tourney. Most every team was loaded and the booking through Baba was so meticulous that points were distributed for victories, defeats, and draws. Different results could lead to different opponents for a team as the brackets moved. Until the very end, no fan could be sure who would collide for the title.

In 1981, it was Brody and Jimmy Snuka, an incredible piece of talent who had formed a smashing tag duo with Frank, against Dory Jr. and Terry Funk. "That night, Frank became a true superstar in the business," marvels Funk. The action hit new levels of excitement. When the triumph went to Brody and Snuka, it all clicked.

And especially when Stan Hansen, who until then had been a star for Inoki, came out of nowhere to nail Terry Funk with a devastating lariat ("clothesline" in today's terminology, only twice as stiff from Hansen) while Terry was on the floor, knocking Funk cold. Hansen was added into the mix on Baba's side as he made the jump from Inoki. "That match and Stan coming over was so incredible," says Terry. "We knew immediately that we had five years of great stuff that would draw and draw and draw."

By 1982, it also led to Brody and Hansen forming one of the most famous (if not *the* most famous) tag team units in wrestling. Not only were they unstoppable forces on their own, now they were often together as an incredible duo.

Late in 1982, Dory Jr. began booking in the Carolinas for Jim Crockett Jr., the son of Jim Sr. and the man who had taken over the lucrative territory after John Ringley had been in charge. Naturally, Dory and Terry wanted to bring in Brody and Hansen, but Crockett Jr. eventually nixed the program. Apparently, the "Bolsheviks" in the group concerned Crockett. "It was either real smart or real dumb on his part," says Terry. "If we'd had those guys in, Crockett would have lost control of his business. So that was smart. But he'd have made a *ton* of money. So that was stupid."

Another premier talent who had crossed paths with Frank over the years was Jack Brisco. Brisco won both the NWA professional title and the NCAA collegiate crown when he was at Oklahoma State. "Frank was a good guy. We hung out together in Japan and never one time had a cross word," says Brisco. "We drank a few beers and he told me how he hated promoters!"

During that short run in the Carolinas, Brody and Brisco tangled on December 26, 1982, in Greensboro, North Carolina. After the introductions, Brisco turned to remove his jacket. "I heard a rumbling coming toward me," he says. "I actually felt the ring shaking. It was Brody, running as fast as he could, and Frank crashed into my back and nearly knocked me out!

"I was trying to get my wind back and he was on top of me, pounding away. I snapped at him, 'You son of a bitch!'

"And Frank kept saying, 'I'm sorry, Jack. I'm sorry!' while he kept beating on me. He was just messing with me, having some fun because he knew I could take it." The two got into gear together and had a fabulous match that brought down the house.

The ride got bigger and better for Frank Goodish. However, as Terry Funk admits, "Frank could create disarray. He pushed some people a certain way and just ate up others. It was about the money."

"Frank saw himself as invincible. It was part of his personna, part of who he was," says Gary Hart. "He had to be that way."

"It was a power trip for Frank, and he loved to play. A way to tell some promoter: 'Without me, you can't draw.' Even though Frank couldn't get the first count, he would still fight for his money," agrees Buck Robley.

"It was his business. It was his life," says Pete Ortega. "Frank loved that power game."

In North America, however, professional wrestling was about to undergo an earth-shaking transformation. At the end of 1983, Vince McMahon, Jr. was poised to pounce as the National Wrestling Alliance crumbled. As cable changed television forever, territories became obsolete: the opportunity to have one dominant national promotion was at hand.

The war for control — and it was a war — would be bitter, nasty, and dirty. Promotions would die. Careers would be altered or, worse, destroyed. Yet somehow, through all the turbulence, one basic principle survived: a star is a star. Putting fans in seats and money in the box office is what counts. Gimmicks only go so far. Even in the midst of chaos, a select few thrived: those with the inner drive, the unbreakable spirit, the outlaw mentality.

Frank Goodish, as Bruiser Brody, had it all. As others floundered, he thrived.

CHAPTER FOURTEEN

Barbara Remembers . . .
MARRIAGE AND A SON

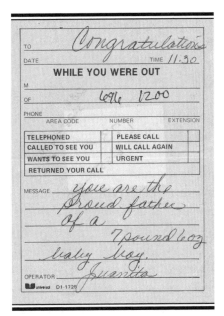

Before we decided to get married — get that official piece of paper — Frank was heading for Japan on one of his many trips. His parents were living in California with one of his sisters at the time. We decided to visit Las Vegas together, then move on to Los Angeles where I could stay for a couple of weeks after he left for his six-week tour of Japan.

Getting married in Las Vegas seemed like a good idea. It was just for the two of us, and we weren't making a big thing out of it. I researched, because Frank naturally wanted to find the best deal. We found a wedding chapel that picked us up in a limo from the hotel, took us downtown to the court-house for the license, and then back to the chapel for the ceremony. It was, apparently, the same chapel where Frank Sinatra and Mia Farrow were married — their picture was up on the wall. The chapel also provided witnesses, so we went ahead and said our vows.

After the ceremony, the minister gave Frank an envelope, which he put in his pocket. That night I asked him what he tipped the minister. He looked at me and pulled the envelope out. Poor Frank — he had not realized that was what the envelope was for! He really felt bad about it, angry with himself for not understanding.

There was no real honeymoon. Within 24 hours I was with relatives and he was on a plane headed toward Japan. We always said one day we would have the honeymoon we never had . . . but sometimes tomorrow never comes.

By the time we were expecting our first child, both of us were more aware that the income from wrestling could disappear at any time. Frank knew as well as anyone: there are no guarantees. That's one of the reasons he was always so careful with a dollar, always wanting receipts. He wasn't just being tight — he was just aware of all the pitfalls, the inevitability of injuries. There were also big expenses — something that was true for everyone in wrestling — men like Frank had to pay for their own accommodation and food when they traveled for work.

Even when the promoter paid for a flight into a territory, there was still the cost of getting from the airport or the hotel to the arena. The cost of gas if he worked around Texas and drove to shows was usually his as well. There were the everyday costs of keeping a home up too.

In addition, the yearly tax bite was huge. There were estimated payments to be made, because no one withheld federal tax. Wrestlers also had to pay self-employed social security tax. There really wasn't a lot left. Sometimes there were negative weeks, when there were more expenses than income. That's why towns like St. Louis, Dallas, and Houston were important: because they drew big crowds and paid well.

And it is definitely why Japan was so important. With that money, Frank could invest and make plans.

We had no insurance when Geoff was born. Promoters certainly did not provide it, so that was another expense for the boys. And because of the risk of injury, the cost of insurance was astronomical. At the time, we saved — just in case.

The hospital wanted insurance before they would admit me. Fortunately, they had a pre-birth plan where you could put money aside regularly so that there was enough to cover all the costs. That was what Frank and I did.

It was hard, being alone when I was pregnant. Frank tried to help. I spent some time with his sister Gayle in Los Angeles, while Frank was once again in Japan. He really had wanted to help before we left, so he went around unplugging appliances — the television, the coffee maker, the washer, the dryer. He didn't realize that the freezer was on the same plug as the washing machine.

I came home a couple weeks before he returned from Japan to a freezer full of spoiled meat. (The chicken was the worst.) There I was, alone, pregnant, and cleaning. We had to throw the freezer out because we couldn't get rid of the smell. But honestly, Frank truly believed he was helping.

Frank's mom has told me stories about him growing up. He was always an independent young man. She said that he was a steak man and enjoyed spaghetti with her special homemade sauce.

In Sydney, his breakfast of choice was spam and eggs. I remember fixing him that meal; I would open the can of spam, cut it into small squares, cook it for a few minutes in a frying pan, put scrambled eggs in, mix it up, and then serve it with toast. I had never heard of spam before I met him.

I know the boys would get on his case about the cans of tuna and green beans he would carry on the road. The funny part is that at home at night he would eat it as a snack. Tuna and green beans. Right out of the can! He listened to his body because it was the tool of his profession. Once it went, he would not be able to perform. He always wanted to give them a match they would remember. I cannot stress enough how seriously he took his work.

Of course, Frank was away often. Luckily, we also made friends with several of the San Antonio Spurs, in particular Kevin Restani and his wife Claire. You form a bond with people who have to travel for their work and understand how difficult it can be.

I met Claire at the gym where I worked out. Frank was out of town so much, and Pete and Rowe worked during the day, so I had a lot of time to myself — which can be very lonely when you are in a new country.

I had finished my workout that day and was relaxing in the pool. Claire and I just started talking. We were both new to San Antonio and it was uncanny because our lives were so similar since both of our husbands were on the road all the time. We had so much in common that a friendship came naturally.

I went to the Spurs games several times and sat with Claire and the other wives. It was good company, as we all had the same situation with our husbands in the public eye.

When I had Geoff on November 7, 1980, it was actually Kevin Restani who was the first to come to see me in the hospital. I couldn't get in touch with Claire, but Kevin happened to be home and got the message so he came to the hospital. All the nurses went crazy when this tall gentleman who played for the Spurs came to see me. When Frank finally got there, they were all in shock about these big men coming to visit the new mother.

Frank was on the road, wrestling in Kansas City and St. Louis, when I gave birth. He had left on Thursday, so I had dropped him off at the airport. Then I went to the gym to do some low impact exercise. This was followed by a doctor appointment, nothing unusual, just my weekly check-up. I still had a couple of weeks to go, and I got a clean bill of health from the doctor. The last thing he said was, "See you next week."

Well, in the middle of the night, I felt a little strange so in the morning I called my wonderful friend and neighbor Dede Middleton. She said to come to her house as she was getting her children ready for school.

After a while she looked at me and informed me she was going to take me to the hospital. I was telling her *no* — they would just send me home again. Dede got very persistent. She said she had three children and she could see the signs, so she bundled me in her car. I am so grateful, as it was a half hour ride to get there and Geoff was born not long after I arrived.

I had given her some numbers where Frank could be reached. I knew he would have worked Kansas City and would be on his way to St. Louis. She left messages for him at the Lennox Hotel, where the office was in St. Louis. Dede stayed with me until she had to go home to take care of her own kids.

I still have the messages that Frank received. The first one tells him I'm at the hospital and the next one informs him of the birth of his son. I found them when I was going through his belongings after his death.

Remember, there weren't cell phones back then. Frank flew right home, getting in late Friday. He left again Saturday morning for a show and then couldn't get back into town until Monday morning. I had to tell the hospital that I couldn't check out until Monday because I had no one to pick me up. I just couldn't bother Dede again. They wanted me to check out Sunday, but I had to stay one more night.

Frank came Monday and took me home with the new baby. But he had to leave the same day, as he had a match in Fort Worth. I remember that night I did not sleep at all. Here I was in the house alone with a brand new baby! I was terrified, and I remember looking at that tiny bundle all night.

When Frank finally got home that Tuesday, it was amazing. He could not take his eyes off of the child. I can still see Frank just sitting there and gazing at our son for hours on end. We just sat and looked at Geoff.

Having Geoff changed Frank's life. He was never one to share his feelings: he held a lot inside. Frank didn't want to show vulnerability, especially, I think, because he was in wrestling. But fatherhood changes men. It put wrestling into perspective for Frank. I don't know if he would have related to a daughter as well. After all, he was something of a male chauvinist, and besides, he already had three sisters.

As busy as he was wrestling, Frank tried hard to do the normal things with his family. Especially when Geoff learned to talk, Frank would call home more often just to hear Geoff speak. Frank wanted to provide for his family, so he had to be on the road, especially Japan. But he made sure the time he spent really was quality. Just seeing him and Geoff horsing around was great.

It wasn't unusual for a call to come through in the middle of the night telling me that Frank was arriving at the airport in the wee hours of the morning. I can remember getting Geoff out of bed and putting him — still sleeping! — in the back seat, and then driving thirty miles to the airport. Every moment together was worth it.

Once, months after Geoff was born, Frank and I tried to get away. After making sure Geoff would be taken care of, we made plans to meet in New Orleans where Frank was wrestling. This was the very first time since Geoff had been born that Frank and I would be alone. It was a big deal.

Frank was coming from Dallas. I was coming from San Antonio. But when I got to New Orleans, his flight was first delayed and then cancelled. We had no way to communicate from two different airports. What a mess! All I could do was stay at the airport and meet every flight — and I think there were five! — that came in from Dallas. Finally he got in.

The problem was that it was so late that everybody had to rush right to the show. We had a little time afterwards, and got to go to the French Quarter, but it wasn't relaxed like we had hoped. The next morning, he had to rush for another flight to wrestle in a different city and I had a later flight back to San Antonio.

I remember once he had been on the road, probably including Japan, but he needed some papers and just didn't have time to get home. I flew to Dallas and met Frank as he got off another flight. We actually had a couple of hours together then at the airport. It was so important, though, to both of us, to find even a couple of hours together.

How unfortunate it was that Frank and Geoff did not have more time together as father and son. I remember that their favorite game was He-Man and Skeletor, which were Geoff's favorite action figures when he was a child. Of course, Geoff was He-Man and Dad was the bad dude Skeletor. They would always refer to themselves as those names in telephone conversations and letters.

Another favorite game they played was Transformers. Dad was often working in Japan and would always bring back the latest Transformer. When Frank would arrive home while Geoff was in school, Frank would set up a treasure hunt with the gifts.

He would send Geoff into the bedroom, where there was a note on the bed. It would say something like, "He-Man, look in the bathtub. Skeletor is waiting." Then in the bathtub would be another note to look somewhere else. Thus, Geoff would end up all over the house looking for clues.

Finally, Geoff would find the gift. Oh my, the look on his face! I don't know who had the most fun, Geoff or his dad.

After that, Geoff knew that Dad would be very tired from his trip and Geoff would be very quiet around the house. He would play with his new toys until Dad had recovered from his jet lag.

Geoff really is his father's son. Although he was not around Frank for long, the traits are unmistakable even today. His eyes tell it all, the way he looks at different things. And his mannerisms: it's uncanny.

I can remember them in the garage, where Frank was sitting on the workout equipment and carving pumpkins for Halloween. Other times, when Frank would be doing his workout, Geoff would go into the garage and try to be quiet. He knew the time at home was very short and he wanted to get as much time with his dad as he could.

They picked out a puppy together. We had seen an advertisement in the paper for a Sharpei, and Frank liked the breed because they were just becoming known in the United States. He liked that they were unusual with all their wrinkles. I remember the two of them looking at all the puppies and this one started following Geoff, so that was the one they picked, as he had picked us. They named him Darcy.

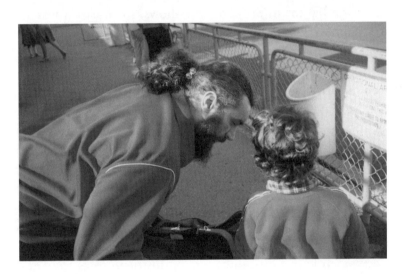

I also have fond memories of them wrestling on the floor. Of course, Frank would "put Geoff over." I once asked Geoff if, when he was older, he would ever consider wrestling. His answer was a loud "*No!*" His reason was because Dad was never home. That's when I understood that he knew his life was not normal, and that he wished his Dad had been home a lot more. He missed not having his father around for birthdays, Father's Day, and every event that he would go to and see his friends with their Dads there.

Frank attempted to work in dates close to home, and these were special. Christmas was always a difficult day for a family in wrestling; with so many big shows around the country at that time, Frank was always booked. So our holiday was really the night before.

Dallas was a big town for Christmas shows, so at least it was a shorter trip for Frank. We would have to do something Christmas Eve and early in the morning Christmas. There was no time to cook a big meal. Then it was off to the airport to say goodbye to Dad.

I can remember Frank trying to put together toys for Geoff and all the fun when we watched our son unwrap his gifts. I'm glad I have those pictures of the two of them together. When I look back, I can visualize the two of them playing on the floor in the front room of the Boerne house.

He would put Geoff to bed on Christmas Eve and, as every parent can relate, there was usually some item that had to be put together and ready for Christmas morning. You always had it, whether it was a bike or a scooter or anything, hidden somewhere until the night before. Here was Frank on the floor, trying to use those big hands to put a child's bike together.

As we women know, men don't look at instructions as women do. We don't have to take it apart and put it back together again. Frank several times had to do just that while trying very hard to keep his cool and not destroy whatever part he was left with. What made it all worthwhile was the next morning, having the completed item next to the tree and seeing Geoff's face when he awoke. It was one of Frank's special times with his son.

Frank used to tell me that when he walked through the doors at the airport, he would change character from Frank Goodish to Bruiser Brody and then when I picked him up, it was the other way around. Bruiser Brody would stay at the other side of the doors while Dad and Frank would appear.

Christmas Day, of course, meant that trip to the airport so Dad could go wrestle somewhere. Hi . . . bye.

CHAPTER FIFTEEN

THE WORLD
IS CHANGING

Beginning in 1984, the professional wrestling world was about to experience possibly the most gut-wrenching change of any sports-related industry ever. Vince McMahon, Jr. and the World Wrestling Federation adroitly used the natural greed of wrestlers, the weaknesses of existing promotions, and the revolution in production techniques, cable, and pay-per-view television to help eliminate most vestiges of competition. Some, perhaps most, of the methods were ruthless and unethical, which finally made wrestling comparable to the rest of the business world. . . .

One by one, the old territorial promotions began to disappear. In most cases, McMahon raided the office's talent. In other circumstances, he snatched the television time slot away with big money offers to the stations involved. Vince's television package was truly state-of-the-art, especially when the company established its own production facility.

WWF programming became *the* television wrestling show to see. Their syndicated package gobbled up favorite time slots in almost every market and it had so much talent at its disposal that no other show could match it. Cable was becoming stronger and the WWF had its weekly place on USA Network. The home run, of course, was when the WWF landed a series of specials on NBC-TV. This moved the perception of the WWF to another plateau.

Since the talent level was so high and the new tools of production so eye-catching, the territorial TV programs that survived looked minor league at best. When the WWF ran an arena card in a town, the lineup was loaded with recognizable talent from top to bottom. The locals usually took it on the chin until they folded. Adding closed circuit and eventually pay-per-view for major events like WrestleMania simply completed the trend. A regional operation could not compete as the national "elephant" would pay more money and snatch away the best of everything from the smaller offices.

Cross-promotion through McMahon's New York contacts made pro wrestling seem mainstream, hip, and new. The media compliantly accepted whatever pablum Vince offered about the dark old days of wrestling, when supposedly only a limited audience was interested in grappling. The business itself was so fragile after the retirement of Sam Muchnick that the death of the National Wrestling Alliance made McMahon's goal of having it all much easier to achieve. Nonetheless, his business tactics were often unsavory and left many a career buried in the rubble.

Not, however, that of Bruiser Brody. With Japan as his foundation, Frank Goodish found success by cherry-picking territories and towns in need as the WWF onslaught progressed. As the territories dried up, Goodish discovered and added a lucrative (for him, at least) market of independent promoters around the country. The rebel did quite nicely.

Early in 1984, an ominous event occurred: the sudden death of David Von Erich, a charismatic and exciting performer who was growing in his understanding of the business. Perhaps that tragedy was a foreshadowing of all the catastrophes which would be linked with professional wrestling from that point on.

For Goodish, it was a terrible blow because David had been a close friend, almost a "little brother." Frank often teased David with the nickname "Spider," because Von Erich "was all arms, all legs, no body."

David had been reeling, drinking too much and using painkillers, as he broke away from the stern hand of his father Fritz to make his own mark in Florida and then on to his own tour of Japan. In addition, David's personal life had been shaken by a divorce and the crib death of his infant child.

On February 10, Goodish, along with referee Joe Higuchi and wrestler Gerry Morrow, went to David's room when he didn't arrive for that night's card. They found David on the bed, telephone book in hand. He was dead. A distraught Goodish later called me and said, "I don't want to believe it. He had so much to live for. This had to be an accident."

In that room, Goodish thought of his long relation with David's father and his friendship with the other boys. Then he took the remaining pills and flushed them down the toilet before tossing the bottle. Frank saw no reason for the family to suffer further agony with the media and the business. He protected his friend as best he could.

Perhaps it was a tragic mistake, an accidentally lethal mixture of booze and drugs. Unfortunately, for three other Von Erich brothers (Kerry, Mike, and Chris) the results definitely pointed to suicide. The drug culture, particularly with steroid abuse and painkillers, would claim many more victims in the next two decades.

Japan was, however, still the bulwark of Goodish's business. He was at the top of the pay scale in All Japan, earning approximately $12,000 per week. The tag team combination with Hansen was dominant, getting the high-profile matches against the Funks or Baba and Tsuruta. Often he also joined forces with "Crusher" Blackwell. When the time came for the big one-on-one duels, Brody was always on top as well.

At the same time, Verne Gagne's American Wrestling Association had taken some major blows from the WWF expansion. Verne had been a top attraction himself for many years throughout the Midlands and was essentially the AWA. Gagne himself had moved into other towns at times, failing terribly in Los Angeles but displacing the existing promotion in San Francisco in 1981. One of the ways McMahon rationalized his actions was that if he didn't make the attempt to go national, Gagne would. In addition to grabbing talent like Hulk Hogan, Jesse Ventura, David Schults, and

Bobby Heenan from Gagne, McMahon had also taken key people from Verne's television, such as Gene Okerlund and behind-the-scenes production personnel.

Gagne's first inclination, after Vince's raid, was to fight. He had a core group of wrestlers, but it was shrinking and needed a shot in the arm. As a partner in the St. Louis operation, he had seen the impact Brody had on business. Undoubtedly worried because of the big man's reputation, Gagne rolled the dice and booked Frank. The marriage was rocky at best.

"Frank booked himself with Gagne," says Buck Robley, "although we talked about it a lot. He said it was so easy to get over, but always a fight. There were lots of problems. He caused a few scenes."

Gary Hart feels that the headaches stemmed "from a dressing room that was really a clique. They just always did things the same way. Lots of those guys had been there for years and were practically office. You know how Bruise was with cliques! His idea of a clique was two people at most and he did things his own way.

"I know he liked the television exposure he got," said Hart. "I don't think there was a real problem with Gagne, but he always called Verne 'that frieeeend of Dick The Bruiser,' and when he said 'frieeeeend' that way, you know Bruise was careful." Of course, Frank had had his money disputes with Dick, who owned Indianapolis and was also a partner of Gagne in Chicago.

Terry Funk thinks Frank may have pushed things too far with Gagne: "He hurt Verne's pride, gave him no respect." Frank's attitude offended some of Gagne's longtime talent, at least what was left after Vince Jr. swooped in, but he helped lure houses and keep the AWA alive while others were already starting to fall. One of the best foes for Brody was "Crusher" Blackwell, and that rivalry drew some meaningful cash. Thus, the relationship with the AWA bumped along into the start of 1985 and would have yet another life in 1986.

In 1984, the rapport Frank and I shared became even stronger. I was working for the WWF and had the inside news. Frank knew virtually everything else from the other side because he worked in the most lucrative cities, including AWA towns, for anyone who needed a star to pop a town fast and draw serious money.

The coming and going of various wrestlers, front office operators, and television outlets made for an intriguing soap opera. Through me, Frank also became a friend and mentor for an eager young wrestling journalist named Dave Meltzer. What Meltzer wrote in his *Wrestling Observer* earned the wrath of all sectors of promotion in the mid 1980s. Meltzer had no intention of hurting wrestling; he simply wanted to cover it — from a journalistic viewpoint — as the fascinating business that it was.

"Kayfabe," the industry term for keeping the inside details of wrestling from fans and outsiders, became obsolete as much through Vince Jr. himself, who testified before various state legislatures in order to avoid athletic taxes for his company, as through anything Meltzer said to a much smaller but more devoted audience. Those readers were going to buy tickets unless they were personally driven away from wrestling. They just wanted the inside scoops common in baseball, football, and basketball coverage.

Since Frank and I both majored in journalism in college, we clicked with Meltzer. We urged Dave to somehow fight through "the con" and get the facts. In the long run, such coverage would actually help wrestling while keeping Vince and others in line (perhaps a tiny bit) when they resorted to the shady side of promotion. The *Wrestling Observer* today still has tremendous, if unacknowledged, power behind closed doors.

In the mid-1980s, between the three of us — Goodish, Meltzer, and me — we probably had more knowledge of what was happening, how and when, than most anyone save for Vince himself and some of his top manipulators.

A fair portion of the so-called horror stories about Brody refusing finishes or even no-showing cards came during this era. It was an ironic twist, especially taken from the Goodish perspective. Here was a promoter who had never faced real competition before in his territory. Now, thanks to the NWA's death and the WWF's surge, drawing a house and maybe even staying in business were at issue.

Despite what has been written, no one has actually come forward with proof that Brody walked out on a show through the crowd to put heat on the promoter. In fact, Gary Hart insists, "That is just a flat-out lie. We all heard stories of stars like Johnny Valentine, 'Bearcat' Wright, 'Thunderbolt' Patterson, and maybe a few others having done that. But who knows if those stories were even true. I had some promoters call and complain after they'd had an argument with Frank, but nobody that I know of ever had Frank do that to them."

Robley, who was often in the middle if Frank had aggravated some manipulating promoter, made the same claim: "He might no-show somebody he was really peeved at, but, to my knowledge, he never walked out through a crowd. Never!"

Frank told me the stories about Patterson and Valentine supposedly doing that, getting angry about money and walking out through the fans so everyone knew the wrestler was really there no matter what the promoter would announce (injury, late flight, etc.). Frank got a kick out of a guy willing to do that, but I don't remember him ever doing it. But I do think he considered it an option if a promoter tried to change the deal on guaranteed money.

Dave Meltzer says, "I heard of Dick 'The Bruiser' and Ernie Ladd doing that. My memory says that [Brody] threatened to do it when there was a money problem on an indie show, but he got his money so he didn't."

In recent books, plenty of the authors/wrestlers have claimed to be the toughest guys ever in wrestling. Many have bragged about refusing to "do jobs," about not cooperating with promoters or opponents. They claimed that they changed finishes, bullied bookers, and that they did it because it was "what was right for business." Several of those parties also became bookers or promoters.

Why was it acceptable for them to have refused to "do business" when they wrestled and then criticize Brody because he did the exact same thing? Why was it not "bad for business" for these wrestlers/bookers/authors to have stiffed the request to lose, or do a finish a certain way, since they felt it might hurt their personal drawing power, but it was "bad for business" for Brody to do just as they did?

The word "hypocrite" comes quickly to mind to describe some of those who verbally attack Brody today.

Hart angrily defends Brody against those who have criticized how he handled his business. "So much of it is lies just to get some individual over. It's a cheap shot now that Frank's gone. Some were just jealous that Bruise wouldn't let them use him as a pawn; they are angry that he stood up for himself."

With Brody, Goodish created a character who could catch the paying customers' attention immediately. He could fill the building, putting money in the bank for all concerned. It was and is a funny thing about wrestling: thanks to McMahon, the cat was out of the bag and everyone knew that the results were predetermined. But then, as now, who wins still matters to the fans. For the couple of hours they spend enjoying the fascinating world of pro wrestling, the audience wants to believe victory matters. Therefore, common sense would seem to dictate that if a promoter has a stellar attraction, it would be wise not to ask that superstar to go down in defeat, to "do a job," unless a future plan was clearly in view for all concerned.

Why take some of the luster off that star with a defeat? Why cut into his ability to draw a big crowd the next time, whenever that may be? To the fans, winning and losing matters if they are to have an emotional investment in what happens. From Frank's position, not only was he protecting his own status, but he was also guarding what was left of the old line promoters' chance to make money.

Furthermore, stories about and photographs of American matches involving a personality like Brody always found their way to Japan. There was no way in the world, no chance in heaven or hell, that Frank Goodish was going to allow a photo, tape, or even a story showing that he had been beaten by a lesser foe disrupt his Japanese status.

From the moment Brody was established in Japan, Frank vigorously protected that position in what he did in North America. Sensing the shifting winds in the business, guarding his Japanese status became even more important. Robley said that was often a simple reason that most promoters accepted. "I can't do it because of Japan," the big man would bark.

Bobby Jaggers said he was in many dressing rooms when finishes were brought to Frank. "If he didn't want to do something a certain way, he'd say 'Wouldn't this be better' and give an idea or two," Bobby says. "He looked to the future, because he knew he had to be strong and so did his opponent for when Frank came back. Not that there weren't arguments — he had plenty. He would push hard! In the end, though, he wanted everybody strong so they could make money."

Of course, one other thing needed to be protected, from Frank's point of view: his name. He was Brody. The name alone, by word of mouth almost as much as by his wise use of various television shows, meant dollars. Brody delivered the goods, both in gate receipts and action. And, somewhere floating around deep in the background, was a potential run with the WWF and Hulk Hogan.

While lots of territorial stars were devalued and pushed down the ladder as the WWF sucked up everything and everyone, a few special talents remained unique and independent. Bruiser Brody was at the top of that list, and it was something Frank Goodish was not about to let be toppled.

Not that this stubborn attitude hadn't appeared years earlier. But it made sense — to Frank at least — to "do the job" for a solid, well-paying promotion like St. Louis in 1979, but *not* to "do the job" for an American Wrestling Association that was wavering on the brink of bankruptcy in 1986. This "outlaw" could see how the game was being played.

And, as Terry Funk claims, sometimes Frank just liked to create the chaos as part of his reputation. Brody did indeed love to play the power game. Matt Farmer asks a logical question about the complaints some made about Brody: "If I was a promoter or booker and had problems with a talent like that . . . Wouldn't the sane thing to do be not to book him?"

It sure would, unless he drew money nobody else could or the stories were occasionally blown out of proportion.

More often than not, the issue also came down to money and what Goodish perceived as "right." Mark Nulty, who worked with the office in San Antonio, shakes his head even today about one incident with promoter Joe Blanchard. "It was for a really big card on the Fourth of July, and a run of dates over the rest of the week," explained Nulty. "Brody versus Abdullah the Butcher and a scaffold match between Eric Embry and Bobby Fulton, where Embry would win with Fulton taking that big bump off the scaffold. And we drew a big house.

"Afterward, Fulton got paid $500. Like all wrestlers, Bobby was skeptical and wasn't sure if that was fair or not, so he went to Frank to ask his opinion," says Mark. "Well, Joe Blanchard had also paid Frank $500. Frank got angry and no-showed every other card we had on that run."

As Nulty notes, pay was subjective in many territories and Blanchard, who had a good heart, felt it was fair to pay Fulton as much as the big names since Bobby was taking a nasty bump from way up high. He could just as easily have paid Fulton $300. But in Frank's mind, the top attractions got paid the most, especially when their addition made the gate receipts jump accordingly. Goodish said later that while he liked Bobby personally, "the kid took the bump, he got paid $500, and Bobby Fulton still can't get over."

Nulty said he saw both sides of Brody. Sometimes he was truly a bully and other times he was a champion for the underdog. Once, a likeable, eager youngster named Fred Ottman was trying to break in around San

Learning to be a father generated new emotions – even for Bruiser Brody.

Frank Goodish has his mechanical skill tested.

Brody, with Larry Matysik in the background, was a surprise hit at the birthday party for J.R. Obrecht.

Would Bruiser Brody put over this opponent – his son Geoff – with no argument?

Like father, like son.

TOP: Despite the fresh scar of a ring battle, it was Christmas for Frank, Geoff, and Barbara.

BOTTOM: In New Zealand, Frank and Geoff join Barbara's father and her Aunt Evelyn.

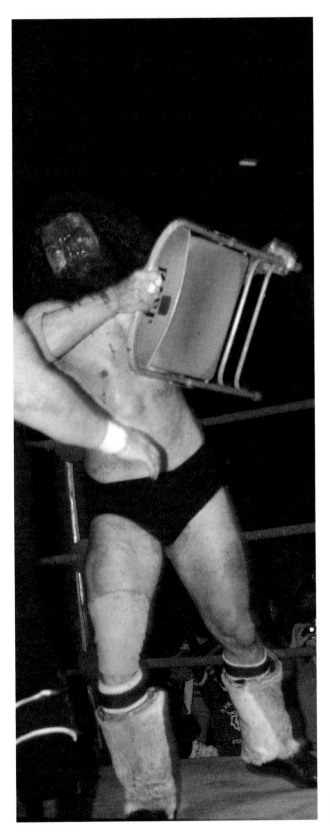

Brody at his most dangerous – with blood in his eye and a chair in his hands.

ne chain was closely identified with Brody in Japan.

OPPOSITE: Brody is delighted to be punishing Jumbo Tsuruta.

Two Hall of Famers in action: Brody nails Dory Funk, Jr. with a drop kick.

Battered but not beaten, Brody wonders where his next foe is.

OPPOSITE: Bruiser Brody and Stan Hansen were *the* ultimate warriors in the eyes of Japanese fans.

Fitting into a sleek sports car is no easy chore for Brody at an auto show in St. Louis.

OPPOSITE TO
Legendary promoter Sam Muchnick presents his "troph
to Brody at The Fabulous Fox Theater in St. Lou

OPPOSITE BOTTON
Jimmy Snuka knows it's over when Brody unleashes t
big knee dro

Crusher Blackwell has the edge on Brody — for the moment.

Can Ric Flair stop Brody with the figure four leglock?

Brody and Flair meant box office success anywhere in the mid-1980s.

Antonio, but Ottman was clumsy and had all sorts of difficulties. In the dressing room one night, Mark recalls a salty and experienced grappler verbally tearing apart the downcast newcomer: "This is wrong; that is wrong. You can't work a lick. You just suck in there."

Suddenly, Goodish, who had been quietly observing the scene, stood up and walked over to Ottman. "It's always the little guy telling the big guy how to work, kid," Frank said loudly. There was no more picking on poor Fred.

Another time around 1986 in the same dressing room, Brody was booked after a long absence from San Antonio as the town and territory were in the process of dying. Business had been worse than horrible and none of the boys were making a dime, but with Frank back there was a decent house that night. He was booked with Ray Candy, a big 300-pounder who really had gotten no push but was in many of the feature bouts around the horn. Candy was told he would be doing the job for Brody and exploded angrily.

"That's bullshit! Here I am going out every night for no money in this territory," griped Candy as wrestlers in the dressing room ran for cover, expecting the worst from Frank. "You come in once a month, get a pay day, and leave while we're stuck here trying to get a house. Where are you gonna be tomorrow? Tokyo?"

Goodish nodded easily. He understood that Candy had a legitimate gripe in a difficult situation. "You're right, brother. Let's do a double count out," Frank suggested. Then he gave Candy plenty of offense in the ring so that Ray stayed strong in the town.

Robley pointed out that once in a while the horror stories got out of hand and perhaps became more controversial (and maybe less accurate and more creative) with each retelling. The reputation of causing trouble occasionally fed on itself, like all rumors. Nonetheless, Robley admits, "There were plenty that were true. Frank loved stirring up that stuff.

"Still, no promoter had a bitch about Frank and me," Robley insists. "We revived dead territories. I'd go in for a few weeks, build something up and give ideas, then Frank would get there and pop some houses. We'd take our money and go, but they made money too. They were always glad to see us when we came back a second time."

That was obviously true when Frank made a second run with Gagne and the AWA in 1986. After bouncing ideas around with me, Frank laid out a plan that would culminate in a match sending Brody and John Nord against Verne's son Greg and Jimmy Snuka at the huge Met Center in Minneapolis on April 20.

The key was that Adnan Al Kassey (who was Billy White Wolf in another life for the WWF) managed Brody and Nord. Verne became involved as a ringside presence for his son's team. "It's all ego," Goodish laughed back then. "Give them a spot where the kid wins and Verne beats up Kassey at the finish. They'll bite."

Nord did the job for Greg and the AWA reputedly drew close to 20,000 fans. Everyone made money. The next night Brody was in Fort Worth, Texas, battling Terry Gordy as Fritz's World Class group struggled to stay in the fight. To top it off, after all their difficulties with Frank, Kansas City had him at Memorial Hall the following Thursday as that promotion desperately clung to life.

The outlaw was paid well.

There was still another reason for Frank to become even closer with me and his old St. Louis success. Beginning in late 1984, I made contact with a couple of reliable, honest, independent promoters in the Midwest. Working separate from the WWF, I found a spot where both Frank and I could profit and have fun to boot. It also gave me another peek into how Frank's mind worked.

Before the McMahon invasion actually shrank the business by putting the territories under, there had been little independent groups that got virtually no attention from the NWA or AWA honchos. When the "indies" discovered potential talent, the established forces grabbed them as quickly as possible. Now, suddenly, they provided a ground-level avenue to make money for some big stars.

The youngsters working for the independents got ignored, because the WWF locked up the more experienced matmen from the NWA, AWA, and other older groups. That fresh talent didn't get an opportunity to blossom because it was either the independents or the WWF with nothing in between. And the WWF at that time wanted more seasoned hands on board.

Therefore, for an independent promotion to headline someone like Brody gave them a chance to draw a crowd. It was a thrill and a learning experience for those young wrestlers on the cards to meet a legitimate international superstar. Of course, Frank Goodish was brutally honest when discussing their chances with those eager wrestlers.

Also, the more relaxed atmosphere around an independent show provided more interaction between fan and performer. Even more, Frank took pride in going against a less experienced, less talented opponent and generating an exciting match that thrilled the paying customers.

After one show in central Illinois, Frank and I were driving home and Frank got tired of the wrestling chatter. "I'm not like all those others guys," he complained. "I read the *Wall Street Journal*, the *New York Times*, and all the newspapers. Let's talk about business, the stock market, or maybe politics and the Middle East. Let's talk about our kids — seriously. Wrestling can drive you nuts with all the lies!"

Once I, along with my wife, Pat, and daughter, Kelly, met Frank at the airport so the big man could kill time between flights and we could discuss some business. Kelly was perhaps three at the time, and — like most youngsters — notoriously shy around strangers. But she clicked easily with Frank, who was also charmed. Kelly tentatively touched Frank's beard and Frank laughed, "Give it a tug. It's okay." And they laughed together.

Another time Frank stopped at my house to eat and relax before we headed to a show. Kelly was maybe six by then and already getting interested in sports. She was tossing a softball and looking for someone to play catch with her. Frank happily went into our backyard and was on his knees urging Kelly to throw the ball. It was relaxed fun, watching this beast who frightened fans and foes alike laughing as he chased a ball wildly thrown by a six-year-old girl.

Ronnie and Dede Middleton, Frank's neighbors at home in Boerne, Texas, also knew how terrific he was with kids. The Middletons had two sons, David and Lath, and a daughter, Sandy. They all loved the giant who made wrestling fans roar and saw how close he was with his own boy Geoff. "All kids adored him," recalled Dede when we talked years later. "He was so big and so gentle; they would just hang all over him."

Dede, who was very close to Barbara, still laughs about "Frank, Ronnie, and the kids getting into the bumper cars at the Kendall County Fair. Ronnie is big, but can you imagine someone Frank's size sticking himself into a bumper car? It was hilarious. When Sandy was maybe four years old, Frank would put her in his wrestling boots and they'd come up to her waist!"

Frank was not mechanically inclined, Dede reports. "Ronnie was always helping him start the lawn mower. And Frank didn't like to go up ladders. He'd have Ronnie, or more likely Barbara, climbing the ladder and he'd be on the ground giving directions."

The Middletons really only saw Frank as a friend and neighbor. "Once we had a big snowstorm, which was unusual in our part of Texas. Ronnie and Frank used a rope to tie this big piece of plywood to a four-wheeler. They pulled it all over the subdivision so they could give the kids rides in the snow.

"Frank kept his personal life personal. Whatever he did in wrestling, we never saw it," Dede says. "Don't mess with his family, his money, or his friends. I still have the big, huge rocking chair he sat in at home. Barbara gave it to me when she moved. She is a wonderful, strong woman."

The conversations Frank and I had on our road trips became wide-ranging. Wrestling, like it or not, was both our business and our passion so no matter what subject started the talk, generally it was wrestling that finished it. When the business was in turmoil as Vince Jr. put territorial promotions out of business during the mid-1980s and moved inexorably toward becoming a monopoly, it was Frank Goodish who sensed the truth.

"Vince Jr. is going to win this battle in the long run," Frank stressed as we talked about those who held out hope for the territory system which thrived under the National Wrestling Alliance from the late 1940s through the 1970s. "His style of wrestling is different, and it may not always be what some of us want or like.

"If he has all the television, though, new fans are going to grow up thinking: *this is what wrestling is.* They won't even know what Sam did, or Verne, or Paul Boesch, or Baba. Wrestling will be whatever Vince says it is," Goodish predicted.

He smiled wryly. "I may have to revamp my image. Get a flat top, trim down to 240, wear silver tights, and call myself the Space Invader."

Goodish also was able to rationalize my frustration at how I ended up with Vince and the WWF. I griped plenty about the difference in philosophy between my beloved St. Louis and the WWF. In one of our regular late night — often it was 2 a.m. — phone calls, I cynically wondered how Vince Jr. could put up with my barely hidden bitterness.

He told me, "Better to have you inside the castle, pissing out, than outside, pissing in." Afterward, I realized that Frank meant it as a compliment but, as usual, the big man's method of making his point was colorful.

In private, Goodish told me that his elbow was a wreck from the way he landed on it when unleashing the big flying knee drop that made the crowd gasp. A doctor had warned him that his elbow had been broken and he would eventually need to have the joint replaced. Feeling in his fingers was dwindling; they tingled and a couple of fingers even wanted to draw up into a ball. The pain was constant, so Frank gobbled aspirins regularly by the mid-1980s.

His hip was also damaged from that move. The way this huge man got into the air — well, he had to land on some body part. His hip and elbow took the brunt of the trauma.

By that time Frank was not lifting nearly as heavily. Flexibility and endurance, more and more, became his targets. And as he did more cardio work, Frank's weight leveled at around 270 pounds. It was not uncommon for us to meet at his St. Louis hotel before a show, and I'd have to wait for him to do hundreds of free squats before we'd leave his room.

After the event, some food, and probably a long drive, the search was on for bags of ice to nurse Frank's hip and elbow. And Goodish, who knew I never used marijuana, would admit that smoking it helped relax the muscles and joints so the pain was less excruciating. Yet, in deference to a friend, Frank never carried the pot with him when we were together.

Years earlier, on April 27, 1979, Brody had come to Kiel Auditorium and was as sick as a dog. He had felt bad since coming back from a Japanese tour a few weeks earlier. Sam Muchnick didn't think Frank would be able to wrestle that evening in St. Louis, but Brody gave an explosive performance in a quick victory over "Ox" Baker.

Shortly after, Brody hospitalized himself. Eventually he dropped more than 20 pounds. Because he was still an awesome physical specimen, most fans likely never noticed.

Of course, by the mid-1980s, everyone was talking about steroids and Frank said that he used steroids during the late 1970s. Frank felt this was why he had been so sick back in 1979. "Hell, back then nobody knew what they could do to you. They definitely helped make me bigger and recover faster when I worked out," he admitted.

But then he related how sick he had become returning from Japan, how he had cramped up and collapsed in the aisle of the airplane. "I thought I was going to die," Frank said. Apparently, although his muscles were huge, he had been feeling uncomfortable and ill much of the time in that period. He knew something wasn't right.

"You're on the road and it's hell," Frank claimed. He said he'd tried all sorts of drugs and steroids. That trip back from Japan and its aftermath convinced him to check himself into the hospital. The doctors believed he may have picked up a parasite — some test results were unusual. But Brody thought it through himself. He came to the conclusion that steroids were destroying his body. He quit, cold turkey.

Wrestling, Frank decided, could wreck his body just fine on its own — he didn't need steroids making things even worse.

When Frank heard talk about wrestlers forming a union in hopes of medical coverage and some type of retirement, he grumbled. "Bullshit!" Goodish snapped. "Great idea, but wrestlers can't even agree on where to go for breakfast. They bitch and moan and complain — and then cave in for every promoter or look the other way when some promoter cheats them out of money."

Frank pointed out that promoters ran the talent ragged in territories, where the boys often worked every night, and it was similar at the time in the WWF. Usually pay would come weekly for dates a week or two before. "Half of the guys or more couldn't even tell you what town they were in a week ago Tuesday," griped Goodish, "much less what the house was and how much their cut should have been.

"Keep the talent busy and most of them won't be able to figure how much money they have coming. But the promoters always get their cash!" he emphasized. "Think they mind if some of the wrestlers are drinking too much or hung up on drugs? The more messed up a guy is, the harder it is to keep track of how much money he is due.

"All of us wrestlers are losers," Frank declared during one memorable road trip. "Failed in football, failed in basketball, failed in college or school. Nowhere else to go. How many actually tried to go right into professional wrestling? Maybe Jack Brisco or a couple others. Look at me — I got bored trying to be a sports writer and I failed in football."

Angrily, Frank snapped, "Most wrestlers are sheep. For all their big talk, they go right over the edge of the mountain like a herd of sheep. I won't do that. I'll stand up and fight.

"The idea is to make as much money as you can with as little work," he suddenly laughed. "But, brother, this is hard work."

I argued. Surely Frank had to get some satisfaction, some thrill, out of performing in the squared circle? "Well, yeah, it's athletics. It is a sport. Only the best survive and make money. I love the crowd and making them scream,"

BIG TIME ★ WRESTLING

SPORTATORIUM – Cadiz & Industrial – DALLAS

June 3, 1979   ED WATT, Matchmaker   50c

BRUISER BRODY BACK AFTER HOSPITAL STAY TO GET LEWIN IN BIG MAIN EVENT SHOWDOWN

Brody Eager To Prove Hart Very Wrong! Anxious To Tackle Lewin!

Even 320-pound Bruiser Brody can be hospitalized, especially when a heavyweight grappler, not known for his restraint, is hitting him with a metal pipe, plus his fists, and finally loading him on a stretcher, destined for three weeks of hospitalization!

That is a brief summing up of what has happened — when Mark Lewin, reportedly at the command of his manager Gary Hart, attacked Brody with the bell ringer's pipe and sent him to the hospital several weeks ago.

In the ensuing weeks, Hart stated more than once, for all to hear, that he thought Brody was broken in body and spirit and would never return to the ring!

Tonight, Hart should see Brody in the ring ready to return all the shots given him by Lewin! Barring injury or unknown possibilities nothing in the world would keep Brody out of this match!

Hart says Brody has lost, probably thirty pounds, and that Lewin will go after him again and probably make Brody leave the ring! Hart insists that Lewin could punish Brody almost at will!

"Brody couldn't take it before and this time he will probably give up again," explained Hart!

Brody agrees that his conditioning program and the artfulness of his doctors enabled him to return to the ring but he concedes nothing otherwise and advises Hart and Lewin that he is more than ready for action!

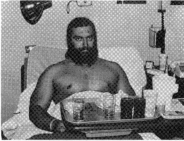

BRUISER BRODY

TOMORROW NIGHT! TEXAS DEATH MATCH! FRITZ vs LEWIN!

Fritz Von Erich beat Mark Lewin in a fenced ring in Ft. Worth but trying to leave the caged ring, Fritz was pushed back by Lewin's manager Gary Hart. Then Hart and Lewin took their licks against Fritz when to the surprise of all Bruiser Brody — last seen there leaving on a stretcher — returned and got into the action!

Tomorrow night the same four are involved. It will be Fritz vs Lewin in a Texas Death Match — and it will be Fritz' Iron Claw against Lewin's sleeper-

Brody will be in Fritz' corner — and Hart, presumably — will be in Lewin's corner. Brody says there may not be any deaths in the ring but there is a good chance there might be one just outside the ring if Hart makes a mistake.

Brody feels he will not have to interfere — that Fritz can handle Lewin by himself. But if Hart tries to make it two on one, then it will be Hart and Lewin against Fritz and Brody and that is a tough twosome!

HERE NEXT SUNDAY! SPOILER VS OX! U.S. TITLE! Page 3!

MGR. HART & MARK LEWIN

KERRY VS HART? Page 4!

Frank acknowledged. "But this is a damn tough way to make a dollar!"

Terry Funk, years later, made a similar point: "Anyone who'd been around knew the idea was to make as much as you could in as few dates. Inside that ring, though, Frank always gave one hundred ten percent and busted his ass. Every single time."

Another evening, as we discussed the ways different wrestlers worked and how some guys simply did not understand the basics, Frank laughed about "how dumb some babyfaces can be." Of course, part of Brody's image in the squared circle was that he could not be slammed or knocked off his feet. He might stagger, he might be lifted a few inches into the air, but Bruiser Brody wasn't going to go down to just anyone.

Brody incorporated that fact into his solid ring work. Trying to overcome the indestructible bad guy, making him wobble but not fall — this was Brody's method of selling for a comeback. It fit into what the fans believed Brody was.

If Brody were performing as the babyface, it would be a smaller but clever heel trying to outsmart him . . . or a heel nearly as big and rugged trying to bulldoze him. Stopping the heel from slamming him was one way to start his fiery comeback. It was, and is, Ring Philosophy 101.

Because he had that reputation, when someone (a guaranteed main event performer like Brody himself) would actually lift or floor Brody, the crowd would pop. A new star could also be made if he could damage Brody — but only because Frank jealously guarded his image every time out and only sold when it mattered.

So, Brody simply chuckled about some wrestlers. If they paid attention to what was going on, Frank declared, they'd understand what would and would not work. "If I'm in a match and some 230-pound babyface calls for a back drop and tosses me to the ropes," smiled Frank, "I just watch him bend over and then shove my boot into his face. Some of them are just so stupid they deserve to be double-crossed.

"You can't draw a dime if you don't do the right thing at the right time," Frank emphasized, echoing a belief all great workers have. "It has to mean something."

On another long, late night drive, Frank got into his investment philosophy. He liked to play the market and was, not surprisingly, aggressive. He also added some advice, which he himself didn't always follow but recognized to be true. "Don't worry about how much money other people make," instructed Frank. "You can't spend other people's money."

Gerry Cohen was an investment adviser in San Antonio, where he met Frank at one of Cohen's seminars. Goodish became Cohen's client in early 1987, but the two became closer on a personal level after the stock market crashed late in the year. At that time, one particularly horrible piece of news came when a man went to his broker's office in Florida and shot the broker to death.

"Naturally, everyone in the business was looking over their shoulder after that happened," Cohen remembers. "Frank called me right after it happened and he was growling. 'Don't worry,' Frank said. 'You don't know me very well, but I'm not the kind of guy who would walk in and shoot you.'"

Gerry was uncertain how to respond, and answered something like, "Yeah, that's good."

Then Frank said, "No, I'd just come right in and break both of your legs." After a long pause, Frank began laughing, knowing his broker had fallen for the joke, and soon both were chortling. It broke the ice and the two became close.

"Frank was such a neat guy. He was very organized and knew what he wanted to do, which is half the battle," Cohen explains. "He was a sophisticated investor, but was open to suggestions. He knew where he was going and was really bright. Frank was much more detailed and organized than most clients."

Cohen continues, "He was delightful. He could barely get in through the door he was so big. Some people are just fun to work with, not like the other kind. Frank was fun. He had a sense of humor, had a smile on his face, and made everyone feel that way before he left."

On one trip to St. Louis, Goodish was shaking his head when he came off the airplane. Actually, he was more Brody while traveling, wearing a sweat suit, pants rolled up to the knees, and with his long hair pulled back and scarred forehead very evident. "Out in public," he said, "I've got to play the part. Anyone who recognizes me would expect it."

This flight, however, was marked by a seatmate who surprised Brody. Frank liked to study his financial information on trips, usually picking a stock prospectus or two to digest. He was just settled in as he felt the man next to him eyeing the hair, the scars, and Frank's size. Since Frank wanted to concentrate, he didn't encourage conversation.

The gentleman, in a suit and tie, could not restrain himself. "Just curious what you do for a living," he said.

Brody answered, "Professional wrestler." Then he kept reading.

The new buddy hesitated, then said, "Yeah, I've watched that a few times. Looks pretty rough." Brody grunted, but kept trying to concentrate on his material.

After a few seconds, the guy had to ask, "That's all fake, isn't it?"

Now Frank could have gotten angry. He could have tried to explain that "fake" is far from correct for such a bruising endeavor. He could have tried to deflect the conversation into some other area. But Frank Goodish wanted to read and study.

Therefore, in hope of ending the conversation such as it was, Frank agreed, "Yeah, it's fake."

More silence. Aahh, maybe the ploy worked! Then, very seriously, the fellow said, "Oh, I don't know. Look how banged up your head is. You guys really get hurt." And he began arguing the exact position Frank would have likely taken if he hadn't wanted to read.

Frank was resigned to reality. He put away his reading and just gave in to the moment. The two talked wrestling throughout the flight. "I got a lesson in human nature," sighed Frank.

Brody was always adamant, whenever he worked a small independent show, that the size of the house didn't matter, at least not after he had his money. "I don't care if there are 50 fans or 500 or 5000. I owe them something because they paid to see me. I'm giving them everything I got."

Being interrupted while eating seldom bothered Frank either. Often it appeared as though someone lower on the social scale got even more attention from Frank than a socialite. "Doesn't matter how much money someone has or how big a job he's got," explained Frank. "Every person deserves respect. He's got his pride. Who does it hurt to be nice to them?"

Goodish liked working on the small, indie cards. The pay was very good — and always guaranteed in advance — and having a meaningful star at the top helped small operations turn a profit for the promoter or organization handling the affair. In addition, youngsters got a chance to start somewhere. And those kinds of opportunities were drying up quickly.

"The only worry I have is when I sign more autographs in the dressing room than I do for fans," Frank said. He and I developed excellent rapport with the likes of Herb Simmons in Illinois, while Goodish discovered other small promoters willing to pay guarantees in different parts of the country. It kept wrestling alive on that grass root level while the business was undergoing cataclysmic changes.

It was also a profitable, low-pressure spot for the big man to fit between tours of Japan and his other cherry-picking outings. One here, three there, every month, every two months . . . it all added up.

Around St. Louis, we often sold shows to people like Simmons or Larry Irwin in Centralia, Illinois. Herb Simmons, in fact, was a key part of the effort with his promoter's license and many contacts. The money for us, plus that for the other wrestlers, was built into the basic cost of the program.

Depending on how much money the sponsor was willing to commit, the main event could be Brody versus Blackwell, Brody versus Abdullah the Butcher, Brody versus "Killer" Brooks, Brody versus John Nord, or Brody versus any of a large number of established grapplers who had learned to trust us. They were also finding that as the WWF marched on, chances to get a payday elsewhere were drying up.

For more money, more established names were used on the undercard. For a tighter budget, more local youngsters who had shown spark and fire were added to the lineup. In smaller venues, Frank often tackled The Assassin, a promising 300-pounder known as Joe Zakibe to his parents. No transportation, cheaper pay, easier nut to crack for the sponsor. Additionally, The Assassin had a colorful manager called Big Daddy (Roger Bailey on tax returns) who Frank loved to chase.

The responsibility of marketing was squarely on the local promoter's shoulders. While we advised and helped in every possible way, some cards simply stiffed. We and the performers got our money, but occasionally the local sponsor took a hit. Many shows sold out or drew good receipts, in which case the promoters were joyous. We wanted them to succeed so they'd come back and run another card in a few months.

For instance, before a card in conjunction with the horse races at Fairmount Track, we concocted the idea of having Frank train with the jockeys and the thoroughbreds. Local television broadcaster John Pertzborn liked the concept and did an interview with Frank for the evening news.

The video displayed Brody pulling a horse cart on the track. The next cut was to Brody, with a jockey perched on his back, trotting alongside one of the horses. It was eye-catching stuff. The management at the track was so pleased that they scheduled a second wrestling bill later in their season.

Another time, before a sellout for the well-liked Simmons, I said, half-jokingly, "Maybe we'll get a bonus over the guarantee."

Frank was offended. "No, no!" he protested. "Herb deserves to have it all. He never cried on the bad ones; he paid us our money. He earned the right to celebrate tonight!" And this was from a hard-nosed businessman who would scrap with any big-time promoter for every last cent.

Ronnie Middleton remembered a similar situation when Ronnie rode with Frank and Gary Hart to a little show in Fredricksburg, Texas. "I just hung on the fringe and it was fun hearing all the talk, meeting the other wrestlers. It was nice that Frank trusted me enough to include me," remembers Middleton.

At the end of the show, Ronnie noticed the promoter handing out envelopes to all the wrestlers — except Frank. Ronnie couldn't help himself and he asked Frank why he didn't get an envelope. "Aahh, he just didn't have enough money. I'll get it later,"

Frank shrugged.

Friendships formed, of course. Herb Simmons found a genuine human being in Frank Goodish. On August 1, 1984, Brody tackled Bob Sweetan for Herb in Belleville, Illinois, and that was the first of many satisfying nights with Herb. The success probably opened Frank's eyes even more to the entire idea of working independent shows.

"I was surprised how down-to-earth Frank was," Herb says. "I was involved with Tony Casta, who was running shows at the South Broadway Athletic Club in St. Louis and I asked Frank about appearing there. He asked what kind of crowd we drew. I told him that it was a strong local audience, and almost always sold out with 500 or so people.

Herb was surprised at the big man's answer. "Frank asked, 'Why bring me in with that big ticket when you don't need me? Why pay my big check?' He was honest about it and didn't try to just get a chunk of money. He always treated me with respect."

Hal LaPorte was an amateur photographer doing an internship for a local community college. At one of the shows in Belleville, he got to meet Frank. "He was a hero to me and my sons, Eddie and Jeffrey," says Hal. "When we went behind the curtain, we half expected him to be mean and violent. That's what he was in the ring.

"Instead, here was this brute of a man who was a gentle giant," Hal recalls. "He took the time to talk to us, explaining all of his travels and how much he missed his own son. I had been asked to photograph Brody with a youngster who was terminally ill. While we waited, he just was so kind to us.

"When they brought that boy in a wheelchair, Brody stopped dead in his tracks," LaPorte remembers. "He actually took a step back, probably just the idea that he had a son who could be like this too. Then he asked us to back away and he talked alone quietly for a long time with the boy. He was visibly moved by the boy's courage and I was able to snap a picture."

The boy died soon after and it was a few months until LaPorte met with Frank at another card. "I showed him the picture," Hal says. "He asked me to keep it for myself, that it was personal. But now, it seems this is a part of the man people should know." (The picture appears earlier, on page 25.)

Hal LaPorte, a very perceptive gentleman, adds, "He didn't use wrestling to gain your approval. That wasn't him. That wasn't Frank. He offered me his hand in friendship and I am proud of that."

Frank also gave Hal a chuckle one day when they met in a St. Louis airport hotel. Frank was talking with a couple of other friends along with LaPorte in the lobby. Naturally, thanks to Brody's visual impact, every bystander took a long look at this ruffian who seemed so civilized.

Realizing that Hal was noting how everyone was staring at him, Frank caught Hal's eye. With the hint of a wink, Brody shrugged, "It's not everybody that can be as good-looking as I am." Needless to say, Hal had to laugh.

Larry Irwin owned a funeral home in Centralia and Frank actually picked up Irwin's name from the Kansas City office. As that promotion was dying, Irwin ran a few spot shows and earned a reputation for honesty and efficiency under difficult circumstances. Goodish gave the name to me, I made the contact, and we two Larrys hit it off immediately.

The entire group clicked and Irwin also became an admirer of Frank Goodish, the brain behind Brody. "I was surprised how smart he was," says Irwin. "At first, he was in character, talking about 'rasslin'.' Then, as we got to know each other, suddenly he was seriously discussing the financial problems of the business and what wrestling had to do to change and thrive. I really admired Brody. He was brilliant — when he let you see it."

Frank did Irwin a favor he never forgot. Bill and Sherry Baker, in little Irvington, Illinois, were good friends of Irwin, and their son J.R. was a big Brody fan. For J.R.'s 12th birthday, on March 5, 1988, Larry asked if Brody would go to the youngster's birthday party before a show that evening in Centralia. I was surprised when Frank agreed, because it made his trip in even more rushed. Frank shrugged and said, 'Larry's been a great friend.'"

An adult today, J.R. Obrecht is a senior loan officer with a prominent mortgage company and he still remembers quite clearly that birthday party. "Brody came in out of the blue. He was so huge that when he walked down the stairs, it was like his head would go through the ceiling," he recalls.

"In the ring, he was a big monster with no feeling. But here, in my basement, my friends and I saw a different side," J.R. continues. "He knew he was being stared at and he knew his audience. He'd give us a little gimmick and then his real self. He was so gentle that nobody was scared. He answered questions and actually talked to us."

That night, J.R. was at the card in Centralia. "I told everyone what had happened, and nobody would believe that 'King Kong' Brody was at my birthday party," smiles J.R. "But for maybe 20 minutes, I knew I was his little man."

J.R.'s father passed away a couple of years later, but that memory of the birthday party and a different perspective of Frank Goodish is still crystal clear.

The dry sense of humor that Irwin had was also unexpected from a funeral home owner. It led, however, to Irwin finding what was perhaps the big man's true Achilles' heel. After a show in Centralia, we were all having pizza in the office of Irwin's funeral home. It was probably 2 a.m., the conversation was ranging over many subjects, and Frank decided he wanted to know more about the funeral business. Always curious, he asked how bodies were prepared for funerals.

Irwin explained the practice of keeping frozen spare body parts, just in case. Frank was startled. "No," he growled, "you're kidding!"

"Follow me!" Irwin ordered. The three of us walked through a dark, spooky hallway in a real funeral home with real corpses in real caskets on either side. We reached the garage and Irwin opened a large freezer. "Here are the legs," he announced.

Frank turned sharply and, nearly trampling me since I was hiding behind him, made a bee-line back to the office. Irwin couldn't stop laughing. "I knew he wasn't that tough. I should have shown him the eyes."

It may have been that night, I am fairly certain, when Frank brought up a touchy subject on the drive back to the St. Louis hotel. "Have you ever considered what will happen if you die and leave Pat alone with Kelly?" Frank asked. "Get your business in order so they are taken care of.

"I've been thinking about it, about Barbara and Geoffrey, and doing some planning. You should too," instructed my big friend. "And I don't want to be buried in any pine box! In New Zealand, where Barbara is from, most of them do cremation. That's what I want. That's the way to go. Go for the burn!" I was a bit startled that Frank was being so serious.

Frank was also serious when the promising talent around St. Louis asked him for advice. As usual, he was blunt. He could see wrestling contracting and opportunities disappearing. If it came down to just the WWF, there would be hundreds fewer wrestlers making a living than when there were 30 or more different promotions.

He told Roger Bailey, the extroverted manager "Big Daddy," who had potential, "Don't give up your day job." He counseled Rob Phillips, who had the looks and athleticism to go somewhere, that if he had other options, which he did, he should look at them seriously.

Goodish helped Don Stock, who was billed as "Nuko," get a taste of what the business was becoming by getting him dates in San Antonio. Stock found out it wasn't at all what he had hoped for; indeed, it was what Frank had warned. Joe Zakibe, the Giant Assassin whom Frank often wrestled, listened and learned.

Zakibe describes how impressive it was when "Brody came into the dressing room, put down his bag, and made it a point to personally introduce himself to every wrestler there. 'Hi, I'm Frank. What's your name?' he asked," Zakibe recalls. "Frank went out of his way to make everyone comfortable. I'd been around plenty of wrestlers with big reputations who thought they were above the new guys and the independents. They'd barely acknowledge you."

Not Frank, big Joe went on. "He sat in the middle of the room and talked to everybody. He always watched the matches but never forced his opinion on anybody. If you asked him something, he'd tell you his opinion."

When Brody was booking and working in World Class as the masked "Red River Jack," he realized he couldn't wear his usual furry boots. He was on a card with The Assassin just before he headed to Texas and asked to borrow Joe's boots. Zakibe was happy to do it, as he had access to another pair of boots.

Wrestling being the on-the-road business it was, though, meant Frank couldn't return Zakibe's boots for a couple of weeks, until they were together again on a Herb Simmons' show. "Frank came right to me, gave me my boots, and was really apologetic it took longer than he had figured to return them," Joe says. "He told me that he was sorry and offered to pick up the tab if I'd had to miss any dates. Frank didn't have to do that, but he did."

Zakibe also remembers Frank giving Joe a tip before one of their bouts. "He said, 'When I hit you with the chair, it's got to look good for the people, so I'm going to crack you hard.' Then Frank said I should drop down on the floor and roll onto my back, because the concrete would cool off the sting from where he hit me. It helped," Joe laughs, "but you know, it still hurt like hell."

Ron Powers (Plummer) came along a little later, but he too picked up hard truths from Frank. Gary Jackson, who got the nickname "Night Train" from Frank because Gary reminded the big man of football star "Night Train" Dick Lane, absorbed every lesson Frank could teach. Like Zakibe, both Jackson and Powers had the ability to make it, but unfortunately landed in territories that were on their deathbeds, so the wrestlers couldn't make enough money to stay in the business full time.

Sadly for them, and for many others Frank talked to elsewhere or never even met, his prediction of dwindling opportunities for young wrestlers came true.

Terry Funk has a sense of why it was that Goodish could be so analytical about wrestling. "He lived *in* wrestling," says Terry, "but he didn't *live it*." In other words, Frank was not fooled by either his own hype or the hype of wrestling itself.

He knew the difference.

There was plenty of hype, however, when we were the masterminds behind an eye-catching independent extravaganza at the ornate Fabulous Fox Theatre in St. Louis on March 4, 1988. Through my connection with Geri Couch, who had been the assistant manager at The Checkerdome during the 1983 war, wrestling, of all things, went on the stage.

Originally an enormous movie theater, the Fox had been remarkably renovated into a home for stage plays and musical theater including traveling Broadway shows and concerts in a setting holding over 4000 people. The place sparkled from top to bottom and had an incredible giant chandelier hanging over the audience.

Some setting for wrestling! It was reminiscent of the Khorassan Room at the Chase-Park Plaza Hotel where Sam Muchnick had started his television wrestling show in 1959. In fact, Sam happily agreed to present a "Sam Muchnick Trophy" to the winner of the main event between Brody and Blackwell.

The night before the event, after we had been making promotional appearances at radio and newspaper spots around the metropolitan area, we were the guests of Geri Couch and Fox management for dinner. A

Stevie Ray Vaughn concert followed. Later, we pondered our one remaining question. What should Sam present to the winner of the feature event?

Relaxing in the dining area which overlooked the lobby, we talked of a plaque (boring) or a proclamation (not visual enough). Sue Nickrent, the Fox's bright stage manager at the time, was chiming in with ideas when everyone spotted the solution to the dilemma. Down below was a large, golden, shiny ash tray or spittoon. Sue laughed at us, but she delivered the goods. The next evening Sam Muchnick had a polished, gleaming, unique, three-foot tall trophy to give the victor. (Yes, the winner was Brody.) That same "trophy" is probably filled with sand in the lobby of the Fox right now.

The logistics of presenting the action actually proved easy. The orchestra pit was brought up to the level of the stage to accommodate the ring. A few rows of ringside seats were on the sides of the squared circle. The wrestlers, including Blackwell, John Nord, Kimala the Ugandan Giant, Chris Adams, The Fantastics (made up of Bobby Fulton and Tommy Rogers), Ron Powers, "Spike" Huber, Steve Regal, and even the midgets, were enthralled, roaming through the historic Fox dressing rooms before putting on a show that thrilled every spectator.

That night, though, also showed the gentler side of Frank Goodish. Geri Couch had suggested doing a promotion with local Scout groups. Frank jumped at the chance when I proposed he speak to some of the units before the doors opened.

Therefore, the giant who would bang heads with 450-pound "Crusher" Blackwell talked with and amazed the youngsters. He spoke about life, about choices, about making mistakes, about their future. In fact, Frank got so wound up that he went long and fans were surprised, pleasantly, at what they saw as they spilled into their seats.

Then he went into the dressing rooms and put in the finishes that we had agreed on for all the talent. I laid out the production plans with Fox technical people and coordinated the box office with Geri Couch. Finally, Brody went into the ring for a blockbuster battle with Blackwell.

Wrestling at the Fox was indeed a night to remember, if for nothing other than the many facets of Frank Goodish that it showed.

St. Louis was, of course, a spot where Frank always had the chance to spread his wings and fly. Not long before the Fox show, he and I were guests of Muchnick at the prestigious Baseball Writers' Dinner. In the

1930s, before he got involved in wrestling, Sam had been a much-respected sportswriter.

All that history helped give Muchnick a special niche on the St. Louis scene, so it was a "big deal" to be at Sam's table for the affair. Dressed in a suit (yep, that's right), with his long hair pulled back into a neat ponytail, Frank made a tremendously favorable impression on his fellow guests who included a doctor, a prominent lawyer, and a couple of famous baseball scouts. Muchnick beamed, for it also made wrestling look good to the general business world.

Even as early as 1979, I had set Frank up to do a series of zany television spots for popular appliance store owner Steve Mizerany, which led to lunches with more serious business folk after the commercials were recorded.

Brody was also booked to sign autographs at a major auto show in the convention center. While those putting on the affair were cautiously optimistic about what a wrestler would bring to their effort, they were shocked when Frank was swamped with a huge line of fans to meet him all day long.

In addition, Frank had been an in-studio guest for several radio personalities, but none were more important than Bob Costas. That particular one-hour interview on the all-powerful station KMOX was followed by a classy dinner at a fine restaurant.

Frank was just as much at home joining me for casual visits with owner Bart Saracino and a huge plate of seafood pasta at Bartolino's on Hampton Avenue in St. Louis. The full range of his personality was amazing.

In all cases, this man, as Frank Goodish or as "King Kong" Brody, got the chance to show off parts of his individuality that nobody would have thought existed. It's no wonder that in the spring of 1988, he told me, "I wish we'd met years earlier." From my point of view, Frank was one of a select group (including Brisco, Gene Kiniski, the Funks, and maybe a couple more) who could uphold, in varied situations, Muchnick's idea that wrestlers were in fact serious professionals to be respected.

But major challenges were awaiting the professional business acumen of Frank Goodish.

CHAPTER SIXTEEN

Barbara Remembers . . .
LIFE IN TEXAS

At home in Boerne late at night, Frank and I would sit at the kitchen table and discuss different wrestling angles. I was the "mark." If I felt it was good, he knew it would work. I only knew the wrestling business because it was his profession. Frank could talk openly and honestly with me. He could tell me anything and everything associated with the business as it would never leave the house. I was someone he could confide in about personal and professional things.

I knew about the people he trusted and about those he did not trust. They would call the house, because it was his office. I became the receptionist, bookkeeper, travel agent, and booking agent as well as wife, mother, and housekeeper. And I was the chauffeur, too, between the airport and home.

Before or after we would talk, I often heard Frank making those late night calls to people like Buck, Larry, and Gary to talk about the various ideas. A lot of business was conducted after midnight! Pete was someone else Frank could talk with, although Pete wasn't in the business. As I've said, Pete was a man's man, and Frank liked his input.

I felt like I knew everyone who called the house, even though I met but a few. I recall a time when Frank came home and I was not allowed to answer any calls. It was before the time of everyone having answering machines. He also did not believe in credit cards at the time, either.

After a few days, there was a frantic knock at the door. When I opened it, there stood one of my friends. I was in a pre-school carpool with her. She had driven to the house because she had been trying to contact me. When she could not get any answer, she became very concerned. I was not one to change my patterns.

After that, Frank realized he had to do something. He put in another phone line for me, for family and friends, so the same thing would not happen again.

I remember Vince McMahon, Sr. calling when Frank talked about maybe working for New York around 1980. Frank admired Vince Sr. and knew he could do business with him as he had an open relationship with the man and enjoyed his conversations with him. It never came about, though. I wouldn't be surprised if the two of them are looking down on us and discussing the incredible change that wrestling has taken over the years, mainly due to Vince Sr.'s son.

Talking ideas through with the few Frank trusted helped him understand better what might happen. Verbalizing it all helped to get it straight in his head. He always had theories and plans.

Also, Frank always wanted to look at the tapes of his matches and especially of the interviews. He wanted to be sure that he was telling a story that got the fans excited and interested.

Frank particularly wanted to review his bouts from Japan, because it was so important. He would often come home with tapes of all of his matches. We would sit and watch everything, while he would critique himself and ask my opinion. "That didn't work," Frank would sometimes say.

He gave everything a lot of thought and didn't do things on the spur of the moment. It was part of Frank's work ethic, taking that extra time to talk, plan, and review. It's what goes into your business to make you successful.

More than a few times Frank told me, "If they would let me do it right, it would make them more money too." He really did want to do things right when promoters asked for favors, but he didn't want to tarnish himself or the business. I know he had arguments, and I worried about him but trusted that he knew what was best for himself.

When he worked as the booker for Fritz, things were good. Frank got to see the other side. It was actually part of the growing process that probably started when Geoff was born.

Another thing that I think changed Frank was the death of David Von Erich. This was personal — David wasn't just an acquaintance, he was part of Frank's life. It brought the reality of death home. It triggered something in his planning and really started him concentrating on investing even more than before.

Frank was devastated and he felt helpless when David passed away. He couldn't understand why and how this had happened. A death to someone close changes who you are.

I seldom actually saw Frank wrestle live, and neither did Geoff. Often, when he was booked in Texas and could drive to a town, Geoff and I would ride along, just so we could be together. If the arena was in a place like Austin or Corpus Christi, where it was scenic and safe, we would walk around outside. If it was somewhere real small, however, we would stay in the back of the building until it was time to leave.

One time, the venue was so tiny that Frank had to change into his wrestling clothes in the street by the car. Believe me, there was nothing glamorous about it. But you appreciated any time you could all be together.

Once, though, Frank flew me to St. Louis in 1983 when he was wrestling Ric Flair at The Checkerdome. There was a huge crowd, and the fans were incredibly excited. It was kind of fun to just blend in with all of them. St. Louis was incredible and I could see why he thought so much of the town. His sister Gloria was living in the St. Louis area and she was there. I got to meet Mrs. Baba for the first time — she was there because her husband was wrestling on the card. And I also met Larry, and his wife Pat, for the first time.

It was an important match for Frank, because it went back to Japan on television. He said, "It proved I can wrestle." He and Ric went for a full hour.

Japan was very important to him, but it took a lot out of him physically and mentally. I always monitored his calls, especially when he came back from Japan, because he didn't want to talk then. It took a couple days for him to get back to being himself.

I remember one time when Frank had back-to-back Japan trips. He thought that because there was such a short time off between tours, rather than going to the States for a few days and then heading right back to Japan, he would send me and Geoff to New Zealand to visit family. Then he would take the opportunity to go to New Zealand, rather than the States, to visit us and finally meet my family.

Frank was always thinking. This way he could visit New Zealand and the Japanese company would be paying for his fare.

It was so great for me to be able to introduce him to all my relatives, and of course, they all loved him. "What a charmer," they told me after he had left. I had an opportunity to show him around all the places from my childhood, and it's a memory I will not forget.

Unfortunately, the time went all too fast and it was time to put him back on the plane. Geoff was not too happy when Dad had to leave, because it was a time when Geoff had Dad almost all to himself. There was no phone ringing, and he was away for a short time from the American wrestling scene. I do believe, looking back, that that was the only true vacation we had as a family.

In December 1985, I had been visiting his sister in Los Angeles, and I flew to San Francisco to meet him when he returned from a tour of Japan for Antonio Inoki's company. He arrived, walked toward me, and held up his hands. "I'm broke," he said.

Frank explained that he and Jimmy Snuka had walked out on the last day of the tour. The boys always got paid after the last match before heading back home, but they didn't get paid this time since they had left before the last match. It was a matter of principle, Frank told me. He had integrity and would not let anyone make him do what he knew was not right for himself or the business.

It took until August of 1986 for them to settle their dispute. Geoff and I went with Frank to Hawaii, where Inoki and Frank met and then did an angle on the beach for the Japanese media to set up a match between them. In the end, Frank and Jimmy got back all the money they were supposed to have been paid. Then Frank went back to work for Baba, who he always respected greatly.

Of course, Geoff and I didn't mind being in Hawaii. We arrived a couple

Brody was certainly a hit at this birthday party in Irvington, Illinois.

days before Frank and checked into the hotel on the beach and waited for him. Geoff was very young at the time. While waiting for Frank to arrive, we went to the room to freshen up, and when I came out of the bathroom, Geoff had put his shoes, clothes, and my handbag in the safe and closed it. We had to get the hotel management to find a way to open it, so we were trapped in the hotel room for a while when Frank finally got there.

When Frank had all that time without the long Japanese trips, he opened up even more and became a husband and father in the true senses of the words. Because he was not working a lot, it was easier for him to get home more and especially when Geoff had special events.

The teachers at Geoff's school were in awe. He would always come when Geoff had a school activity, if he could. This huge, frightening-looking man would arrive and join in the classroom. He would even sit on those tiny chairs. As soon as he opened his mouth, and this very polite voice came out, the teachers melted. He always knew the exact thing to say to put people at ease. He could be quite a charmer.

I'm sure some would chuckle at seeing Frank when he was on his riding mower, cutting our grass when he had time.

Frank knew that his wrestling career could be over at any time. The injuries mount up, especially with the way he wrestled, being such a big man. It was part of what he did, a price you could accept for being part of the business. He rehabbed from so many injuries.

Frank made lots of visits to orthopedic doctors. He did not want to show weakness and hardly ever said anything, but I'm sure he was hurting more than I realized.

A couple of orthopedic doctors said he should retire, but he would just change his workout routine and rehab himself. He actually created a hotel workout with a huge number of chair squats.

When a physician told him to "keep off it," he never cancelled dates. He would work hard to surprise the doctor. He had tremendous inner strength and will power.

But he knew he would never be young again. His body was going to break down eventually, so he looked to the future and even life without wrestling. Lots of times, though, he would ask, "Where's the ice?"

One doctor told him he "would never wrestle again," thanks to his knees and especially his elbow. He told Frank that the joints could not be saved. The doctor said Frank had to stop because the damage was really bad and asked if he wanted to lead a normal life. He told Frank, "You're done."

But somehow Frank struggled through the pain and changed how he worked out and wrestled, and soon he was jumping off the ropes again.

Wrestling had changed and Frank had to book himself differently. Of course, he had dates all over the country, he still had Japan, he never closed the book on Vince Jr., and he came up with many ideas of what else he could do.

And we decided to have another child.

Unfortunately, though, it wasn't to be. I got pregnant but had a miscarriage. Originally, Geoff and I were going to make a trip with him while he wrestled in Puerto Rico. We decided, however, that wasn't a good idea for me and that he would go alone.

Frank never showed much emotion, but I saw how much he had mellowed, at least as it concerned his family. I was sad, of course, and sitting alone on our porch just before he left. He came and sat next to me, put his arm around me, and consoled me. Frank never would have let his emotions show that much years before.

He said, "It's okay. Are you feeling okay? We can try again. It will all work out."

CHAPTER SEVENTEEN

ADAPTING, MANIPULATING, AND PLANNING

While Bruiser Brody had flourished in Japan, that lucrative market became mired in a tense, topsy-turvy situation in the mid-1980s. In the overall scheme of things, for Frank Goodish, it made the independent market even more valuable, especially in 1986 and 1987.

While Goodish was pulling down $12,000 a week headlining for Baba, Antonio Inoki was not asleep at the wheel. From Inoki's perspective, Baba had stolen Stan Hansen late in 1981. In 1985, Inoki found the opportunity to return the favor by stealing none other than Bruiser Brody.

It is likely that Frank disregarded his own advice about not spending other people's money. In Japan, no matter how high up on the card, a star was often locked into a certain position financially. Apparently, Frank found out that some new talent (notably The Road Warriors) were coming in for Baba and All Japan at the same pay Frank himself was getting.

Regardless of how analytical a person is, ego always comes into play — at least a bit. To Frank, it was an insult that he had worked his way to a certain spot and pay scale that was now being matched by someone on their first tour. As Pete Ortega often said, "Frank always wanted more."

Now the door was open for something to happen. Relations with All Japan became frayed. After much quiet contact, the end result was Bruiser Brody jumping to Inoki and New Japan for an astronomical figure of $16,000 per week. Considering what was starting to happen with some prime markets in North America, it was a deal Frank could not refuse.

On March 21, 1985, Brody was in the New Japan ring at Korakuen Hall in Tokyo to challenge Antonio Inoki for a match. He had just completed a tour for Baba and All Japan. The shock waves reverberated around the wrestling world. In Japan, it was equivalent to Shaquille O'Neal departing the Lakers to join the Heat.

Only a couple of weeks later, on April 18, Inoki and Brody were both counted out outside the ring after a wild duel at the Sumo Hall in Tokyo. Taking advantage of every buck out there, Frank then headed to Australia, bounced back for a few dates in Texas, even clashed with Jerry Lawler in Memphis, stopped in Florida, and was back in Japan by late in June. It was a whirlwind run.

New Japan and Inoki, though, were not the tight, detailed operation of Baba and All Japan. Stan Hansen sounded the warning. "What Baba said was what was there. With Inoki . . . you better not count on everything being gospel from him," he says. "I understand why Frank made the deal, because the money was great. But I was afraid there would be problems."

Even though Frank's old partner Jimmy Snuka was also with Inoki, there were indeed problems. In many ways, headaches about finishes and simple details like transportation and hotels played on the big man's mind. It was not that smooth, efficient effort that Baba had provided.

More pressure was added as Goodish attempted to broker a deal between New Japan and Fritz Von Erich so Fritz's World Class group could funnel talent to Inoki's company. In the midst of all that behind-the-scene tension, Brody had a pair of historic one-hour draws with Inoki — one in Honolulu and one in Tokyo.

Between trips to Japan, Frank got back to little ol' Belleville, Illinois, for a tussle with "Ox" Baker that was actually secondary to what happened after everyone had been shooed out of the Fairgrounds Exposition Hall on August 29, 1985. In Japanese wrestling, Lou Thesz is on a par with Babe Ruth, and Lou was the referee for the match between Brody and Baker.

The whole point of the visit to Belleville was for a photographer to get shots of Thesz, the ultimate wrestler and technician, training Brody, the ultimate wildman and brawler, to be ready for his showdown with Inoki. Those pictures would play big in the Japanese press.

On a personal level, Frank loved it because he truly liked and respected Thesz. With only a few bystanders, including me and Herb Simmons, the two rolled around the mats as the photographer snapped her pictures. The bumps and flips were impressive, especially considering Thesz's age.

Afterward, with me in the car, Frank was shaking his head about Lou. "How old is that guy? Over 70? He must have been a panther in his prime, because he's tough as nails even now," Frank enthused. "When he grabs your wrist, it's like a vise. You better go where he wants you to go, or he's going to break your wrist."

A memorable moment, but nothing could save the deal with Inoki. Like All Japan, New Japan had their big tag team tournament in December. On December 11, 1985, the night before the finals, Brody tangled in a one-on-one test with Seiji Sakaguchi, who was a tough guy and Inoki's number two star. The bout turned stiff, very stiff, and eventually got out of control. If it wasn't a "shoot," it was close, and Frank at one point used his chain to take a shot at Sakaguchi's knee.

More trouble was also brewing as it involved the arrangement between Inoki and Von Erich. Big money was involved and Frank had expected a significant finder's fee. As the argument grew, and Goodish feared he was not getting the cash he was due, the tension built. Plus, the climactic match in the tourney pitted Brody and Snuka against Inoki and Sakaguchi.

Hansen felt that the trouble "was all about finishes." Barbara recalled that Frank in no way liked what they wanted him to do, perhaps lose the fall as a "punishment" for the squabble with Sakaguchi. Even more, was Frank's antenna up because of the danger of an ambush in the ring after that scrap with Sakaguchi?

Nobody could have expected what Brody, who had to be boiling with all the different issues, engineered on December 12. As Barbara mentions in the previous chapter, Brody and Snuka walked out on the finals and headed home.

Was it courage or insanity? It was certainly standing up for what they believed. Brody got on an airplane and went back to the United States. Since nobody got paid until the end of each tour, Frank got off the flight and had not one penny to show for the weeks of work, tension, headaches, sweat, and blood.

Goodish praised Snuka. "Jimmy is all man. He stood side by side with me, fought in the ring, and had the courage to walk out when we believed that was the right thing to do."

Eventually, after all sorts of maneuvering, a deal to appease all parties was struck.

It took until August 8 and 9, 1986. The site for the face-to-face was Hawaii, where Frank was still concerned that some treachery could develop. Instead, everything went as planned.

Brody and Inoki met on the beach to settle their dispute, and got into an argument. Amazingly, of course, the Japanese press was there to record and photograph it all. Pictures were all over the Japanese print media. Even wary and at odds with each other, the two had plotted a way to work an angle.

Brody got the money he felt he was due and also included Snuka in the deal. Inoki got a showdown with Frank, which turned into a one-hour stalemate, on September 16 in Osaka. Brody fanatic and wrestling student Matt Farmer recalls that match being "a big deal with tape traders at the time." Brody also did a hot double count out with Tatsumi Fujinami, thus helping to elevate the status of Fujinami, on September 19 in Fukuoka.

But Brody was finished with Inoki and never performed for New Japan again, perhaps ducking a later booking where he sensed the danger of a betrayal either in the ring or on the money. Unfortunately for Frank, his earlier departure from All Japan also appeared to have burned his bridge with Baba. Going into 1987, the Japanese foundation was no longer in place for Frank Goodish. At least, though, thanks to his tough negotiating in a nasty situation, he had money in the bank.

Yet the telephone never stopped ringing. While various Japanese manipulations went on secretly, Frank had bookings from Dallas, Kansas City, and the AWA hardly without even blinking. One simple fact remained — Bruiser Brody could draw a house and he could draw it fast. That's what promotions needed in 1986 and 1987. In addition, the independent market was lively and Brody was the first on any dream list for talent.

During one trip to the AWA, Frank came across a new piece of talent that really impressed him. "Played football, really athletic, independent," said Goodish of a gentleman named Leon White, who was soon to become Van Vader and have runs in Japan and with both the WWF and WCW.

The independent business really put the icing on the cake for Frank. From Manchester, New Hampshire, to the Delaware State Fair. From Collinsville, Illinois, to Winnipeg and Brandon, Manitoba. From Montreal, Quebec to Valley Forge, Pennsylvania.

In addition, Frank had all his regular stops and Puerto Rico was popping up more and more. Abdullah the Butcher was a regular rival and the feud guaranteed money at the gate. Matt Farmer recalls, and his results verify, that Brody stopped in Portland on September 23 and Seattle September 24 to join Rip Oliver for tag team brawls against The Road Warriors

Bruiser Brody was like a local politician, knocking on every door available. He still was able to pick up enough television to blend with his personal outings and keep the legend alive and strong. It was flying below the radar of the national media, which only saw the WWF, but it was valuable nonetheless.

One night after a bloody duel with Kimala in Kansas City, Buck Robley had to take Frank to the hospital. When Brody bladed, the action had been so intense and the crowd so hot that Frank actually sliced his forehead, across his eyebrow, and opened his eye lid. "Bled pretty damn good," Frank mused later.

He also did a couple of favors for Gary Hart. One involved dates booked with the Savoldis to appear in the Northeast. Gary was working as Frank's manager for the shows. "It was a three-day run," explains Hart. "The first two nights, they told us they didn't have enough cash to pay but they'd catch us later. Frank was starting to seethe, but we gave them the benefit of the doubt.

"The third night, they never came to the dressing room. We waited until we were the last people to leave the building. But we knew what hotel the Savoldis were staying at," Hart goes on. "We got to the hotel and Frank rummaged around in one of the dumpsters until he found a big ol' two by four.

"Then we ordered a couple pizzas and sat in the hallway outside their room," Hart says. "It was 4 a.m. until they showed up.

"We got all of our money!" he roars. "Bruise was not taking excuses."

Another situation happened in Frank's old stomping grounds of Dallas. Totally exhausted from booking earlier in the 1980s, Hart had left World Class and moved to the Carolinas as a manager. Somehow George Scott, who had a strong reputation as a booker, had landed with Fritz. When Carolina was burned out for Hart as the manager of Kabuki, he came back to Texas and was involved with turning Chris Adams, a handsome and strong babyface, into a heel. Gary was not, however, doing any booking with Fritz.

Maybe Scott felt that Hart was a threat. Nobody really knows, but Scott scheduled the "blow-off" of a rivalry between Brody and Abdullah, managed by Hart, into a cage match at Reunion Arena in Dallas on December 25, 1986. What he didn't tell the talent was that it was announced on television as a "loser leaves town" showdown.

Frank found out when Scott asked him to come up with a finish for the event. Scott wanted Brody to win, so that Abdullah — and Gary Hart — would have to leave if the stipulations were followed as George intended. Frank refused to give an idea. "You're the booker," he told Scott. "You figure it out."

Then Goodish went to Hart and told him of Scott's ploy. "Scott's trying to fuck you and get rid of both you and Abby."

Hart was hurt and angry, having been part of the World Class scene for a decade. Nothing developed until the night of the card, though, when Scott came into the room where Goodish, Hart, and Abdullah were. "Tell them what you think for the finish," Scott told Frank. Brody snorted and told Scott, "George, you tell them the finish. It's up to you."

Scott mumbled and fumbled before leaving the room. When he was gone, Frank told his buddies, "What if I lose? I'll do the job."

Hart argued, "You can't put yourself in a position where you have to leave." But Brody insisted.

"They bled buckets for 15 minutes and then Frank slipped on a banana peel so that Abby could pin him," Hart says admiringly. "He did that because he was my friend."

Hart added, "Those of us who really knew the man, who spent time with him, who were in his home — we knew who Frank Goodish really was. He wanted to do what was right to make money for everybody involved. But nobody could control him; you could only maybe direct Bruise!"

What happened with Hart and Scott also led to Frank becoming a booker (Scott was gone quickly) with World Class, which was a hurting operation. The experience was stressful. With goofy interviews being done by the likes of the Dingo Warrior (Jim Hellwig, soon to become the Ultimate Warrior) and even Kevin Von Erich, Brody actually found himself having to jump in at the end of the promos to snarl, "What he meant was . . ." and try to clarify a garbled story in 30 seconds.

Frank said, "Thank goodness I don't have to deal with anyone like me." Hart admits that booking, with all the details and personalities, was not Frank's forte, but he tried since Fritz had asked him.

At the start of 1987, Frank was working with a mask and was billed as "Red River Jack" for World Class. Of course, everyone knew "Red River Jack" was Brody. Once, though, to prove to the heels like Abdullah, John Nord, and Hart that Brody wasn't "Jack," Frank had a big, burly, youngster wear the mask as "Red River Jack" and then Brody came out too.

That extra "Red River Jack" was Mark Calaway, who was training with Don Jardine and hanging around the action in Dallas. He wanted to be a wrestler. Today, of course, Mark is better known as WWE's Undertaker.

At one point Frank came up with the gimmick — one made famous by Undertaker years later — of having a hearse driven right to ringside during his matches in San Antonio. That way, the battered opponent of Brody could be tossed right into the appropriate vehicle.

During his travels, Frank also came across Paul Heyman, another personality who would be the guiding light for Extreme Championship Wrestling before joining WWE. Frank was immediately impressed with the youngster who called himself Paul E. Dangerously. "Good, sharp mind," pronounced Frank, before predicting a bright future for Paul.

It wasn't so bright, however, at one card featuring both Brody and Paul E., who was managing Frank's foe, in Georgia. The office for the card was set up in a trailer, and Frank arrived early as fans were beginning to gather. Paul also was coming in; he spotted Brody and yelled, "Hey, Frank! How are you? What's going on?"

Paul E. offered his hand — and Goodish smacked Paul, knocking him down the trailer steps. Obviously, Paul still had something to learn and Frank tried to teach him. "It's one thing to go out quietly and eat together, but it's another to come right up in front of fans. Can't let that happen, brother!" Goodish explained.

Lots of young wrestlers got to see the gory violence produced by Brody and Abdullah on cards all over the country. In St. Louis, one newcomer brought up Brody's chase of Abdullah, how somehow he never seemed to catch the bulky Butcher. Abdullah was not exactly a candidate for the hundred-yard dash at the Olympics.

Frank laughed and gave the lesson. "When you chase a big man, he's going straight ahead in a line. If you're quicker, and you look like me, you have to get those arms moving and zig zag, side to side. That should keep him just a step ahead of you," he explained.

Moments after a bout began against The Assassin (Joe Zakibe), Frank went after The Assassin's manager, "Big Daddy." Roger Bailey might have had a good race with Abdullah in that hundred-yard dash. Brody gave an example of "the chase" executed just perfectly, saving "Big Daddy's" hide. It was at a small building in St. Louis, the Carondelet Sunday Morning Club, where Roger tried to escape Brody's wrath with a mad dash through the exit door and into the parking lot.

The problem was, zigging and zagging, Brody was hot on "Big Daddy's" heels along with plenty of excited fans. Roger hissed, "Run me into that tree."

Brody snapped, "Run back!" Thus, "Big Daddy," going in a straight but wobbly line, desperately ran back into the building with Brody, still zigging and zagging and flailing, right behind him. By the time they got back to the ring, The Assassin was semi-revived and managed to block Brody from "Big Daddy" and take more punishment. Roger could take a deep breath of relief.

It was punishment that Lex Luger apparently feared he would be taking that led to a bizarre incident with Brody in Lakeland, Florida, on January 21, 1987. Frank had been booked into a few bouts previously with Luger, and things just didn't click. Luger, with one of those "pretty" bodies just ripped to shreds, as they say, was getting a big push during desperate times for promoters. A few called Luger "the new Hulk Hogan."

Apparently, Lex believed his own hype, because he wouldn't sell for Brody, who was the heel. Therefore, since the babyface (Luger) didn't sell, no heat had been built for a comeback. In turn, that meant Brody was not about to sell for Lex. When the pair were slated for a cage match, Frank was in no mood to put up with any of Luger's attitude.

Luger came out strong, firing punches, and Frank essentially stood there and looked at him. Unnerved, Luger backed off and then came back with much stiffer punches. Brody took some of the blows off his shoulders, moving subtly, and still didn't sell or even react, except for once taking Luger down. Again, Luger put more into his punches and took a frantic look at the referee.

Bruiser Brody just wasn't budging and Luger could not make him move. Brody hooked Luger's head, gave him a hard squeeze, but then released him. Brody looked totally relaxed and Luger was visibly shaken, huffing and puffing.

He threw a couple of punches, to no effect again, before he backed off with the realization that whether or not Luger wanted to sell for Brody was shortly *not* going to be an issue. Discretion became the better part of valor, because it was clear to the winded Luger he was about to be hurt for real. Luger darted for the cage, crawled over the barrier, and sprinted to the dressing room.

By the time Brody booted open the cage door and got back to the dressing room, Luger and his gear were long gone. All in all, that was a good decision on Luger's part. Of course, the story spread like wildfire throughout wrestling. Depending on one's point of view, it was either another example of Frank "not being professional" or it was a good lesson for a cocky hotshot who hadn't yet paid his dues.

Frank Goodish was surely adapting to the new reality. More Puerto Rico dates, always a trying journey, were added as most regional promotions in the states and their television shows died. He was literally all over the map, yet somehow finding more time to be at home in Boerne, Texas. Now the itinerary was from Montreal, Quebec, to Jackson, Mississippi, to Bricktown, New Jersey, to Saskatoon, Saskatchewan, to Reading, Pennsylvania, to Marietta, Georgia, to Centralia, Illinois to Winnipeg, Manitoba.

There was even a tour to Israel based on the fame of Brody and the Von Erichs and on the strength of the World Class show, which was hugely popular only a year or so previously before it disintegrated.

"He was running out of TV spots and had to do something different," says Robley.

Brody had learned how to play this new game, as every date was for guaranteed money with people he could trust. Frank recognized that nobody can stand against change. The key was to adapt and eventually use the transformation to his advantage.

What was left of the old guard was pretty much run by Jim Crockett, Jr. out of North Carolina. Jerry Lawler stayed alive, somehow, around Memphis. Different people were trying their luck, with zero success, around Dallas, as personal tragedy and the recognition that wrestling was changing irretrievably drew Fritz Von Erich away from the business. Of course, Vince Jr. and the WWF got stronger every day.

Yet, against all those odds, Bruiser Brody still meant something — something huge. A living myth! He was like wrestling's Mad Max looking for survivors after the apocalypse. Brody was clearly part of wrestling lore.

Financial adviser Gerry Cohen recalls visits with Goodish. "He would talk about 'what Bruiser is going to do,' referring to himself in the third person," Gerry describes. "Frank was proud of Bruiser, this incredible character he had created and made famous. He was pleased Bruiser had the reputation he did about being independent."

Of course he was proud, and with good reason. Like Frank Goodish, Bruiser Brody stood up for what he believed and went his own way.

How much of Brody was Goodish? And how much of Goodish was really Brody? Frank once said he could summon that Brody energy and use it in business situations, maybe for a strong retort or an intimidating stare. Indeed, Brody was a wrestling character honed by Goodish, but there was more.

It was not a role that had no relation to who Goodish was. It was not an empty role that someone had to inhabit as an actor would. At some deep, inner point in his soul, there was a blend of Brody and Goodish. Frank knew that Brody could open doors for him, and he realized when to display that character. When someone saw Brody, he was seeing at least some portion of Goodish, a part of his personality that helped make Frank who he was.

But Frank also recognized when Brody was not welcome, nor appropriate. He understood himself, his personality, and his character.

In addition, the fertile imagination of Frank Goodish was at work, and not just with regards to wrestling. Frank had ideas, and he worked them out talking with Barbara and me. Huge plans, big ideas — but I'll get to that later.

One day, Frank called wanting to talk about his conspiracy theory concerning Baba and Inoki. He acknowledged immediately that he could be wrong, that he could be reading too much into things. "Inoki and Baba are supposed to be enemies, and I know there's been legitimate heat between them for years," Frank said. "But this is big business, big money, we're talking about."

Completely serious and rational, Goodish went on to detail how it would be in the best interests of both Baba and Inoki to hold a ceiling on the money they paid to wrestlers — especially foreigners. A bidding war could spiral out of control and end up costing both men serious money.

Wouldn't it be wise, therefore, for some highly discreet contact between them, to hold the line on what either would pay the likes of Brody, Hansen, or The Road Warriors? Both sides would continue to try to lure talent from the other, but a silent pact could be mutually beneficial.

Frank wasn't angry as he speculated. Maybe there was a touch of paranoia — not surprising, considering the experiences he'd had. He would hate a de facto salary cap, naturally, and would try everything in his power to bust through that barrier. But if it was insurmountable, he'd accept the reality and try to work for the best deal possible.

That quiet and reasoned day, I actually sensed a grudging respect for the Japanese promoters — if, in fact, there was truth to the theory. After all, Frank was ultimately a businessman. He was attempting to understand both sides of the issue so that he could respond in a way that would do the most good for him and his family.

When someone can draw real money, no bridge is ever totally burned. With hushed diplomacy in particular on the part of the Funks and possibly Hansen as well, the doors of communication were reopened between Frank Goodish and "Giant" Baba. The war in North America had caused Jim Crockett, Jr. and what was a mere shell of the NWA to pull Ric Flair from All Japan dates, and Baba needed a superstar. A smart businessman who had always been fond of Frank, Baba realized that Brody was an icon in Japan. There was money to be made.

In October 1987, Frank made a short swing to All Japan (cutting short that trip to Israel) and the details were ironed out. The money wouldn't be as good as it had been, but was nonetheless substantial. "Frank was going to get back to the same level he'd been very fast anyway," Terry Funk reports.

Goodish himself knew what had to be done. "Baba has to trust me again," admitted the big man. "I need to give him a reason to trust me."

"Baba was one of a kind," declares Hansen. "There were none like him." Baba accepted Brody back into the fold.

With Jimmy Snuka back as his partner, Brody went into All Japan's famous tag team tournament starting November 21, 1987. Dave Meltzer was in Japan and remembered seeing one of the tourney bouts which sent Brody and Snuka against Abdullah and TNT (Savio Vega, today involved in the promotion started by the late Victor Quinones in Puerto Rico).

"Brody was *really* over," stresses Dave. "The people just went crazy for him, as well as for Abdullah. Brody was just as strong as ever — in fact, stronger. That was obvious. They brawled all over the building."

In Japan, unlike in North America, liability for injury to the fans wasn't a big deal. The audience went running when the bloody donnybrook carried into the seats. Meltzer remembers running himself just so he wouldn't get trampled.

"The jump to Inoki and back to Baba had actually made Brody an even bigger star than ever," Dave explains.

Baba saw it as well. Brody and Snuka went to the finals of the tourney before losing to "Jumbo" Tsuruta and Yoshiaki Yatsu (who had a big reputation at the time in Japan) when Snuka was pinned. Not Frank. The request wasn't even made.

An interesting tease during that tourney may have come on November 22, 1987, at Korakuen Hall where Brody and Snuka went to a wild double count-out against Hansen and Terry Gordy. Was the groundwork perhaps being laid for Brody versus Gordy or, in particular, Brody versus Hansen?

When Brody returned to Japan, he immediately defeated Tsuruta (who was the dominant player at the time for All Japan, as age was starting to take its toll on Baba in the ring) to win the company's National championship on March 27, 1988, at Budokan Hall in Tokyo. It was a classic battle.

Even more important to Frank, however, was the favor he would do for Tsuruta on April 19 at Sendai. Frank was firmly convinced that putting Tsuruta over in the right way would cement his relationship with Baba once again. So concerned was the big man that the match looked good that he sent a videotape of the duel to me for my opinion. The struggle was everything Frank had hoped, with stiff and believable action leading to a clean one-two-three finish that left both performers at the top of the heap. It was everything a fan, or promoter, could expect from two superstars at the top of their games.

With All Japan back in the picture, some stability was added for Frank when most in wrestling were finding complete instability. "The way we had done business was coming to an end," says Robley.

In his unique case, though, Frank could still pick up the valuable and numerous independent outings, aggravate himself with high tension dates in Puerto Rico, ponder what might happen if he went to the WWF, and brainstorm ideas in totally different areas. There was more time at home and Geoffrey was growing up. Yet the business situation was definitely stressful.

In May 1988, Frank had a layover at the St. Louis airport and visited with me for a few hours. I found him thoughtful and distracted. "Geoff just wrote a little essay for school about what he and Mom would do if Dad never came back from a trip," Frank explained.

"I was really proud of how mature it was. He said 'We would be sad, but we'd get through it and go on because that was what Dad would want.' That's really smart for Geoff's age." Frank hesitated before adding, "But it kind of scared me."

Could the term "mellowing" ever be applied to one as intense as Frank Goodish? "He was not mellow," claims Stan Hansen, "but he was realizing there was a little more to life. I think the deal with Inoki humbled Frank a little, because he was always so sure of himself."

On May 21, 1988, Frank worked for a group known as U.S. Championship Wrestling in Malden, Massachusetts, a Boston suburb. He clicked personally with the owner, Richard Byrne, who had been trained by Wladek "Killer" Kowalski and had worked for both the McMahon family and on independent shows around the world.

Byrne says, "Frank was a stand-up guy. I realized that the people who complained about Frank were not guys who stood by their word. Frank did. He was a pretty amazing guy as I got to know him a little."

During the time Byrne spent with Goodish, Frank made clear that "the most important thing was his family. Geoff was starting to play baseball and he said he wouldn't take any bookings that interfered with his son's schedule," Byrne recalls. "He said he wanted to see Geoff play ball."

Byrne's group taped four shows for local television that day. On one card, Brody had "a bit of a situation" with a younger worker by the name of Bruce Battalion. According to Byrne, Battalion wasn't "green" but just didn't get it either. Battalion understood that Brody was going over in a big way and Frank worked like a feather while he battered the guy from pillar to post.

Unfortunately, at one point Battalion stood right up instead of selling and threw a punch to Frank's face. "All the guys were watching on the monitor in the dressing room and everybody held their breath," Byrne recalls. "Frank just pounded him then. Battalion's chest was bleeding and his eye was closed. He looked like a train had hit him head-on." The need to sell wasn't there during that beating.

"The kid was confused afterwards and I tried to explain what he did wrong," says Byrne, who now owns a chain of karate schools. "Then I went to Frank and said that I was sorry he had a problem in there."

Frank just shrugged it off and said to Byrne, "Either the boy is going to get out of the business or he learned a lesson." Once, 14 years earlier, Frank Goodish was the student. Now he was the teacher.

And so much for "mellowing"! Or maybe not — perhaps Goodish could "mellow" outside of the squared circle.

On July 9, 1988, Frank stopped by his old stomping ground of St. Louis to do an autograph session at a bar and grill owned by Herb Simmons in Cahokia, Illinois.

Frank had a relaxed, enjoyable time bantering with the fans and eventually ended up staying late into the evening as he and Herb talked.

Simmons asked whether all the travel and the danger inherent in the business bothered him. "Frank said it did bother him, that it was tough and he hated not being with his son," Herb says. "He said that was the business he was in, though, so he had no choice. I've thought about that night over and over ever since." Then Frank headed off to Puerto Rico by way of an independent shot in Georgia.

On the trip, Frank could consider how all of the years in a brutal, demanding endeavor like wrestling had given him an unrivaled perspective from which to consider his future in wrestling, perhaps in business or other areas, and certainly with Barbara and Geoffrey. Frank Goodish was confident there was much more of his story to write.

CHAPTER EIGHTEEN

Barbara Remembers . . .
WHAT MIGHT HAVE BEEN

I learned two important things after Puerto Rico. First, tragedy teaches you who your real friends are. Second, you can't help thinking about what might have been. That stays with you forever, especially on days like Father's Day when I think of Geoff and how different his life would have been if his Dad had been around. I know, though, you can't turn back the clock.

It was really hard afterward. Even a simple chore like going to a grocery store could be difficult. People I was acquainted with would see me, and then they would suddenly disappear. People don't know, a lot of the time, how to approach the subject of death with someone who has lost a loved one like I did. So they pretend they don't see you. All you want is someone just to say hi.

If you are ever in that situation and don't know what to do, just go up and say a few words of kindness. A kind word is worth more than anyone can put a price on.

For sure, Pete and Rowe Ortega are real friends. They were just great after what happened and I arrived back from Puerto Rico. Although they had moved out of the area, they came to see Geoff and me. They asked me if they could do anything to help. It was the school holidays so their two children, Travis and Tanya, were out of school. I suggested that when they went back home, would they mind leaving the kids with me for a week.

I knew just having a household with three kids in it would help Geoff tremendously. He would have someone to play with and it really helped me get through the pain of losing Frank. You get caught up in the moment with so much to do during the day. Little by little, you gain strength by keeping the mind busy. I learned to make lists every day and, even if only one item was checked off at the end of the day, it was a step in the right direction. All you really want to do is go to bed, pull the covers over your head, and hope you'd had a bad nightmare and that you'd soon wake up.

When I was taking care of the kids, I could forget a little and that was good for me. Kids have needs — and this reminds you that they are the future.

Isn't it funny? Frank picked me and he picked Pete. All the people he picked to be close to him also got along with each other very well. We're just able to open up with one another. It's like he planned it, though obviously he couldn't. I guess it's just one of the mysteries of life why different people who grew up so far apart from each other can really connect when they meet. In this case, it was Frank who somehow brought us all together.

Stan Hansen was another. He went out of his way to help Geoff after what happened. Geoff often went to visit Stan and his family, who were living in Mississippi at the time. Once they took Geoff along on what the Hansen family called a "magical mystery tour." They just drove all over several states, from Texas to Missouri, and stopped at places that were interesting and exciting. What a great adventure for Geoff!

He was always there to call and check on us. Geoff visited them often. It gave Geoff another adult friend he could rely on and that was important at the time.

Another time Geoff and I took a trip to see Stan and his family. Our car was old and not dependable enough for the drive from Boerne to Mississippi, so I rented another. We stayed the first night in Houston and went to the Astros baseball game compliments of Rick Johnston, a friend who helped Frank with business. He joined us at the game with his own son. If I remember, they played the Atlanta Braves and that was the team Geoff was following. Rick is another person who has helped me over the years since Frank's death.

The next day we got as far as Louisiana, where we stayed the night before reaching Stan's home. That was some trip, with just the two of us on the highway! We had a great time with Stan's family and I really appreciated the company. His wife is one of the nicest people I know. It's amazing that three of Frank's closest friends — Pete, Stan, and Larry — are all married to wonderful women.

Larry told me he asked Stan why he did what he did for me and Geoff. Apparently, Stan thought for a little while and then told Larry he was motivated because Frank was his friend and that Geoff was Frank's son. He said he could imagine his own son at the same age as Geoff and how he would feel. I bet nobody ever thought Stan Hansen was like that when they saw him in the ring!

Recently, Stan and I talked about what Frank would have thought of how common cell phones have become. I think Frank would have been aggravated by having promoters able to reach him so easily. He wanted to plan talking to them when he wanted to. More importantly, can you imagine him trying to punch numbers in on those tiny keys with his huge fingers?

I asked Stan how many cell phones Frank would have broken by now. Stan just dryly said, "Pretty damn many," and we both laughed.

At the end of August after what happened in Puerto Rico, Geoff and I were brought to Japan for a memorial service and a show in Frank's memory. Baba's wife Motoka was wonderful to us. All Japan was big business and a truly professional organization. Most importantly, it was an opportunity for Geoff to discover how Frank was regarded in Japan.

Frank had always said, "Barbara, you would not believe how it is in Japan. I cannot describe it to you how it is for wrestling and for me in Japan." He loved going there and thought the fans were wonderful. We could see why once we got there and felt their emotion.

This was one of those times you take the opportunity offered to you. I was still in shock, not quite believing what had happened, but I knew in my heart that it was something I had to do for myself and Geoff to see how his dad was thought of by the Japanese people.

Originally, they were going to have us depart from Dallas for Tokyo, which was easiest since we were close to San Antonio. Frank, though, had always gone Japan Airline from Los Angeles and I just wanted to go the exact route that he had gone countless times. I remember landing in Tokyo and seeing all the lights. What a city! Mrs. Baba was there to greet us, along with the wonderful gentleman she had assigned to look after us and be our translator. If I remember correctly, his name was Wally.

They checked us into the hotel and Geoff was thrilled because there was a McDonalds right by the hotel. What a neon city. They even had a press conference for me. That was hard, because they would ask questions and everything had to be interpreted. When I answered, it also had to be interpreted from English to Japanese.

Our interpreter took us under his wing and was with us all the time we were in Japan. Geoff even had his own interpreter! He thought it was great, because they would take him shopping. Whatever he wanted, they would buy for him. I was thinking, "How the heck am I going to get all of this on the plane?"

Stan was over there at the same time, so we went together to the circus which was playing. Geoff and Stan went backstage to meet the clowns and they painted Geoff's face. All night he walked around with his clown face on.

They took us to Tokyo Disneyland and we got to ride the bullet train to Osaka. What an experience that train was. Baba's organization treated us with great respect and we did feel like very important people. Frank would have been very happy. It was certainly our 15 minutes of fame in Japan!

Of course, it is wrestling. We appeared in the ring for a big ceremony. There was only Geoff and myself. I was holding a picture of Frank and they dimmed the arena lights. I remember that it got very quiet and then they did a ten-bell salute for Frank. Everyone started chanting "Brody, Brody, Brody." In respect, all the boys were standing outside the ring with Baba.

Flowers and streamers were everywhere. It was a big deal as only a top-notch Japanese promotion can do. They were taping it for television as well. At the end of the ceremony, naturally they did some angle for business. Luckily, Stan had warned us so we were ready and understood.

When we arrived back in the States, school had already started for the year but the principal at Geoff's school was very accommodating. She made sure that Geoff was in class with his best friend so that the transition would be easier. The people at the school were all quite helpful, knowing this seven-year-old had just lost his father under terrible circumstances.

Geoff was always a good kid, but most of the time it was just the two of us, even before Frank's tragedy. That's why sports were so important, just to have the company of other children. Soccer was the first one, at age four. I helped out as assistant coach, because I was always there at practice and most of the kids were dropped off before and picked up after. It gave me something to do while Frank was on the road.

After what happened in Puerto Rico, sports were maybe even more important. Geoff has played everything: baseball, basketball, football, and soccer. Basketball was the sport he enjoyed most, and he went on to play varsity as an underclassman. We used to go to the Spurs' games, which was a big deal. To this day, Geoff is still an avid fan of the Spurs.

When he was playing little league and middle school sports, I would car pool for a lot of the kids living in the country. The facilities were in the middle of nowhere. If they didn't have a ride to and from, a lot of kids couldn't play. Their parents had to work and it was hard for them.

I was working at a job that was very flexible and I could work around Geoff's schedule. I am very grateful to William Kirkwood, who was the best boss anyone could have had in my situation. He and his lovely wife Mary, both of whom are incredible photographers, were so helpful. They would allow me to take my work home when we were busy so I could be there for Geoff. I can remember waiting for him while he finished practices and doing my own work in the back of the station wagon I was driving at the time. I had that wagon with *seven* seat belts in it so I could safely transport all the kids.

Our neighbors, Ronnie and Dede Middleton, were always there to help when they could and were a great support for Geoff and me. Once I got scared, thinking I'd heard someone prowling around outside the house. I called Ronnie in the middle of the night and he came right over to make sure everything was okay.

Frank's mom and three sisters (Gayle, Gloria, and Kathy) are the most wonderful people I know. His Aunt Francie is also terrific. Even today they make me feel I am still part of the family. Gayle, his oldest sister, has been a best friend since the beginning and we have always had a great friendship.

My own mother, of course, passed away before I could even tell her about meeting Frank. After that and after Geoff's birth, I visited my father several times because I did not want the same thing to happen. The time to do it is when they are alive and can enjoy the precious time you have. Geoff had a lot of good times with his "Papa," which was what he called my dad.

We think we have all the time in the world, but life has other plans, as we come to find out. I think Geoff's visits prolonged my dad's life as he had something to look forward to. Every time we said goodbye like it was our last one. Finally, the day came that it was the last goodbye, but I have no regrets as Geoff gave him a lot of joy and I got to know my dad better.

The day before my dad died, Geoff and I were in Boerne sitting at the table after our meal. I had this feeling that I needed to call my dad. I stopped what I was doing and made the call. We both had a lovely conversation with him, but after we finished the call we both looked at each other. Geoff said, "Papa doesn't sound good." He passed away 24 hours later.

I am thankful that I made that call. Ultimately, it was goodbye. I did not go over for the funeral, because I had set up everything on my visits. Everyone knew I had done my visiting when he could appreciate it — there was no point in going after he passed, when he'd never know.

The immediate family I have left now is small: a niece, Christine, and three nephews — Andrew, Grant, and Craig. They all have children, and I try to visit when I can.

In the end, I discovered that you have to look within yourself to find happiness, because no one has the power to do it for you. We sometimes go through life with the illusion that other people are going to make us happy, so we keep searching. We have the power all the time, because if we find peace within, we project to others.

Special people can help — like Pete, Stan, and Larry, in my case — but you can't expect others to do it for you. Frank always knew this, I suppose. That's why he knew I could cope with all the separations and I made it easy for him to have his lifestyle without worrying about me being alone most of the time.

And that's why he was planning for the future. Whatever it would be, I would be supportive. He always had a plan.

As much as Frank was happy when he went back to Baba, he was worried about Japan. Frank had set the bar so high by the things he had done in the ring, he knew it would be difficult to stay at that level. He knew his body was hurting. With the type of match he performed, a big man like Frank paid a hard price.

I believed he would never have given up Japan, but never say never. Frank always told me was that he never said no in any negotiation until the very last second if there was any chance at all. I guess that's why I wonder too about Frank and the WWF.

He always had tremendous respect for Vince Sr. Frank was also a good businessman and he really understood what the son, Vince Jr., had done. We talked a lot about Frank going to the WWF. He thought the business had changed and the WWF was the last place to really make money in the United States.

It was getting to that time when he might have been ready to make the move. For Frank, it was all about the right timing. He knew he was the only big man who hadn't been used up. He knew he could draw big money against Hulk Hogan. I know it would have been a challenging situation for him to balance All Japan against the WWF.

Just recently I caught Hogan's reality show with his family on television. I see so many similarities between Hulk and Frank. What an incredible match that would have been. Two strong-willed giants with the integrity and determination to stand up for themselves.

I could also see how Frank was growing into a real father during those last couple of years. He had more time and he loved being with Geoff. Instead of just being home for a day or two, and sleeping for most of the time, he could get on a more normal schedule. Frank was excited about what Geoff did in school and enjoyed seeing his boy play baseball.

The extra time made him a better husband too, because there wasn't quite as much pressure with the constant travel. He was still on the road a lot, but he could balance it better. As usual, he was thinking and planning.

One big thing was Brody Athletic Management (BAM). I know he and Larry talked about it constantly. Frank knew so many athletes, including players for the San Antonio Spurs in the National Basketball Association. He was confident about negotiating and even helping athletes manage their money. He also understood about the toll all that travel can take.

They were just getting started, but Frank was really excited about doing something outside of wrestling. In fact, he bought a wrestling ring from a lady whose husband had worked with Joe Blanchard's promotion in San Antonio. Frank's idea was to take the ring, set it up at different schools, and talk to the students about the dangers of drugs.

He said that when some people make that kind of talk, it was difficult to hold the kids' interest. If they were just there in a suit or slacks, they looked pretty normal. If he had a wrestling ring to talk from, he could let them see Bruiser Brody to get their attention. Then he could talk seriously to them and maybe they would listen.

Frank even wanted to do skits from the ring. He had made connections with a local college professor, who was going to write the material and also help make sure it would have approval of all the educational people who had to say okay. There were a lot of hoops to jump through, but Frank wanted to be positive he did it right. I imagine the professor was surprised to see someone who looked like Bruiser Brody and talked like Frank Goodish!

He even had politics in the back of his mind. I just smiled a few years ago when I heard about Jesse Ventura becoming the Governor of Minnesota. I know the concept of BAM and the work he wanted to do with children might very well have led to something in politics. He was so happy when he met people like the professor or a banker and they listened seriously to his ideas.

I don't know exactly how wrestling might have fit in as time went on. It would always have been a big part of him. But the thought that he could do something he enjoyed and that he believed was important, while being able to spend more time at home with his family, seemed to have him excited.

I was excited for that as well.

Two memories will also be with me forever. One is when we would take him from home to the airport so he could leave to wrestle. Frank Goodish would get out of the car. By the time he got through the entry, it was obvious he was Bruiser Brody just from the walk and the attitude. It was almost like he pushed a button and became a different person. We could actually see him become this dangerous character.

My happiest memory, however, would be when Bruiser Brody came home. Geoff and I would be waiting for him at the airport. He would walk through that gate and Brody would just disappear. It was almost like magic. There was Frank Goodish, so glad to see us and with that giant smile for me and our son. That image will always be with me.

CHAPTER NINETEEN

WHAT MIGHT HAVE BEEN

What could have been. What might have happened. These are valid considerations when it comes to the life and times of Frank Goodish, or Bruiser Brody. It almost seems unfair to play that game, considering what happened to him. But it's impossible not to wonder what might have developed with such a powerful personality as Brody in the mix around 1990.

The opinions are as varied as the many facets of Goodish's personality. Most, of course, deal with what Frank might have accomplished with the World Wrestling Federation (now World Wrestling Entertainment) or, for that matter, World Championship Wrestling. Such a narrow focus ignores the other options and ideas that had already bounced around inside that big, imaginative Goodish brain back in 1988.

Wrestling, though, fires the imagination first. What would have happened had Brody tangled with Hulk Hogan? What explosions might have been triggered between Brody and Vince McMahon, Jr.? What if Brody had headlined WrestleMania? How much money would Frank Goodish have made with the WWF? Or would he have walked out?

Consider the alternative. What if Brody had gotten into the fracas by dealing with WCW? What if I had struck my deal with WCW, Brody had also landed with that company, and the two of us had somehow manipulated our way into power? In that corporate world and barrel full of wrestling sharks, what chaos — or success — might have developed?

The first reaction of almost anyone to the idea of Brody with Vince Jr. and WWF is that there would have been fireworks, battles, and a brief marriage at best.

Bobby Jaggers, for one, believes that "Frank would have lost his individuality. He would have constantly been fighting with Vince's stooges in the dressing room."

Jim Ross, on the other hand, sees things differently: "If Frank were alive today, he could probably still write his own ticket. And only the good Lord knows how much money my old friend would have earned over the past many years if fate had not dealt him such a bad hand."

Still, Ross adds, "Frank would have challenged Vince intellectually. Their collaboration would have equaled big money, even though their relationship might have been volatile at times."

Terry Funk has no qualms saying that Brody would have been dynamite with WWF. "Brody would have been a superstar for Vince and he would not have been a problem," stated Funk. "I thoroughly believe he would have been a huge asset to that company.

"He would have made tons of money and that's why Frank was in this business," Terry points out. "He would have timed his move to Vince when Vince needed him most."

That, of course, was most often Frank's modus operandi, as someone like Buck Robley completely understood. At some point, all parties involved would have decided that there was too much money on the table in Hogan versus Brody to walk away and not try to make it work.

Robley, who says he had once taken dates on Frank's behalf with WWF and then cancelled them later, contends "Vince knew Frank was coming

Frank sharing a meal with Buck Robley.

in the end. After everything was said and done, there was too much ego for it not to happen.

"Frank was the last big name that Vince didn't control and the WWF was the last place that Frank hadn't made money with," says Robley. "Vince would have paid and Frank would have had a big run there, just not very long . . . or unless something went wrong that Frank didn't like."

Gary Hart is more skeptical. "I don't think he would have made the move in the end," he contends. "Back in the mid-80s, Frank slept overnight at my apartment. In the morning, he woke up and saw my son Jason playing with some WWF action figures. Jason asked if Bruiser Brody would ever wrestle these guys.

"And Bruise very matter-of-factly answered, 'Oh, I'd never wrestle for those people.' Jason remembers that to this day," Hart adds.

"He still had big money coming from Japan. His personality would not have fallen into their format. Vince had a way of demeaning talent that wasn't developed by him," Hart points out. "They would have tried to treat Bruiser Brody like they did Bill Goldberg. [WWE essentially took all of the edge away from the very physical Goldberg through silly scenarios and finishes.] Do you think Bruise would have stood for that?"

Both Robley and Hart are in agreement when asked about what might have happened if a booker tried to make Brody something other than what he was. Trouble with a capital T! Hart snickers, "If they could have put Brody into that wwf box, all they would have had was Jim Duggan."

Victor Quinones felt Frank would have gone to the wwf. "He was a businessman. Frank would ask 'What's in it for me?' If the answer was right, I think he would have gone," said Quinones.

Stan Hansen is less than optimistic that something could have developed between Frank Goodish and Vince McMahon, Jr. "Maybe it could have happened if Frank would have made tons and tons of money and if he really felt this was his last opportunity for a big run," says Hansen.

"wwf took the individual out of the guy, though, and if Vince tried to do that with Frank, it would not have worked," Hansen states firmly. "I'm skeptical. It would have been hard to fit Frank into their mold. I have a hard time seeing him fit in. Plus, he still had Japan and that was so different. The Japanese take it serious. They don't laugh at wrestling there and Frank liked that."

Bryan Alvarez, author of *The Death of WCW* and operator of website f4wonline.com, says, "I believe Brody would have gone to wwe and made a lot of money headlining against Hogan. One thing I've learned over the years about Vince McMahon is that he thinks he wants his wrestlers to toe the line and be good company men. But when people actually behave like that he walks all over them, whereas if you speak your mind and stand up for yourself, he develops a strange sort of respect for you."

Alvarez identifies Hogan, Steve Austin, and the Ultimate Warrior as having walked out on Vince. "In every single case, Vince ended up bringing them back and pushing them to the moon," Alvarez explains. "Brody had the kind of personality that would have resulted in a very volatile, but probably very lucrative, relationship with McMahon. I suspect he'd have had at least one very good run against Hogan in the late 80s."

If he had gone to the wwf, what about the question of whether or not Frank would have "done the job" for Hulk? Consider the following queries, and one potential answer becomes clear. Did Frank have any problem putting over the nwa champion in St. Louis, where he got equal money to the titleholder and it was a stable promotion? Did Frank have

Brody and Abdullah used weapons long before anyone "invented" hardcore.

any problem giving a one-two-three for Giant Baba and Jumbo Tsuruta in All Japan, where he got the big money he had been promised and it was a solid promotion?

Of course, Frank was comfortable there was no double-cross hiding in the weeds with Muchnick or Baba.

Mark Nulty, owner of wrestlingclassics.com, broke into the business helping Joe Blanchard promote in San Antonio and got to know Goodish fairly well when Frank worked there. In 1987, they shared a flight from San Antonio to Fort Worth and Frank was very introspective.

"I know how old I am," Frank told Nulty. "I can't do this forever. I need to be smart about my opportunities."

Mark was surprised and asked if Frank Goodish and Vince McMahon, Jr. could really work together and trust each other. "Yes, if it's in both of our financial interests to trust each other," answered Frank. "I'm the one guy left who hasn't been tarnished. It would be nonsense to ask me for a job before I fought Hogan."

What about actually doing the job for Hulk? "When the time is right, there would be too much money at stake for me not to do it," said Frank to Nulty. Of course, this chat with Mark was during the interim between New Japan and All Japan so the cash had even more appeal. Still, there was a bottom line to consider that Frank had never ignored.

J.J. Dillon worked in the office for Vince for several years after a long run with wcw. At first, he hesitated and considered the Brody reputation. Then, Dillon said, "Frank would have been a huge success in the wwf. I'm not saying there wouldn't have been some speed bumps! But it's just like with Steve Austin or Ultimate Warrior, or even Hulk. If there were a need, he'd be back. Vince wanted to make money and so did Frank."

With his brain clicking on all cylinders because such a lucrative reward was waiting, why would Frank Goodish have provided anything less than what was needed to cash in? His long-term vision could have been another issue, but what are the odds that anyone would have been expecting a life-time marriage between the wwf and Brody?

Gary Hart describes it best. "Not everyone's soul is for sale. Bruise may have sold his body, but never his soul."

Hansen adds, "Look at all the big names who were so disappointed after they went to the wwf. They all made big money, unheard-of dollars. But afterward, every single one was cussing out Vince and saying how they hated it." Unless, of course, they were still seeking a payday from him.

Frank Goodish was a businessman in the end. As he had gained more experience, fought his own way through the savagery of the wrestling business, he understood all of that. He would have weighed every element carefully. The odds are he would have seen only one way to make it work.

Wham, bang, and thank you, ma'am. Pop the promotion. Nothing different from what Brody ever did and both sides would have been pleased. Imagine the angles and promos building up to such a monumental collision. Think of the visual impact of Brody storming around the square and Hulk muscled up for combat.

Would the blood have flowed? Would the story have been told? It's ridiculous to believe that two dynamic performers who understood their own characters so well would not provide a classic confrontation.

Especially with Vince, Hulk, and particularly Brody seeing all those dollar signs.

If Frank Goodish had decided it was best for Bruiser Brody, and *if* Vince McMahon, Jr. could have accepted Frank Goodish exactly as he was, even if Vince were trying to figure out what made this complex character tick, Frank would have done the job.

WCW would have been more unlikely. Although if I had, indeed, made my own deal when approached by Jim Herd in late 1988 after Frank's death, interesting dynamics would have been at play. Herd, the new mogul for wrestling when Ted Turner's company took over the bankrupt Jim Crockett, Jr. operation, knew me since he had been a director I had doing play-by-play for the famous *Wrestling at the Chase* television show in St. Louis.

Herd later became the General Manager of KPLR-TV and dealt with me and, particularly, with my mentor Sam Muchnick on a regular basis. Additionally, Herd's boss with WTBS was Jack Petrik, who had been general manager for KDNL-TV in St. Louis and also knew Muchnick and me.

The negotiation between me and Herd eventually fell apart, but I always wondered what I'd have done to make it work had Frank Goodish been alive, active, and helping me to manipulate. The thought of me, highly influential in the office and on booking, with Frank, a main star and dominant in the dressing room, is an enticing one, to say the least.

Yet I also knew the WCW promotion was loaded with sharks, seasoned manipulators who maneuvered for their own personal interests when dealing with unknowing corporate types. The biggest problem WCW had was that ultimately nobody was in charge and there was no real philosophy of what they wanted wrestling to be. That opened the door to a new height of backstabbing, all to the detriment of a successful promotion.

The question would have come down to how much control we could have gotten. One inside and one outside might have been entertaining and effective. If it had worked, the dynamics of a dysfunctional company might have been altered — at least for a short while.

At the World Wrestling Federation, in the end, Vince McMahon, Jr. was the boss. Right or wrong in anyone's opinion, he made the final decision. At WCW, even if Herd agreed, and then Petrik agreed, there was still another layer of administration to say yes or no. There were others, equally ineffective, who replaced Herd and Petrik before the ultimate collapse.

Likewise, the idea of a booking committee became more prevalent at WCW and soon many hands were in the mix. Gary Hart asks, "Now how would anyone in their right mind think that Bruiser Brody would deal with a booking committee?"

Robley notes that "there was money to be made at wcw. Lots of angles Frank could have done. But can you imagine Frank putting up with all that stuff for very long?"

But to underestimate the wide range of Frank's business instincts, particularly as they were developing at that time, would be an error. More and more, he was grasping the similarities and the differences between wrestling and the so-called normal world. He could charm and actually fit in nicely with corporate types, who were always fascinated to see the depth in Frank Goodish. There were two sides, if not more, of a complex man.

Likewise, I was totally at ease in an office setting. Think about the history of St. Louis. Had we been together in that turbulent wcw scene, maybe the door to Ted Turner himself might have cracked open. Certainly a very long shot, but who knows? Look what unexpected insanity did happen in that company.

Bryan Alvarez claims, "Brody probably would have gone to wcw in the early 90s and lasted less than six months. Too many really stupid people." He adds, "I suspect had he done the program with Hogan, wcw would have thrown tons of money at him during the wrestling boom, and at that age he'd probably have put up with more than he would have in the 80s simply because he was running out of time to make super huge money for his family."

Dillon points out that "Frank was right up there with someone like Kevin Nash in recent years as far as knowing how to manipulate people in this business. He was not intimidated by anyone at all and Frank certainly knew how to be assertive. He would have gotten what he wanted from wcw. They would have given it to him."

But forget wrestling for a moment, because Frank Goodish did. He, more than anyone else, knew he couldn't bang heads in the ring forever. Frank grasped the reality that the power and the money were far from the spotlight.

Financial adviser Gerry Cohen says, "Frank understood the business. He treated it like a profession. He was so organized. He knew he wasn't immortal, unlike many professional athletes, so he was way out in front. He thought about 'what am I going to do after wrestling is over' and 'what is life going to look like for me.' He wasn't going to allow himself to be some second-rate gym bum."

Having seen first-hand the difficulties wrestlers had, and the much more organized and successful approach of some other professional athletes, Frank popped the idea of an athletic management company. He and I put our heads together and out came the perfect name — Brody Athletic Management. Use the initials for the visual impact — BAM.

Obviously, the concept was in its infancy but it made all the sense in the world. At the time, Hulk Hogan was about the only grappler who had representation and it was working well for him. Clearly no union was about to evolve to protect individual rights for wrestling's top talent. Who better to go into a board room fracas than Frank?

Wrestling, though, would not have been the thrust of BAM, but more a sidelight. Frank had all sorts of contacts with other pro athletes, as I did too. Frank's feeling was that adding the correct legal and financial representation, along with my public relations skills and Frank's own talents and aggressive nature, could allow BAM to carve out a corner in the much larger field.

Take that a step further. Frank understood how much wrestling, with its concentration on interviews and personality, mirrored politics. Once again, Goodish was comfortable with bankers, investment experts, and lawyers. "They're always surprised to find out Frank Goodish is not Bruiser Brody," Frank said once. "I can give them a little Brody if I have to, but there is a lot more to Goodish than Brody."

Frank had already begun his strategy as he consulted with area business people and was laying the groundwork to visit schools for talks with the youngsters. New ideas jumped up almost daily.

Very carefully, Frank was giving thought to the political option. Does that seem absurd? Did it seem absurd for Jesse Ventura, a wrestling star who became the Governor of Minnesota? Consider Frank Goodish, his hair and beard neatly trimmed but not so much as to make Brody look like a mask.

Consider Frank Goodish, a man of strong opinions and courage, in an interview or a debate. Here was a man who could do a promo in a helmet, sweat pants, and combat boots *or* spend one hour seriously discussing his craft with Bob Costas. Like Ventura, Frank understood the impact of the media and what he had developed with the public. He grasped the power of television and what he'd achieved on that magic medium for many years in many locations before many viewers. As the audience knew Jesse, they knew Frank.

Governer Jesse Ventura. Who would have expected? So why not . . .

Governor Frank Goodish? Or Senator? Or Representative?

What a thought. But it was one that clearly was not beyond the realm of possibility, at least insofar as Frank dreamed and planned. Just think of Frank finding the patience and wit to maneuver in a smoke-filled back room!

The odds of seeing Bruiser Brody gray and shuffling, happy to pick up a few hundred dollars at an autograph show, would be slim indeed. He certainly would never have allowed himself to be a figure of pity. Sedately settling into retirement from wrestling in no way fits the mold of Frank Goodish. The relentless energy and intelligence could never have been satisfied that easily.

Still, considering all of those factors, if his pride in his athleticism could have been personally satisfied, it is difficult to imagine Brody turning down that giant payday here and there in Japan or elsewhere no matter what else he was doing.

Whether he would have been battling Hulk, manipulating with Ted Turner, negotiating for the next great baseball or football star, or running for political office, Frank Goodish was just getting started.

CHAPTER TWENTY

A REAL HERO

Barbara Goodish was so courageous and open throughout the demanding process of writing this book that it would be difficult to praise her enough. She is a strong, private person who found the ability to share emotional parts of her life.

In fact, Barbara is doing well today and is happy with life. She enjoys yoga and Tai Chi. She travels a fair bit, and enjoys exploring each day as it comes. Geoff, so much like his father, lives in Texas and delights in discovering his way in the world as a young adult.

Barbara is also humble and would blush at all the nice things I could write here. Perhaps the best way to capture the type of lady Barbara

Goodish is would be to go back in time and hear something in the voice of her son, Geoff.

A good writer (genes from his sportswriter father perhaps?), Geoff had an assignment in high school due April 14, 1997, when he was 16 years old, to compose an essay on "A Real Hero." What he wrote speaks for itself.

A Real Hero

There have been many "real heroes" in my life. My dad was one of them for the short time I knew him. I also consider myself as a "real hero" for what I have been through. There have also been many others, but I think my mom is the closest to a "real hero" of anybody I know.

One of the hardest things to overcome in a family is the death of a family member or somebody very close to a family. My mom and I had to overcome this when my dad died in 1988. I was only seven years old and just starting to grow up. This was a very hard time for my mom, because it was a very important part of her life. Since my dad was a wrestler, it was not unusual for him to not be around. He got paid very good money, so it was not necessary that my mom have a job. All she had to do was raise me and take care of the house while he was gone. When he died, that all changed. Now, along with taking care of me, she had to get a job, make sure the bills were paid, and put food on the table for the two of us. She has managed to do all this with the help of no one.

Since I was only seven when my dad died, I wasn't much help. I couldn't really help around the house or get a job to help pay for things. Just as things were getting back to normal, her father died. That set her back a little bit and by the time she was getting over it, I was a teenager. Raising a teenager is hard for two parents, let alone one. Teenagers are hard to parent because they don't understand everything and want to do things their way. I was no exception. I was just like every other kid. I got in trouble and did things wrong. She tried to deal with it the best she could. I also played two or three sports and she made sure I got to every practice and game on time.

These are just a few of the reasons that my mom is a "real hero." There are many more that I have failed to mention. My mom has played a very important part in my life and I hope she will continue to, for my sake.

By the way, Geoff Goodish got an "A" on the assignment.

Even at a young age, Geoff showed he was indeed his father's son.

Brody with fellow hall-of-famer, announcer Gordon Solie.

EPILOGUE

What song will they sing when they sing of Bruiser Brody? Is the ballad of Frank Goodish a tragedy? Surely, it has a tragic ending. For his wife Barbara and his son Geoffrey, how else can this tale be interpreted? It was a murder, cold and simple. It was horrible, violent, unnecessary, and wrong.

But ask these questions. Did Barbara develop and display new reservoirs of strength, courage, and determination? Did Geoffrey battle through losing his father to become as strong as his dad? Did life, however difficult, go on and find new energy?

As for Frank Goodish, he did not have a tragic life. He had a sad end, no question. We all, however, have an end one way or another. Wasn't the life of Frank Goodish so much more than the way he died?

Frank had a great, loving, loyal wife who helped him find depths of his soul that he never knew existed. Frank had a terrific son who motivated him to reach even deeper within himself and discover love. Those facts are not tragic. To the contrary, they show the resilience of the human spirit in the persons of Barbara and Geoffrey.

Professionally, his life was a success. Bruiser Brody, or "King Kong" Brody, is a legend who achieved a pinnacle that probably even Frank Goodish never anticipated. He kept his principles in a vicious business and stood firm, whether or not everyone agreed with him. Frank lived the life he lived, without worrying about who was keeping score. He did not compromise his position, thus achieving a personal goal of independence. It came with a price, but Frank Goodish paid it.

How many of us can say that about our careers? Isn't it amazing when or if we can?

Terry Funk said that the wrestling business uses 98% of those in it. It can be a great thing to be used by the business, for the glamour and fun and notoriety and money. Eventually, though, the business eats up 98% of those in it and most do not come out rich, happy, and wonderful.

According to Funk, 2% use the business and come out right. They are secure financially and have a family that loves them. Their lives are in order. Frank Goodish was finally making that happen. He was part of the 2% until the business reached out and snared him at the end.

It would be wrong, though, tragically wrong, to regard the big man only in terms of his last day.

Wrestling in many ways is no different from any other business. There is backstabbing and lying and cheating in all businesses. There is rugged competition, whether it involves car manufacturers or fast food producers or computer companies. What professional wrestling provides is the chance for a single person to stand tall and be in control, as Frank Goodish was at his level.

And, with all due respect to other endeavors, wrestling is so damn much fun!

Brody entertained thousands and thousands of people. He made them *happy*. In this difficult world today, that in itself is good and meaningful. While it was a tragedy that took him, Brody left at the top of his career. He wasn't a pathetic figure, humbled and battered, trying to grab a pay

The fire within Brody burned bright on *Wrestling at the Chase*.

check. Brody remains the monster who blew away the bad guys so that many could be excited and cheer.

Nobody will remember him old and long past his prime, stumbling and puffing. Some young stud didn't spit in his face on television, while he threw a feeble punch that missed. His body wasn't sagging when another ridiculous new gimmick-character squashed him with a leap from the top rope. He didn't act half his age on live television, or beg for votes on a rigged Internet poll. He never wore a toupee into the ring.

Brody was a titan when he left the stage. The mesmerizing illusion, so dangerously real, remains intact.

This is why Bruiser Brody is a mythical, legendary figure that will always live in wrestling. Even years after his passing, Brody stirs the passions of those who remember him and tweaks the curiosity of those who were too young. In Japan, Brody is a powerful image on the wrestling landscape even today.

Around the globe, some wonder why Bruiser Brody did what he did since they do not understand what the wrestling business was and actually in some ways still is. Others question how he could survive and succeed.

Yet Frank Goodish as Bruiser Brody found a way — *his* way — to do it.

Pete Ortega says, "Frank did it his way, on his terms. He loved his wife and son."

Ronnie Middleton says, "It was a terrible loss for Geoff, especially at that age and because his dad was so dynamic. But Geoff is a good kid, very smart, and he's doing well. Frank . . . well, Frank was just a neat guy and a great friend."

Stan Hansen, who, along with Pete, did so much for Barbara and Geoffrey, notes, "He loved his son above all else."

Terry Funk says, "The bottom line to Frank was making money for his family. He did it in the way he wanted to do it."

Jim Ross says, "All of those who came in contact with Frank over the years will probably have a unique story or two to tell of the big, athletic, intelligent man and some of them probably will not be flattering. However, I choose to remember the rookie wrestler who became my friend 30 years ago and who was nice to my umpiring buddies when he did not have to be."

Gerry Cohen says, "If Frank trusted you, he trusted you completely."

Buck Robley says, "It's sad Geoff didn't get to grow up with him around. He loved that kid. Frank was his own man and I hope his son understands that."

Gary Hart says, "If you don't know who you are, you are nobody. Frank Goodish knew who he was."

Father. Husband. Wrestler. Businessman. Rebel. Competitor. Manipulator. Athlete. Independent. Outlaw. Fighter. Thinker. A complex man indeed. He knew it, he accepted it, he had pride in it, and he embraced it.

Parts of the legend will always be shrouded in mystery and fable. The truth, though, is clear. The big man knew who he was, and that was his knowledge and his alone. It is a proud, thunderous anthem that will echo through eternity when they sing of Bruiser Brody!

Frank Goodish would have it no other way.